Education Policy in India

Education Policy in India

1992 and Review 2000 and 2005

J.C. Aggarwal

SHIPRA

(2023, 2016, 2011 Reprint - 3rd Edition)

Rs. 1450 US$ 45

ISBN: 978-81-7541-853-0

2026 Impression, PoD

Education Policy in India:
1992 and Review 2000 & 2005

Published by:

SHIPRA PUBLICATIONS
LG 18-19, Pankaj Central Market,
I.P. Ext., Patparganj, Delhi 110092
+91 11 47322068; 96500 28065, 9810522367
info@shiprapublication.com
www.shiprapublication.com

Preface

The National Policy on Education (1968) marked a significant step in the history of education in post-Independence India. Since the adoption of 1968 Policy, the most notable development has been the acceptance of a common structure of education throughout the country.

The implementation of the policy was reviewed in 1985 and after a nation wide debate, the National Policy on Education–NPE, 1986 was formulated which was approved by the Parliament. A Programme of Action was also prepared for the implementation of the policy.

As stipulated in NPE 1986, it was reviewed in 1992 and some modifications were made. The attempt is made to provide a detailed account of the efforts made in the implementation of the NPE.

While discussing the various dimensions of the NPE, special attention is given to the restructuring of the curriculum. It may be emphasised that curriculum is an important instrument of translating the objectives of education in real terms. In this context, salient features of National Curriculum Framework for School Education 2000, National Curriculum Framework 2005 and overview of implementation of NPE as on date are presented in this book. Appendix lists the Committees, Commissions, Policy statements and other significant Documents on Education in India since independence.

It is hoped that the book would serve as a handy source of information for all sections engaged in the revamping of the educational system in India. The author extends his thanks to all the publishers and authors whose works he has quoted.

J.C. Aggarwal

Contents

Glossary

AICTE	All India Council of Technical Education
ASC	Academic Staff College
CABE	Central Advisory Board of Education
CBSE	Central Board of Secondary Education
CDC	Curriculum Development Centre
CHD	Central Hindi Directorate
CIEFL	Central Institute of English and Foreign Languages
CIIL	Central Institute of Indian Languages
CIVE	Central Institute of Vocational Education
CLASS	Computer Literacy and Studies in Schools
CSS	Centrally Sponsored Scheme
DIET	District Institute of Educational Technology
ECCE	Early Childhood Care and Education
GNP	Gross National Product
HRD	Human Resource Development
ICAR	Indian Council of Agricultural Research
ICDS	Integrated Child Development Scheme
ICME	Indian Council of Medical Education
IEDC	Integrated Education for the Disabled Children
IES	Indian Education Service
IGNOU	Indira Gandhi National Open University
IIT	Indian Institute of Technology
JSN	Jana Shikshan Nilayam
KHS	Kendriya Hindi Sansthan
MLL	Minimum Levels of Learning
MNP	Minimum Needs Programme
MS	Mahila Samakhya
NCC	National Cadet Corps
NCERT	National Council of Educational Research and Training
NCHE	National Council of Higher Education
NCTE	National Council of Teacher Education
NCVE	National Council of Vocational Education
NDC	National Development Council
NGO	Non-Governmental Organisation
NIEPA	National Institute of Educational Planning and Administration
NLM	National Literacy Mission
NPE	National Policy on Education
NPERC	National Policy on Education Review Committee
NSS	National Service Scheme
NTS	National Testing Service
NV	Navodaya Vidyalaya
POA	Programme of Action
REC	Regional Engineering College
R&D	Research and Development
	SIE State Institute of Education
SIET	State Institute of Educational Technology
SUPW	Socially Useful Productive Work
SCVE	State Council of Vocational Education
ST	Scheduled Tribe
TGT	Trained Graduate Teacher
TLC	Total Literacy Campaign
TSP	Tribal Sub-Plan
TV	Television
UEE	Universalisation of Elementary Education
UGC	University Grants Commission
UNDP	United Nations Development Programme
UNESCO	United Nations Educational, Scientific and Cultural Organisation
UNICEF	United Nations International Children's Education Fund
UPE	Universalisation of Primary Education

1
Framing National Policy on Education in India

Thinkers in Ancient India conceived an intimate relationship between education and life. The objectives of education were summarised in a triple formula which gave a wide and lofty framework to the system of education.

असमतो मा सद् गमय ।
तमसो मा ज्योतिर्गमय ।
मृत्योर्माअमृतं गमय ।

Lead me from falsehood to truth !
Lead me from darkness to light !
Lead me from death to immortality !

The ideas of truth, light and immortality constituted a triune unity, each subsisting in the other.

India has a long tradition of education, both of formally organised institutions such as Universities of Nalanda and Takshila, as well as the less formal, such as hermitages where great teachers took charge of their wards. Education provided in these institutions was free of charge.

In the Mahabharata (i.70), there is a description of Kaurava's hermitage. It was situated on the banks of the Malini, a tributary of the Sarayu river. Numerous hermitages stretched round the central hermitage. At this Ashram, there were specialists in each of the four Vedas, in Phonetics, Metrics, Grammar and Niyukta. There were also philosophers well-versed in the science of the Absolute. There were logicians. There were also specialists in the physical sciences and arts. In this forest university the study of every available branch of learning was cultivated.[1]

Years ago, Sir Alexander Johnston wrote a letter to Mr Charles Grant (1746-1823) President of the Board of Control, in the following words : 'Education has always, from the earliest of their history, been an object of public care and of public interest to the Hindu Governments on the peninsula of India. Every well-regulated village under those governments had a public school and a public school-master. The system of instruction in them was that, which, in consequence of its efficiency, simplicity and cheapness, was a few years ago introduced from Madras into England and from England into the rest of Europe. Every Hindu parent looked upon the education of his child as a solemn duty which he owed to his God and to his country and placed him under the school-master of his village as soon as he had attained his fifth year. The ceremony of introducing him for the first time to the school-master and his scholars was publicly recorded and was attended with all the solemnity of a religious observance; a prayer being publicly offered upon the occasion to the figure of Ganesa, the Hindu God of wisdom, which was at the head of every Hindu school imploring him to aid the children in their endeavours to learn and become wise.' [2]

'Education', writes, Dr. F.W. Thomas one of the most distinguished indologists, 'is no exotic in India. There is no country where the love of learning had so early an origin or has exercised so lasting and powerful an influence.'[3]

'Education in India under the British Government', says Hovell 'was first ignored, then violently and successfully opposed, and conducted on a system now universally admitted to be erraneous and finally placed in its present footing.'[4]

'We have to educate a people who cannot at present be educated by means of their mother-tongue. We must teach them some foreign language. The claim of our own language it is hardly necessary to recapitulate. It stands pre-eminent even among the language of the West. It abounds with works of imagination...with models of every species of eloquence, with historical compositions...with just and lively representations of human life and human nature, with the most profound speculations on meta-physics, morals, government, jurisprudence, and trade, with full and correct information respecting every experimental science which tends to preserve the health, to increase the import, or to expand the intellect of man.'[5]

'We must at present do our best to form a class who may be interpreters between us and the millions whom we govern, a class of persons Indian in blood and colour, but English in taste, in opinion, in morals and intellect.'

'The foundation that Macaulay laid of education has enslaved us.'[6]

Gandhiji emphasised that primary education should be imparted through a craft and should be self-supporting. 'I want the whole process of education to be imparted through some craft.'[7]

Gandhiji's views were considered and given a concrete shape in October 1937, in a Conference of National Workers at Wardha. The Conference appointed a Committee of distinguished educationists under the chairmanship of Dr. Zakir Hussain, to prepare a detailed scheme. The report of the Committee published in March 1938, was come to be known as Wardha Scheme of Education. It was approved by Gandhiji and was placed before the Indian National Congress at its Haripura session held in March 1938. The Congress accepted the scheme. The scheme has three important features: (1) Free and compulsory education for seven years on a nationwide scale; (2) Mother tongue to be the medium of instruction; and (3) Education to centre round some form of manual and productive work with due regard to the environment of the child.[8]

The Basic System of Education or the Wardha Scheme of Education or the *Nai Talim* was accepted as the national system of education at the school stage, immediate after independence. After the publication of the Report of the Education Commission 1964-66, the scheme went into oblivion. Many protagonists of this scheme described the report as the 'deathknell of Basic Education'.

After independence the first action of a great significance in the field of education taken by the Government of India was the appointment of the University Education Commission[9] in December 1948, under the Chairmanship of Dr. S. Radhakrishnan, an eminent scholar and former Vice Chancellor of Banaras University, who later on became the second President of India. The Commission submitted its report in August 1949. The report of the Commission is a unique document of great importance as it has guided the development of university education in India till the formation of the National Policy on Education, 1968. While outlining the aims of university education, the Commission said, 'The greatness of a country does not depend on the extent of its territory, the length of its communications or the amount of wealth, not even on widespread education or equitable distribution of wealth, important as all these things are. If we wish to bring about a savage upheaval in our society, a *raksasa raj*, all that we need to do is to give vocational and technical education and starve the spirit. We will have a number of scientists without conscience, technicians without taste who find a void within themselves, a moral vacuum and a desperate need to substitute something, anything, for their lost endeavour and purpose. Society will then get what it deserves. It we claim to be civilised we must develop thought for the poor and the suffering, chivalrous regard and respect for women, faith on human brotherhood regardless of race or colour, nation or religion, love of peace and freedom, abhorrence of cruelty and ceaseless devotion of the claims of justice.'

The second most significant document in the history of the development of education is the Report of the Secondary Education Commission 1952-53.[10]

Writing about the aims of the secondary education in accordance with the needs of democratic India, the Commission observed, '...we shall have to formulate our aims with reference to these broad categories–the training of character to fit the students to participate creatively as citizens in the emerging democratic social order; the improvement of their practical and vocational efficiency so that they may play their part in building up the economic prosperity of their country, and the development of their literary artistic and cultural interests, which are necessary for self-expression and for the full development of the human personality, without which a living national culture cannot come into being.' The recommendation of the Commission, unfortunately remained unfulfilled by and large.

In 1966, an important event in the history of education in India took place. This was the publication of the report of the Education Commission 1964-66,[11] popularly known as the Kothari Commission after the name of its Chairman D.S. Kothari. The report went into all aspects of education and at all levels and suggested a blueprint of educational reforms to be carried out during the coming twenty years. The report appropriately subtitled *Education and National Development* begins with these words, 'The destiny of India is now being shaped in our classrooms. This, we believe, is no more rhetoric. In a world based on science and technology, it is education that determines the level of prosperity, welfare and security of the people.' It concludes with these remarks, 'We must either build a sound, balanced, effective and imagined educational system to meet our developing needs and respond to challenging aspirations or be content to be swept aside by the strong currents of history.'

The Commission identified the three important facets of the big programme that would bring about the desired 'educational revolutions'

- internal transformation so as to relate it to the life, needs and aspirations of the nation;
- qualitative improvement so that the standards achieved are adequate, keep continually rising, and at least in a few sectors become internationally comparable; and
- expansion of educational facilities broadly on the basis of manpower needs and with an accent on equalization of educational opportunities.

For the internal transformation of the system of education the following programmes urged high priority.

(1) Work experience as an integral part of general education; vocationalisation of education at the secondary level; improvement of professional education and research, promoting national consciousness;

(2) Introducing a common school system, making social and national service compulsory; developing all modern Indian languages;

(3) making science education an integral part of all school education and developing scientific research; and

(4) Inculcation of high values—social, moral and spiritual—at all stages of education.

The Report received wide attention and aroused great hopes. Its recommendations had been the major base for the declaration of the National Policy on Education (1968); and the Fourth, Fifth and Sixth Five-Year Plans. More than two decades have passed since the publication of the Report and yet many of its significant recommendations especially on vocationalisation of secondary education, common school system and educational planning on manpower needs have not been implemented.

The Commission recommended that the Government of India should issue a statement on the National Policy on Education which should provide guidelines to the State Governments and the local authorities in preparing and implementing educational plans in their areas. Therfore, in 1967, the Government of India constituted the Committee of members of Parliament on Education to prepare the draft of a statement on the National Policy on Education. Dr. Triguna Sen, the Union Education Minister was the chairman of the Committee which included 29 leading members of all the different political parties in the country. A Drafting Committee under the chairmanship of Shri Ganga Saran was constituted from among the members of the Committee. The Committee arrived 'at the greatest common measure of agreement' and evolved the draft of a National Policy on Education. It was placed before the Central Advisory Board of Education (CABE) which met in 1967 and discussed the formulation of a National Policy. During the discussion it was realized that the policy should be as brief as possible and should define clearly and realistically the new directions of the changes proposed for education at all levels in the country. A general consensus emerged in the course of the Board's deliberations. Thereafter the Government of India passed the issued National Policy on Education (1968).[12] The Resolution inter alia states, 'The Government of India is convinced that a radical reconstruction of education on the broad lines recommended by the Education Commission is essential for economic and cultural development of the country for national integration and for realising the ideal of a socialistic pattern of society.' The Government of India accordingly resolved to promote the development of education in the country in accordance with seventeen principles.

About the educational structure, the policy statement said 'It will be advantageous to have a broadly uniform educational structure in all parts of the country. The ultimate objective should be to adopt the 10 plus 2 plus 3 pattern, the higher secondary stage of two years being located in schools, colleges or both according to local conditions.'

Resolution also envisaged that the Government of India would 'also review every five years, the progress made and recommend guidelines for future development.'

Practically much more should have been done for the implementation of the uniform pattern during these 24 years after the Resolution of 1968. In 1972, the Ministry of Education and Social Welfare appointed a Committee[13] consisting of 11 members to suggest practical steps to be taken for implementation of the pattern for the school and college classes in all States and Union Territories of the country and to estimate the cost of implementing the programme. The Committee was headed by Dr. P.D. Shukla as Chairman and Dr. R.P. Singhal, Secretary, Central Board of Secondary Education as Member-Secretary. The Committee submitted its report in November 1973.

The Report of the Committee provided guidelines for the implementation of the new pattern of Education.

In November 1974, the CABE adopted a resolution

recommending the introduction of the 10+2+3 pattern of education all over the country during the Fifth Plan Period. By the end of 1976-77, this pattern had been introduced in 19 States and Union Territories. It has now been accepted in all parts of the country. According to the modified National Policy on Education, 1992, efforts will be made to have the +2 stage accepted as a part of school education throughout the country.

With the coming of the Janata Government in power in 1977 at the Centre, the first question in the field of education to be raised was whether the Resolution on National Policy on Education (1968) should be reviewed. The new Government declared that it would review all educational programmes including the National Policy. The Government appointed the Ishwarbhai Patel Committee[14] and the Adiseshiah Committee to review the educational programmes in classes I to X and classes XI to XII respectively. The University Grants Commission was also requested to review all its programmes. The draft of the revised National Policy on Education which the Government had promised to the people was released in 1979.

The New Pattern of Education 10 + 2 had been introduced in several schools of the country. The NCERT had prepared new curriculum and textbooks which came under heavy criticism and it was felt that the curriculum was overloaded. The Ishwarbhai Patel Review Committee[15] scrutinised the scheme of studies and suggested some modifications. The Review Committee also defined the concept of Socially Useful Productive Work (SUPW). This, by and large, replaced the concept of Work Experience and Craft Based education.

The National Review Committee (1978-78)[16] on Higher Secondary Education, headed by Dr. Malcolm S. Adiseshiah, Vice-Chancellor, Madras University, reviewed the NCERT's document 'Higher Secondary Education and its Vocationalisation' and recommended a plan of action for vocationalisation of education vocational at the secondary/higher stage. The Report of the Committee is entitled 'Learning To Do–Towards a Learning and Working Society.'

The 1968 National Policy on Education had stipulated a review of progress every five years. Such a review was overdue. In the meanwhile there had been a change of Government at the Centre. The Janata Government, in pursuance of its election manifesto decided to frame a new national education and for this purpose a Draft National Policy on Education (1979)[17] was issued. Since the Janata Dal Government was short-lived, the policy could not be finalised.

In 1985, the NCERT prepared a 'National Curriculum for Elementary and Secondary Education: A Framework.'[18] The document covered four broad areas–emerging concerns and imperatives, curriculum organisation, evaluation and implementation.

On becoming the Prime Minister, Shri Rajiv Gandhi, in his broadcast to the nation on January 1, 1985, declared that a new education policy to 'equip the country both scientifically and economically to enter the 21st century' would be formulated soon. Accordingly the Ministry of Education, Government of India, prepared a document 'Challenge of Education–A Policy Perspective, 1985'[19]

The document was presented to the Prime Minister and the Parliament in August 1985. This contained an overview of the state of education in the country, pointed out the directions of future initiatives based essentially on the views and suggestions from educational planners, teachers, students, parents, intellectuals and citizens interested in education. It aimed at providing the basis for a nationwide debate for facilitating the formulation of the new education policy. It also formed the basis of discussions in the conference of State Ministers of Education, held on August 29-30, 1985. It was translated practically into all regional languages of the country and given wide circulation. In addition, 5,80,000 copies of the document in English, 2,40,000 in Hindi and 4,000 in Urdu were distributed by the Ministry in reponse to requests received from and also to different organisations. As a part of the nationwide debate, 12 National Seminars and 17 Sponsored Seminars were organised by the Government of India and its agencies.

More than 8,000 communications were received by the Ministry of Education. In 1986, the Ministry of Education, now renamed the Ministry of Human Resource Development, Government of India, brought out a revised document *National Policy on Education, 1986–A Presentation* which was discussed in meetings of the State Minister of Education, the National Development Council and the Central Advisory Board of Education. The document was again revised in the light of discussions and the *Draft National Policy on Education 1986* was placed on the table of Parliament in the first week of May, 1986. The draft was debated and finally adopted by the Lok Sabha on May 8 and Rajya Sabha on May 12, 1966. Thus the National Policy on Education, 1986 emerged.

The National Policy on Education (NPE) 1986[20] marks a significant step in the history of education in post Independent India. It contains XII parts and 157 Paragraphs (i) Introductory; (ii) The Essence and Role of Education; (iii) National System of Education; (iv) Education for Duality; (v) Reorganisation of Education at Different Stages; (vi) Technical and Management of Education; (vii) Making the System Work; (viii) Re-orienting the Content and Process of Education; (ix) The Teacher; (x) The Management of Education; (xi) Resources and Review; and (xii) The Future.

With a view to implementing the NPE, the Ministry of Human Resource Development undertook an extensive exercise to prepare a programme of Action.[21] Twenty-three Task Forces were constituted and each was assigned a specific subject covered by the NPE. The Task Forces submitted their reports in July 1986. These reports were discussed in a series of meetings taken by the Minister of Human Resource Development. After these discussions were completed, a conference of Education Secretaries of the State Governments and Union Territories Administrators was convened on 20 July, 1986. Suggestions received during this meeting were considered and the Programme of Action was prepared with reference to the main areas covered in NPE. The CABE met at New Delhi on August 1 and 2, 1986.

The document on the Programme of Action was discussed at this meeting.

The final Programme of Action was presented to Parliament on August 8, 1986.

The Lok Sabha and the Rajya Sabha discussed and approved the Programme of Action on August 22 and 23, 1986 respectively.

It was the first time in the history of independent India that a National Policy on Education was prepared at the initiative of a Prime Minister and that a Programme of Action was planned for bringing about educational reforms.

Among the most important programmes initiated at the school stages are: Blackboard Operation at the primary stage, Pace-Setting of Navodaya Vidyalayas and the Vocationalisation of Education at the secondary stage. In the field of Teacher Education, District Institutes of Education and Training have been set up and selected Secondary Teacher Education Institutions upgraded into Colleges of Teacher Education/Institutions of Advanced Study in Education (CTEs/IASEs).

In the field of Higher Education, some of the major thrust areas are: Strengthening Autonomous Colleges, Redesigning Courses, Academic Staff Colleges for Orientation of Teachers and Eligibility Tests for Recruitment of Lecturers etc.

In 1988, NCERT developed syllabi at the school stage.[22, 23] In this context it is hardly necessary to stress that a detailed syllabi form an important link in the process of curriculum development. The new syllabi were meant for serving as an effective instrument for initiating the desired educational goals. The syllabi were finalised in a national level meeting attended by representatives of State Boards of School/Secondary Education, Kendriya Vidyalaya Sangathan and SCERTs/SIEs.

With a view to implementing the directions contained in the National Policy on Education, 1986 regarding 'Reorienting the Content and Process of Education', the NCERT revised the curriculum in 1988.[24] The revised curriculum is the outcome of the deliberations of a large member of seminars participated by eminent educationists, curriculum specialists, subject experts, principals of schools, teacher educators, legislators, journalists and representatives of teachers organisations. The publication incoporates in it emerging concerns and imperatives, curriculum concerns, basis for the national system of education, factors related to the organisation of the curriculum, allocation of time to different areas, evaluation and examination etc. It also suggests the strategy of implementation.

Two reports[25, 26] on teachers also deserve attention in the context of educational reforms in India. For the first time two National Commissions on Teachers were appointed by the Government of India in 1983. The reports though submitted in 1985 and published in 1986 were made public only in 1987. It is sad to note that these reports have received very little attention of the concerned authorities.

Of course, the recommendations of the Commission on School Teachers regarding the pay scales have led to agitations by the teachers. Mention may be made of the two important observations made by the Commission on Teachers. The Commissions on School Teachers concludes Chapter II with these words, 'Status, by reason of a title or position will become increasingly difficult to come by, we feel. Status, in other words, will have to be earned by the teacher as any other professional worker....So must the new teacher earn status through achievement.' The other Commission concluded Chapter II by stating. 'The National Commission on Teachers in Higher Education would therefore make a fervent plea on the one hand to the Government to appreciate how potent the teacher is in engineering social change and hence to provide him status, encouragement and resources for the purpose and on the other to the teachers to open their minds and hearts to the new possibilities and to discharge their responsibilities with an urgent sense of social purpose.'

The political scenario has greatly affected the implementation of the NPE.

In the November 1989 Lok Sabha poll, Shri Rajiv's Congress Party lost and in December, the Janata Dal Government was formed with Shri V.P. Singh as Prime Minister. The BJP and the Left Parties decided to give outside support to Janata/NF Government.

In pursuance of its election manifesto, the National Front Government appointed on May 7, 1990, a Committee with Acharya Ramamurti[27] as its Chairman, to review the National Policy on Education (NPE), 1986. The Committee submitted its report to the Minister of State in the Ministry of Human Resource Development on December 26, 1990. The report was tabled in Parliament on January 9, 1991. During this period political changes of far reaching consequences took place. Shri V.P. Singh's Government was voted out on November 7, 1990 and Shri Chandra Shekhar became Prime Minister on November 10. Shri Chandra Shekhar's Government lasted for a very brief period between November 10, 1990 to March 6, 1991. Thereafter he worked as a caretaker Prime Minister till June 20. Shri P.V. Narasimha Rao assumed office of the Prime Minister of India on June 21, 1991, after the victory of his party at the polls. It was, therefore, natural that under the changed situation, the Ramamurti Report could not receive government patronage.

The recommendations of the Ramamurti Review Committee Report were examined by the Janardhana Committee appointed by the Central Advisory Board of Education in July 1991. The Janardhana Committee[28] submitted its recommendations in January 1992. The CABE considered the Janardhana Committee Report in the first week of May 1992 and finalised the revised NPE.

The Revised NPE[29] was presented in both Houses of

Parliament on May 7, 1992 by the Human Resource Development Minister Shri Arjun Singh. Apart from tabling the Revised NPE, Shri Singh also presented the Report of the Janardhana Committee (Central Advisory Board of Education's Committee). In his statement[30], the Minister said the NPE, 1986 has stood the test of time and enunciated a comprehensive framework to guide the development of education. He further observed that while that framework continues to be relevant, the development during the last few years and the experience in implementation of the policy have necessitated certain modifications.

In the field of higher education also, a number of committees have made recommendations for carrying out the directions cotained in the NPE.

A comprehensive list of Committees and Commissions appointed on education since 1947 is given in the appendix.

Notes

1. Sri Aurobindo International Institute of Educational Research, *The Good Teacher and the Pupil,* Auroville, 1988.
2. *Oriental Annual* (1836), pp. 31-32, quoted in the *Report of the University Education Commission* 1948-49, Ministry of Education, Government of India, New Delhi, 1950.
3. F.W. Thomas, *History and Prospects of British Education in India*, George Bell & Sons, Cambridge, 1891.
4. A.H. Howell, *Education in British India*, Calcutta, Government Printing, 1872.
5. Macaulay's Minute on Education, 1835.
6. M.K. Gandhi, *To Students*, Navajivan Trust, Ahmedabad.
7. M.K. Gandhi, *Basic Education,* Navajivan Trust, Ahmedabad.
8. Report of the *Zakir Hussain Committee and the Detailed Syllabus*, Hindustani Talimi Sangh, Wardha, 1938.
9. *Report of the University Education Commission*, Dec. 1948-August 1949, Volume I, Manager of Publications, Delhi, 1949.
10. Report of the Secondary Education Commission (October 1952-June 1953), Ministry of Education, New Delhi, 1953.
11. *Report of the Education Commission,* 1964-66, Ministry of Education, Government of India, 1966.
12. *Resolution on the National Policy on Education,* Ministry of Education, 1968.
13 Committee on the ten plus two plus three, *Ministry of Education,* New Delhi, 1973.
14. NCERT, *The Curriculum for the Ten Year School: A Frame Work.*, 1973
15. *Report of the Review Committee of Curriculum for the Year School,* Ministry of Education and Social Welfare, 1977.
16. *National Review Committee on Higher Secondary Education and Its Vocationalisation,* Ministry of Education, 1978.
17. *Draft National Policy on Education*, Ministry of Education, 1979.
18. NCERT, New Delhi, 1986.
19. Ministry of Human Resource Development, Department of Education, New Delhi, 1985.
20. Ministry of Human Resource Development, Department of Education, New Delhi, 1986.
21. Ministry of Human Resource Development, 1986.

22. NCERT, *Guidelines and Syllabi for Upper Primary Stage: Classes VI-VII.*, NCERT. N. Delhi, 1988.
23. *Guidelines and Syllabi for Secondary Stage : Classes IX and X.* NCERT, New Delhi, 1988 at New Delhi on August 1 and 2, 1986.
24. NCERT, *National Curriculum for Elementary and Secondary Education : A Framwork, Revised version,* NCERT, 1998.
25. Controller of Publications, *National Commission on Teachers I* (School Teachers), Delhi, 1986
26. Controller of Publications, *National Commission on Teachers II* (Higher Education), Delhi, 1986.
27. Committee for Review of National Policy on Education, 1986, *Towards an Enlightened and Humane Society,* Ministry of Human Resource Development, New Delhi, December, 1990.
28. Ministry of Human Resouce Development, *Report of the CABE Committee on Policy,* Government of India, Department of Education, New Delhi, January 1992.
29. *National Policy on Education (NPE), 1986 : Revised Policy Formulation,* Minister of Human Resource Development, 1992.
30. *The Hindustan Times* and *Times of India*, May 8, 1992.

2
Revised National Policy on Education

With a view to have a clear perception of the revised policy 1992, it will be quite in the fitness of things if broad outlines of both policies i.e. 1986 and 1992 are given. The following table in a nutshell provides the changes incorporated in the two policies. It is observed that only two paragraphs are added and thirty four paragraphs are modified

Modifications at a Glance

Part	*Title*	*Total No. of Paragraphs*	*Paragraphs Modified*
I	Introductory	15	No Change
II	The Essence and Role of Education	4	No Change
III	National System of Education	13	3, 12,
IV	Education for Equality	14	4, 5 (vii), 6 (i), 11, 12, 13, 14 New Para
V	Reorganisation of Education at Different Stages	41	5, 7, 8, 9, 11, 12, 13, 15, 16, 17, 23, 33, 35, 36, 37, 41,
VI	Technical and Management Education	20	12, 19
VII	Making the System Work	3	No Change
VIII	Reorienting the Content and Process of Education	25	16, 17, 20, 21, 25
IX	The Teacher	6	No Change
X	The Management of Education	10	New Para
XI	Resources and Review	5	4
XII	The Future	2	No Change
Total		158	

Text of the Policy

(The modified paragraphs are given in italics)

Part I
INTRODUCTION

1.1 Education has continued to evolve, diversify and extend its reach and coverage since the dawn of human history. Every country develops its system of education to express and promote its unique socio-cultural identity and also to meet the challenges of the times. There are moments in history when a new direction has to be given to an age-old process. That moment is today.

1.2 The country has reached a stage in its economic and technical development when a major effort must be made to derive the maximum benefit from the assets already created and to ensure that the fruits of change reach all sections. Education is the highway to that goal.

1.3 With this aim in view, the Government of India announced in January 1985 that a new Education Policy would be formulated for the country. A comprehensive appraisal of the existing educational scene was made, followed by a countrywide debate. The views and suggestions received from different quarters were carefully studied.

The 1968 Education Policy and After

1.4 The National Policy of 1968 marked a significant step in the history of education in post-Independence India. It aimed to promote national progress, a sense of common citizenship and culture, and to strengthen national integration. It laid stress on the need for a radical reconstruction of the educational system, to improve its quality at all stages, and gave much greater attention to science and technology, the cultivation of moral values and a closer relation between education and the life of the people.

1.5 Since the adoption of the 1968 Policy, there has been considerable expansion in educational facilities all over the country at all levels. More than 90% of the country's rural habitations now have schooling facilities within a radius of one kilometre. There has been sizeable augmentation of facilities at other stages also.

1.6 Perhaps the most notable development has been the acceptance of a common structure of education throughout the country and the introduction of the 10+2+3 systems by most States. In the school curricula, in addition to laying down a common scheme of studies for boys and girls, science and mathematics were incorporated as compulsory subjects and work experience assigned a place of importance.

1.7 A beginning was also made in restructuring of courses at the undergraduate level. Centres of Advanced Studies were set up for post-graduate education and research, and we have been able to meet our requirements of educated manpower.

1.8 While these achievements are impressive by themselves, the general formulations incorporated in the 1968 Policy did not, however, get translated into a detailed strategy of implementation, accompanied by the assignment of specific responsibilities and financial and organisational support. As a result, problems of access, quality, quantity, utility and financial outlay, accumulated over the years, have now assumed such massive proportions that they must be tackled with the utmost urgency.

1.9 Education in India stands at the cross roads today. Neither normal linear expansion nor the existing pace and nature of improvement can meet the needs of the situation.

1.10 In the Indian way of thinking, a human being is a positive asset and a precious national resource which needs to be cherished, nurtured and developed with tenderness and care, coupled with dynamism. Each individual's growth presents a different range of problems and requirements, at every stage–from the womb to the tomb. The catalytic action of education in this complex and dynamic growth process needs to be planned meticulously and executed with great sensitivity.

1.11 India's political and social life is passing through a phase which poses the danger of erosion to long-accepted values. The goals of secularism, socialism, democracy and professional ethics are coming under increasing strain.

1.12 The rural areas, with poor infrastructure and social services, will not get the benefit of trained and educated youth, unless rural-urban disparities are reduced and determined measures are taken to promote diversification and dispersal of employment opportunities.

1.13 The growth of our population needs to be brought down significantly over the coming decades. The largest single factor that could help achieve this is the spread of literacy and education among women.

1.14 Life in the coming decades is likely to bring new tensions together with unprecedented opportunities. To enable the people to benefit in the new environment will require new designs of human resource development. The coming generations should have the ability to internalise new ideas constantly and creatively. They have to be imbued with a strong commitment to humane values and to social justice. All this implies better education.

1.15 Besides, a variety of new challenges and social needs make it imperative for the Government to formulate and implement a new Education Policy for the country. Nothing short of this will meet the situation.

Part II
THE ESSENCE AND ROLE OF EDUCATION

2.1 In our national perception education is essentially for all.

This is fundamental to our all-round development, material and spiritual.

2.2 Education has an acculturating role. It refines sensitivities and perceptions that contribute to national cohesion, a scientific temper and independence of mind and spirit–thus furthering the goals of socialism, secularism and democracy enshrined in our Constitution.

2.3 Education develops manpower for different levels of the economy. It is also the substrate on which research and development flourish, being the ultimate guarantee of national self-reliance.

2.4 In sum, education is a unique investment in the present and the future. This cardinal principle is the key to the National Policy on Education.

Part III
NATIONAL SYSTEM OF EDUCATION

3.1 The Constitution embodies the principles on which the National System of Education is conceived of.

3.2 The concept of a National System of Education implies that, up to a given level, all students, irrespective of caste, creed, location or sex, have access to education of a comparable quality. To achieve this, the Government will initiate appropriately funded programmes. Effective measures will be taken in the direction of the Common School System recommended in the 1968 Policy.

3.3 ***(Revised Para)*** *The National System of Education envisages a common educational structure. The 10+2+3 structure has now been accepted in all parts of the country. Regarding the further break-up of the first 10 years efforts will be made to move towards an elementary system comprising 5 years of primary education and 3 years of upper primary, followed by 2 years of High School. Efforts will also be made to have the +2 stage accepted as a part of school education throughout the country.*

3.3 (NPE 1986) The National System of Education envisages a common educational structure. The 10+2+3 structure has now been accepted in all parts of the country. Regarding the further break-up of the first 10 years efforts will be made to move towards an elementary system comprising 5 years of primary education and 3 years of upper primary, followed by 2 years of High School.

3.4 The National System of Education will be based on a national curricular framework which contains a common core along with other components that are flexible. The common core will include the history of India's freedom movement, the constitutional obligations and other content essential to nurture national identity. These elements will cut across subject areas and will be designed to promote values such as India's common cultural heritage, egalitarianism, democracy and secularism, equality of the sexes, protection of the environment, removal of social barriers, observance of the small family norm and inculcation of the scientific temper. All educational programmes will be carried on in strict conformity with secular values.

3.5 India has always worked for peace and understanding between nations, treating the whole world as one family. True to this hoary tradition, education has to strengthen this world view and motivate the younger generations for international cooperation and peaceful co-existence. This aspect cannot be neglected.

3.6 To promote equality, it will be necessary to provide for equal opportunity to all not only in access, but also in the conditions for success. Besides, awareness of the inherent equality of all will be created through the core curriculum. The purpose is to remove prejudices and complexes transmitted through the social environment and the accident of birth.

3.7 Minimum levels of learning will be laid down for each stage of education. Steps will also be taken to foster among students an understanding of the diverse cultural and social systems of the people living in different parts of the country. Besides the promotion of the link language, programmes will also be launched to increase substantially the translation of books from one language to another and to publish multilingual dictionaries and glossaries. The young will be encouraged to undertake the rediscovery of India, each in his own image and perception.

3.8 In higher education in general, and technical education in particular, steps will be taken to facilitate inter-regional mobility by providing equal access to every Indian of requisite merit, regardless of his origin. The universal character of universities and other institutions of higher education is to be underscored.

3.9 In the areas of research and development, and education in science and technology, special measures will be taken to establish network arrangements between different institutions in the country to pool their resources and participate in projects of national importance.

3.10 The Nation as a whole will assume the responsibility of providing resource support for implementing programmes of educational transformation, reducing disparities, universalisation of elementary education, adult literacy, scientific and technological research, etc.

3.11 Life-long education is a cherished goal of the educational process. This presupposes universal literacy. Opportunities will be provided to the youth, housewives, agricultural and industrial workers and professionals to continue for education of their choice, at the pace suited to them. The future thrust will be in the direction of open and distance learning.

3.12 ***(Revised Para)*** *The institutions which will be strengthened to play an important role in giving shape to the National System of Education are the University Grants Commission, the All India Council of Technical Education, the Indian Council of Agricultural Research and the Indian Medical Council. Integrated planning will be instituted among all these bodies so as to establish functional linkages and reinforce programmes of research and post graduate education. These, together with the National Council of Education*

Research and Training, the National Institute of Educational Planning and Administration, the National Council of Teacher Education and the National Institute of Adult Education will be involved in implementing the Education Policy.

3.12 (NPE 1986) The institutions which will be strengthened to play an important role in giving shape to the National System of Education are the University Grants Commission, the All India Council of Technical Education, the Indian Council of Agricultural Research and the Indian Medical Council. Integrated planning will be instituted among all these bodies so as to establish functional linkages and reinforce programmes of research and post graduate education. These, together with the National Council of Education Research and Training, the National Institute of Educational Planning and Administration and the International Institute of Science and Technology Education will be involved in implementing the Education Policy.

A Meaningful Partnership

3.13 The Constitutional Amendment of 1976, which includes Education in the Concurrent List, was a far-reaching step whose implications—substantive financial and administrative require a new sharing of responsibility between the Union Government and the States in respect of this vital area of national life. While the role and responsibility of the States in regard to education will remain essentially unchanged, the Union Government would accept a larger responsibility to reinforce the national and integrative character of education, to maintain quality and standards (including those of the teaching profession at all levels), to study and monitor the educational requirements of the country as a whole in regard to manpower for development, to cater to the needs of research and advanced study, to look after the international aspects of education, culture and Human Resource Development and, in general, to promote excellence at all levels of the educational pyramid throughout the country. Concurrency signifies a partnership which is at once meaningful and challenging; the National Policy will be oriented towards giving effect to it in letter and spirit.

Part IV
EDUCATION FOR EQUALITY

Disparities

4.1 The new Education Policy will lay special emphasis on the removal of disparities and to equalise educational opportunity by attending to the specific needs of those who have been denied equality so far.

Education for Women's Equality

4.2 Education will be used as an agent of basic change in the status of woman. In order to neutralise the accumulated distortions of the past, there will be a well conceived edge in favour of women. The National Education System will play a positive, interventionist role in the empowerment of women. It will foster the development of new values through redesigned, curricula, textbooks, the training and orientation of teachers, decision-makers and administrators, and the active involvement of educational institutions. This will be an act of faith and social engineering. Women's studies will be promoted as a part of various courses and educational institutions encouraged to take up active programmes to further women's development.

4.3 The removal of women's illiteracy and obstacles inhibiting their access to, and retention in, elementary education will receive overriding priority, through provision of special support services, setting of time targets, and effective monitoring. Major emphasis will be laid on women's participation in vocational, technical and professional education at different levels. The policy of non-discrimination will be pursued vigorously to eliminate sex stereotyping in vocational and professional courses and to promote women's participation in non-traditional occupations, as well as in existing and emergent technologies.

The Education of Scheduled Castes

4.4 The central focus in the SCs' educational development is their equalisation with the non-SC population at all stages and levels of education, in all areas and in all the four dimensions–rural male, rural female, urban male and urban female.

4.5 The measures contemplated for this purpose include:

(i) Incentives to indigent families to send their children to school regularly till they reach the age of 14;

(ii) Pre-matric Scholarship scheme for children of families engaged in occupations such as scavenging, flaying and tinning to be made applicable from Class I onwards. All children of such families, regardless of incomes, will be covered by this scheme and time-bound programmes targetted on them will be undertaken;

(iii) Constant micro-planning and verification to ensure that the enrolment, retention and successful completion of courses by SC students do not fall at any stage, and provision of remedial courses to improve their prospects for further education and in employment;

(iv) The recruitment of teachers from Scheduled Castes;

(v) Provision of facilities for SC students in hostels at district headquarters, according to a phased programme;

(vi) Location of school buildings, Balwadis and Adult Education Centres in such a way as to facilitate full participation of the Scheduled Castes;

4.5 ***(Revised Para vii)*** *The utilisation of Jawahar Rozgar Yojna resources so as to make substantial educational facilities available to the Scheduled Castes; and*

4.5 [NPE 1986 Para (vii)] The utilisation of N.R.E.P. and R.L.E.G.P. resources so as to make substantial educational facilities available to the Scheduled Castes; and

(viii) Constant innovation in finding new methods to increase the participation of the Scheduled Castes in the educational process.

The Education of Scheduled Tribes

4.6 The following measures will be taken urgently to bring the Scheduled Tribes on par with others:

4.6 ***[Revised Para (i)]*** *Priority will be accorded to opening primary schools in tribal areas. The construction of school buildings will be undertaken in these areas on a priority basis under the normal funds for education, as well as under the Jawahar Rozgar Yojna, Tribal Welfare schemes, etc.*

4.6 [NPE 1986 Para (i)] Priority will be accorded to opening primary schools in tribal areas. The construction of school buildings will be undertaken in these areas on a priority basis under the normal funds for education, as well as under the N.R.E.P., R.L.E.G.P, Tribal Welfare schemes, etc.

(ii) The socio-cultural milieu of the ST has its distinctive characteristics including, in many cases, their own spoken languages. This underlines the need to develop the curricula and devise institutional materials in tribal languages at the initial stages, with arrangements for switching over to the regional languages.

(iii) Educated and promising Scheduled Tribe youths will be encouraged and trained to take up teaching in tribal areas.

(iv) Residential schools, including Ashram Schools, will be established on a large scale.

(v) Incentive schemes will be formulated for the Scheduled Tribes, keeping in view their special needs and life styles. Scholarships for higher education will emphasise technical, professional and para-professional courses. Special remedial courses and other programmes to remove psycho-social impediments will be provided to improve their performance in various courses.

(vi) Anganwadis, Non-formal and Adult Education Centres will be opened on a priority basis in areas predominantly inhabited by the Scheduled Tribes.

(vii) The curriculum at all stages of education will be designed to create an awareness of the rich cultural identity of the tribal people as also of their enormous creative talent.

Other Educationally Backward Sections and Areas

4.7 Suitable incentives will be provided to all educationally backward sections of society, particularly in the rural areas. Hill and desert districts, remote and inaccessible areas and islands will be provided adequate institutional infrastructure.

Minorities

4.8 Some minority groups are educationally deprived or backward. Greater attention will be paid to the education of these groups in the interests of equality and social justice. This will naturally include the Constitutional guarantees given to them to establish and administer their own educational institutions, and protection to their languages and culture. Simultaneously objectivity will be reflected in the preparation of textbooks, and in all school activities, and all possible measures will be taken to promote an integration based on appreciation of common national goals and ideals, in conformity with the core curriculum.

The Handicapped

4.9 The objective should be to integrate the physically and mentally handicapped with the general community as equal partners, to prepare them for normal growth and to enable them to face life with courage and confidence. The following measures will be taken in this regard:

(i) Wherever it is feasible, the education of children with major handicaps and other mild handicaps will be common with that of others;

(ii) Special schools with hostels will be provided, as far as possible at district headquarters, for the severely handicapped children;

(iii) Adequate arrangements will be made to give vocational training to the disabled;

(iv) Teacher's training programmes will be reoriented, in particular for teachers of primary classes, to deal with the special difficulties of the handicapped children; and

(v) Voluntary effort for the education of the disabled, will be encouraged in every possible manner.

Adult Education

4.10 Our ancient scriptures define education as that which liberates, i.e., provides the instruments for liberation from ignorance and oppression. In the modern world, it would naturally include the ability to read and write, since that is the main instrument of learning. Hence the crucial importance of adult education, including adult literacy.

4.11 ***(Revised Para)*** *The whole nation has pledged itself, through* *the National Literacy Mission, to the eradication of illiteracy, particularly in the 15-35 age group through various means, with special emphasis on total literacy campaigns. The Central and State Governments, political parties and their mass organisations, the mass media and educational institutions, teachers, students, youth, voluntary agencies, social activist groups, and employers, must reinforce their commitment to mass literacy campaigns, which include literacy and functional knowledge and skills, and awareness among learners about the socio-economic reality and the possibility to change it.*

4.11 (NPE, 1986) The critical development issue today is the continuous upgradation of skills so as to produce manpower resources of the kind and the number required by the society. Since participation by beneficiaries in the developmental programmes is of crucial importance, systematic programmes of adult education linked with national goals such as alleviation of poverty, national integration, environmental conservation, energisation of the cultural creativity of the people, observance of small family norm, promotion of women's equality, etc. will be organised and the existing programmes reviewed and strengthened.

4.12 ***(Revised Para)*** *Since involvement of the participants of the literacy campaigns in the development programmes is of crucial importance, the National Literacy Mission will be geared to the national goals such as alleviation of poverty, national integration, environmental conservation, observance of the small family norm, promotion of women's equality, universalisation of primary education, basic health-care, etc. It will also facilitate energisation of the cultural creativity of the people and their active participation in development processes.*

4.12 (NPE, 1986) The whole Nation must pledge itself to the eradication of illiteracy, particularly in the 15-35 age group. The Central and State Governments, political parties and their mass organisations, the mass media and educational institutions must commit themselves to mass literacy programmes of diverse nature. It will also have to involve on a large scale teachers, students, youth voluntary agencies, employers, etc. Concerted efforts will be made to harness various research agencies to improve the pedagogical aspects of adult literacy. The mass literacy programme would include, in addition to literacy, functional knowledge and skills, and also awareness among learners about the socio-economic reality and the possibility to change it.

4.13 ***(Revised Para)*** *Comprehensive programmes of post-literacy and continuing education will be provided for neo-literates and youth who have received primary education with a view to enabling them to retain and upgrade their literacy skills, and to harness it for the improvement of their living and working condition. These programmes would include:*

(a) establishment of continuing education centres of diverse kind to enable adults to continue their education of their choice;

(b) workers' education through the employers, trade unions and government;

(c) wider promotion of books, libraries and reading rooms;

(d) use of radio, TV and films — as mass as well as group learning media;

(e) creation of learners' groups and organisations; and

(f) programmes of distance learning.

4.13 (NPE, 1986) A vast programme of adult and continuing education will be implemented through various ways and channels, including :

(a) establishment of centres in rural areas for continuing education;

(b) workers' education through the employers, trade unions and concerned agencies of government;

(c) post-secondary education institutions;

(d) wider promotion of books, libraries and reading rooms;

(e) use of radio, TV and films, as mass and group learning media;

(f) creation of learners' groups and organisations;

(g) programmes of distance learning;

(h) organising assistance in self-learning; and

(i) organising need and interest based vocational training programmes.

4.14 ***(New Para)*** *A critical development issue today is the continuous upgradation of skills so as to produce manpower resources of the kind and the number required by the society. Special emphasis will, therefore, be laid on organisation of employment/self-employment oriented, and need and interest based vocational and skill training programmes.*

Part V
REORGANISATION OF EDUCATION AT DIFFERENT STAGES

Early Childhood Care and Education

5.1 The National Policy on Children specially emphasises investment in the development of the young child, particularly children from sections of the population in which first generation learners predominate.

5.2 Recognising the holistic nature of child development, viz., nutrition, health and social, mental, physical, moral and emotional development. Early Childhood Care and Education (ECCE) will receive high priority and be suitably integrated with the Integrated Child Development Services programme, wherever possible. Day-care centres will be provided as a support service for universalisation of primary education, to enable girls engaged in taking care of siblings to attend school and as a support service for working women belonging to poorer sections.

5.3 Programmes of ECCE will be child-oriented, focused around play, and the individuality of the child. Formal methods and the introduction of the 3 R's will be discouraged at this stage. The local community will be fully involved in these programmes.

5.4 A full integration of child care and pre-primary education will be brought about, both as a feeder and a strengthening factor for primary education and for human resource development in general. In continuation of this stage, the School Health Programme will be strengthened.

Elementary Education

5.5 ***(Revised Para)*** *The new thrust in elementary education will emphasise three aspects : (i) universal access and enrolment, (ii) universal retention of children up to 14 years of age; and (iii) a substantial improvement in the quality of education to enable all children to achieve essential levels of learning.*

5.5 (NPE, 1986) The new thrust in elementary education will emphasise two aspects: (i) universal enrolment and universal retention of children up to 14 years of age, and (ii) a substantial improvement in the quality of education.

Child-Centred Approach

5.6 A warm, welcoming and encouraging, approach, in which all concerned share a solicitude for the needs of the child, is the best motivation for the child to attend school and learn. A child-centred and activity-based process of learning should be adopted at the primary stage. First generation learners should be allowed to set their own pace and be given supplementary remedial instruction. As the child grows, the component of cognitive learning will be increased and skills organised through practice. The policy of non-detention at the primary stage will be retained, making evaluation as disaggregated as feasible. Corporal punishment will be firmly excluded from the educational system and school timings as well as vacations adjusted to the convenience of children.

5.7 ***(Revised Para)*** *Provision will be made of essential facilities in primary schools. The scope of Operation Blackboard will be enlarged to provide three reasonably large rooms that are usable in all weather, and blackboards, maps, charts, toys, other necessary learning aids and school library. At least three teachers should work in every school, the number increasing, as early as possible, to one teacher per class. At least 50 per cent of teachers recruited in future should be women. The Operation Blackboard will be extended to upper primary stage also. Construction of school buildings will be a priority charge on JRY funds.*

5.7 (NPE, 1986) Provision will be made of essential facilities in primary schools, including at least two reasonably large rooms that are usable in all weather, and the necessary toys, blackboards, maps, charts, and other learning material. At least two teachers, one of whom a woman, should work in every school, the number increasing as early as possible to one teacher per class. A phased drive, symbolically called *Operation Blackboard* will be undertaken with immediate effect to improve Primary schools all over the country. Government, local bodies, voluntary agencies and individuals will be fully involved. Construction of school buildings will be first charge on NREP and RLEGP funds.

5.8 ***(Revised Para)*** *The Non-formal Education Programme, meant for school dropouts, for childrem from habitations without schools, working children and girls who cannot attend whole-day schools, will be strengthened and enlarged.*

5.8 (NPE, 1986) A large and systematic programme of non-formal education will be launched for school drop-outs, for children from habitations without schools, working children and girls who cannot attend whole-day schools.

5.9 ***(Revised Para)*** *Modern technological aids will be used to improve the learning environment of NFE Centres. Talented and dedicated young men and women from the local community will be chosen to serve as instructors, and particular attention paid to their training. All necessary measures will be taken to ensure that the quality of non-formal education is comparable with the formal education. Steps will be taken to facilitate lateral entry into the formal system of children passing out of the non-formal system.*

5.9 (NPE, 1986) Modern technological aids will be used to improve the learning environment of NFE centres. Talented and dedicated young men and women from the local community will be chosen to serve as instructors, and particular attention paid to their training. Steps will be taken to facilitate their entry into the formal system in deserving cases. All necessary measures will be taken to ensure that the quality of non-formal education is comparable with formal education.

5.10 Effective steps will be taken to provide a framework for the curriculum on the lines of the national core curriculum, but based on the needs of the learners and related to the local environment. Learning material of high quality will be developed and provided free of charge to all pupils. NFE programmes will provide participatory learning environment, and activities such as games and sports, cultural programmes, excursions, etc.

5.11 ***(Revised Para)*** *The Government will take over-all responsibility for this vital sector. Voluntary agencies and Panchayati Raj institutions will take much of the responsibility of running NFE programmes. The provision of funds to these agencies will be adequate and timely.*

5.11 (NPE, 1986) Much of the work running of NFE centres will be done through voluntary agencies and panchayati raj institutions. The provision of funds to the agencies will be adequate and timely. The Government will take over-all responsibility for this vital sector.

A Resolve

5.12 ***(Revised Para)*** *The New Education Policy will give the* *highest priority to solving the problem of children dropping out of school and will adopt an array of meticulously formulated strategies based on micro planning, and applied at the grass roots level all over the country, to ensure children's retention at school. This effort will be fully coordinated with the network of non-formal education. It shall be ensured that free and compulsory education of satisfactory quality is provided to all children up to 14 years of age before we enter the twenty-first century. A national mission will be launched for the achievement of this goal.*

5.12 (NPE, 1986) The New Education Policy will give the highest priority to solving the problem of children dropping out of school and will adopt an array of meticulously formulated strategies based on micro planning, and applied at the grass roots level all over the country, to ensure children's retention at school. This effort will be fully coordinated with the network of non-formal education. It shall be ensured that all children who attain the age of about 11 years by 1990 will have had five years of schooling, or its equivalent through the non-formal stream. Likewise, by 1995 all children will be provided free and compulsory education upto 14 years of age.

Secondary Education

5.13 ***(Revised Para)*** *Secondary education begins to expose students to the differentiated roles of science, the humanities and social sciences. This is also an appropriate stage to provide children with a sense of history and national perspective and give them opportunities to understand their constitutional duties and rights as citizens. Access to secondary education will be widened with emphasis on enrolment of girls, SCs and STs, particularly in science, commerce and vocational streams. Boards of Secondary Education will be reorganised and vested with autonomy so that their ability to improve the quality of secondary education is enhanced. Effort will be made to provide computer literacy in as many secondary level institutions as possible so that the children are equipped with necessary computer skills to be effective in the emerging technological world. A proper understanding of the work ethos and of the values of a humane and composite culture will be brought about through appropriately formulated curricula. Vocationalisation through specialised institutions or through the refashioning of secondary education will, at this stage, provide valuable manpower for economic growth.*

5.13 (NPE, 1986) Secondary education begins to expose students to the differentiated roles of science, the humanities and social sciences. This is also an appropriate stage to provide children with a sense of history and national perspective and give them opportunities to understand their constitutional duties and work ethos and of the values of a humane and composite culture will be brought about through appropriately formulated curricula. Vocationalisation through specialised institutions or through the refashioning of secondary education can, at this stage, provide valuable manpower for economic growth. Access to secondary education will be widened to cover areas unserved by it at present. In other areas the main emphasis will be on consolidation.

Pace-Setting Schools

5.14 It is universally accepted that children with special talent or aptitude should be provided opportunities to proceed at a faster pace, by making good quality education available to them, irrespective of their capacity to pay for it.

5.15 ***(Revised Para)*** *Pace-setting residential schools, Navodaya Vidyalayas, intended to serve this purpose have been established in most parts of the country on a given pattern, but with full scope for innovation and experimentation. Their broad aim will continue to be to serve the objective of excellence coupled with equity and social justice (with reservation for the rural areas, SCs and STs), to promote national integration by providing opportunities to talented children from different parts of the country, to live and learn together, to develop their full potential, and, most importantly, to become catalysts of a nationwide programme of school improvement.*

5.15 (NPE, 1986) Pace-setting schools intended to serve this purpose will be established in various parts of the country on a given pattern, what with full scope for innovation and experimentation. Their broad aims will be to serve the objective of excellence, coupled with equity and social justice (with reservation for SCs and STs), to promote national integration by providing opportunities to talented children largely rural, from different parts of the country to live and learn together, to develop their full potential, and, most importantly, to become catalysts of a nationwide programme of school improvement. The schools will be residential and free of charge.

5.16 ***(Revised Para)*** *The introduction of systematic, well planned and rigorously implemented programmes of vocational education is crucial in the proposed educational reorganisation. These elements are meant to develop a healthy attitude amongst students towards work and life, to enhance individual employability, to reduce the mismatch between the demand and supply of skilled manpower, and to provide an alternative for those intending to pursue higher education without particular interest or purpose. Efforts will be made to provide children at the higher secondary level with generic vocational courses which cut across several occupational fields and which are not occupation specific.*

5.16 (NPE, 1986) The introduction of systematic, well-planned and rigorously implemented programmes of vocational education is crucial in the proposed educational reorganisation. These elements are meant to enhance individual employability, to reduce the mismatch between the demand and supply of skilled manpower, and to provide an alternative for those pursuing higher education without particular interest or purpose.

5.17 ***(Revised Para)*** *Vocational Education will also be a distinct* *stream, intended to prepare students for identified occupations spanning several areas of activity. These courses will ordinarily be provided after the secondary stage, but keeping the scheme flexible, they may also be made available after Class VIII.*

5.17 (NPE, 1986) Vocational education will be a distinct stream, intended to prepare students for identified occupations spanning several areas of activity. These courses will ordinarily be provided after the secondary stage, but keeping the scheme flexible, they may also be made available after Class VIII. In the interests of integrating vocational education better with their facilities the Industrial Training Institutes will also conform to the larger vocational pattern.

5.18 Health planning and health service management should optimally interlock with the education and training of appropriate categories of health manpower through health-related vocational courses. Health education at the primary and middle levels will ensure the commitment of the individual, to family and community health, and lead to health-related vocational courses at the +2 stage of higher secondary education. Efforts will be made to devise similar vocational courses based on Agriculture, Ma.keting, Social Services, etc. An emphasis in vocational education will also be on development of attitudes, knowledge, and skills for entrepreneurship and self-employment.

5.19 The establishment of vocational courses or institutions will be the responsibility of the Government as well as employers in the public and private sectors; the Government will, however, take special steps to cater to the needs of women, rural and tribal students and the deprived sections of society. Appropriate programmes will also be started for the hanidcapped.

5.20 Graduates of vocational courses will be given opportunities, under predetermined conditions, for professional growth, career improvement and lateral entry into courses of general, technical and professional education through appropriate bridge courses.

5.21 Non-formal, flexible and need-based vocational programmes will also be made available to neoliterates, youth who have completed primary education, school dropouts, persons engaged in work and unemployed or partially employed persons. Special attention in this regard will be given to women.

5.22 Tertiary level courses will be organised for the young who graduate from the higher secondary courses of the academic stream and may also require vocational courses.

5.23 *(Revised Para) It is proposed that vocational courses cover 10 per cent of higher secondary students by 1995 and 25 per cent by 2000. Steps will be taken to see that a substantial majority of the products of vocational courses are employed or become self-employed. Review of the courses offered would be regularly undertaken. Government will also review its recruitment policy to encourage diversification at the secondary level.*

5.23 (NPE, 1986) It is proposed that vocational courses cover 10 per cent of higher secondary students by 1990 and 25 per cent by 1995. Steps will be taken to see that a substantial majority of the products of vocational courses are employed or become self-employed. Review of the courses offered would be regularly undertaken. Government will also review its recruitment policy to encourage diversification at the secondary level.

Higher Education

5.24 Higher education provides people with an opportunity to reflect on the critical social, economic, cultural, moral and spiritual issues facing humanity. It contributes to national development through dissemination of specialized knowledge and skills. It is therefore a crucial factor for survival. Being at the apex of the educational pyramid, it has also a key role in producing teachers for the education system.

5.25 In the context of the unprecedented explosion of knowledge, higher education has to become dynamic as never before, constantly entering uncharted areas.

5..26 There are around 150 universities and about 5,000 colleges in India today. In view of the need to effect an all-round improvemnent in these institutions, it is proposed that, in the near future, the main emphasis will be on the consolidation of and expansion of facilities in existing institutions.

5.27 Urgent steps will be taken to protect the system from degradation.

5.28 In view of mixed experiences with the system of affiliation, autonomous colleges will be helped to develop in large numbers until the affiliating system is replaced by a freer and more creative association of universities with colleges. Similarly, the creation of autonomous departments, within universities on a selective basis will be encouraged. Autonomy and freedom will be accompanied by accountability.

5.29 Courses and programmes will be redesigned to meet the demands of specialisation better. Special emphasis will be laid on linguistic competence. There will be increasing flexibility in the combination of courses.

5.30 State level planning and coordination of higher education will be done through Councils of Higher Education. The UGC and these Councils will develop coordinative methods to keep a watch on standards.

5.31 Provision will be made for minimum facilities and admission will be regulated according to capacity. A major effort will be directed towards the transformation of teaching methods. Audio-visual aids and electronic equipment will be introduced; development of science and technology, curricula and material, research and teacher orientation will receive attention. This will require preparation of teachers at the beginning of the service as well as continuing education thereafter. Teacher's performance will be assessed systematically. All posts will be filled on the basis of merit.

5.32 Research in the universities will be provided enhanced support and steps will be taken to ensure its high quality. Suitable mechanisms will be set up by the UGC for coordinating research in the universities, particularly in thrust areas of science and technology, with research undertaken by other agencies. An effort will be made to encourage the setting up of national research facilities within the university system, with proper forms of autonomous management.

5.33 ***(Revised Para)*** *Research in Indology, the humanities and social sciences will receive adequate support. To fulfil the need for the synthesis of knowledge, inter-disciplinary research will be encouraged. Efforts will be made to delve into India's ancient fund of knowledge and to relate it to contemporary reality. This effort will imply the development of facilities for the intensive study of Sanskrit and other Classical languages. An autonomous commission will be established to foster and improve teaching, study and research in Sanskrit and other Classical languages.*

5.33 **(NPE, 1986)** Research in Indology, the humanities and social sciences will receive adequate support. To fulfil the need for the synthesis of knowledge, inter-disciplinary research will be encouraged. Efforts will be made to delve into India's ancient fund of knowledge and to relate it to contemporary reality. This effort will imply the development facilities for the intensive study of Sanskrit and other Classical languages.

5.34 In the interest of greater coordination and consistency in policy, sharing of facilities and developing inter-disciplinary research, a national body covering higher education in general, agricultural, medical, technical, legal and other professional fields will be set up.

5.35 ***(Revised Para)*** *The open learning system has been initiated in order to augment opportunities for higher education, as an instrument of democratising education and to make it a lifelong process. The flexibility and innovativeness of the open learning system are particularly suited to the diverse requirements of the citizens of our country, including those who had joined the vocational stream.*

5.35 **(NPE, 1986)** The Open Univeristy system has been initiated in order to augment opportunities for higher education and as an instrument of democratising education.

5.36 ***(Revised Para)*** *The Indira Gandhi National Open University, established in 1985 in fulfilment of these objectives, will be strengthened. It would also provide support to establishment of open universities in the States.*

5.36 **(NPE, 1986)** The Indira Gandhi National Open University, established in 1985 in fulfilment of these objectives, will be strengthened.

5.37 ***(Revised Para)*** *The National Open School will be strengthened and open learning facilities extended in a phased manner at the secondary level in all parts of the country.*

5.37 **(NPE, 1986)** This powerful instrument will have to be developed with care and extended with caution.

De-linking Degrees from Jobs

5.38 A beginning will be made in de-linking degrees from jobs in selected areas.

5.39 The proposal cannot be applied to occupation–specific courses like Engineering, Medicine, Law, Teaching, etc. Similarly, the services of specialists with academic qualifications in the humanities, social sciences, sciences, etc. will continue to be required in various job positions.

5.40 The de-linking will be applied to services for which university degree need not be a necessary qualification. Its implementation will lead to a re-fashioning of job-specific courses and afford greater justice to those candidates who, despite being equipped for a given job, are unable to get it because of an unnecessary preference for graduate candidates.

5.41 (Revised Para) *Concomitant with de-linking an appropriate machinery, such as National Evaluation Organisation, will be established to conduct tests on a voluntary basis to determine the suitability of candidates for specific jobs, to pave the way for the emergence of norms of comparable competencies across the nation, and to bring about an over-all improvement in testing and measurement.*

5.41 (NPE, 1986) Concomitant with de-linking an appropriate machinery, such as a National Testing Service, will be established, in appropriate phases, to conduct tests on a voluntary basis to determine the suitability of candidates for specified jobs, and to pave the way for the emergence of norms of comparable competence across the nation.

Part VI
TECHNICAL AND MANAGEMENT EDUCATION

6.1 It is essential to look at technical and management education together, in view of their close relationship and complementary concerns. The reorganisation of Technical and Management Education should take into account the anticipated scenario by the turn of the century, with specific reference to the likely changes in the economy, social environment, production and management processes, the rapid expansion of knowledge and the great advances in science and technology.

6.2 The infrastructure and services sectors as well as the unorganised rural sector also need a greater introduction of improved technologies and a supply of technical and managerial manpower. This will be attended to by the Government.

6.3 In order to improve the situation regarding manpower information, the recently set up Technical Manpower Information System will be further developed and strengthened.

6.4 Continuing education, covering established as well as emerging technologies, will be promoted.

6.5 As computers have become important and ubiquitous tools, a minimal exposure to computers and a training in their use will form part of professional education. Programmes of computer literacy will be organised on a wide scale from the school stage.

6.6 In view of the present rigid entry requirements to formal courses restricting the access of a large segment of people to technical and managerial education, programmes through a distance learning process, including use of the mass media, will be offered. Technical and management education programmes, including polytechnics, will also be on a flexible modular pattern based on credits, with provision for multipoint entry. A strong guidance and counselling service will be provided.

6.7 In order to increase the relevance of management education, particularly in the non-corporate and under-managed sectors, the management education system will study and document the Indian-experience and create a body of knowledge and specific educational programmes suited to these sectors.

6.8 Appropriate formal and non-formal programmes of technical education relevant to their skills will be devised for the benefit of women, the economically and socially weaker sections, and the physically handicapped.

6.9 The emphasis on vocational education and its expansion will need a large number of teachers and professionals in vocational education, educational technology, curriculum development, etc. Programmes will be started to meet this demand.

6.10 To encourage students to consider 'self-employment' as a career option, training in entrepreneurship will be provided through modular or optional course, in degree or diploma programmes.

6.11 In order to meet the continuing needs of updating curriculum, renewal should systematically phase out obsolescence and introduce new technologies or disciplines.

6.12 *(Revised Para) Some polytechnics in the rural areas have started training weaker groups in those areas for productive occupations through a system of community polytechnics. The community polytechnic system will be appropriately strengthened to increase its quality and coverage.*

6.12 (NPE 1986) Some polytechnics in the rural areas have started training weaker groups in those areas for productive occupations through a system of community polytechnics. The community polytechnic system will be appraised and appropriately strengthened to increase its quality and coverage.

Innovation, Research and Development

6.13 Research as a means of renovation and renewal of educational processes will be undertaken by all higher technical institutions. It will primarily aim at producing quality manpower capable of taking up R & D functions. Research for development will focus on improving present technologies, developing new indigenous ones and enhancing production and productivity. A suitable system for watching and forecasting technology will be set up.

6.14 The scope for cooperation, collaboration and networking relationships between institutions at various levels and with the user systems will be utilised. Proper maintenance, and an attitude of innovation and improvement will be promoted systematically.

Promoting Efficiency and Effectiveness at all Levels

6.15 As technical and management education is expensive, the following major steps will be taken for cost-effectiveness and to promote excellence.

(i) High priority will be given to modernisation and removal of obsolescence. However, modernisation will be undertaken to enhance functional efficiency and not for its own sake or as a status symbol.

(ii) Institutions will be encouraged to generate resources using their capacities to provide services to the community and industry. They will be equipped with up-to-date learning resources, library and computer facilities.

(iii) Adequate hostel accommodation will be provided, specially for girls. Facilities for sports, creative work and cultural activities will be expanded.

(iv) More effective procedures will be adopted in the recruitment of staff. Career opportunities, service conditions, consultancy norms and other perquisites will be improved.

(v) Teachers will have multiple roles to perform: teaching, research and development of learning resource material, extension and administration or managing the institution. Initial and in-service training will be made mandatory for faculty members and adequate training reserves will be provided. Staff Development Programmes will be integrated at the State and coordinated at Regional and National levels.

(vi) The curricula of technical and management programmes will be targetted on current as well as the projected needs of industry or user systems. Active interaction between technical or management institutions and industry will be promoted in programme planning and implementation, exchange of personnel, training facilities and resources, research and consultancy and other areas of mutual interest.

(vii) Excellence in performance of institutions and individuals will be recognised and rewarded. The emergence of substandard institutions will be checked. A climate conducive to excellence will be promoted with full involvement of the faculty.

(viii) Select institutions will be awarded academic, administrative and financial autonomy of varying degrees, building in safeguards with respect to accountability.

(ix) Networking systems will have to be established between technical education and industry, R&D organisations, programmes of rural and community development and with sectors of education with complementary characteristics.

Management Function and Change

6.16 In view of the likely emergence of changes in management systems and the need to equip students with the ability to cope with them, effective mechanisms will be devised to understand the nature and direction of change per se and to develop the important skill of managing change.

6.17 In view of the integrated nature of task, the Ministry of Human Resource Development will coordinate the balanced development of engineering, vocational and management education as well as the education of technicians and craftsmen.

6.18 Professional societies will be encouraged and enabled to perform their due role in the advancement of technical and management education.

6.19 ***(Revised Para)*** *The All India Council for Technical Education, which has been given statutory status, will be responsible for planning, formulation and the maintenance of norms and standards, accreditation, funding of priority areas, monitoring and evaluation, maintaining parity of certification and awards and ensuring the coordinated and integrated development of technical and management education. Mandatory periodic evaluation will be carried out by a duly constituted Accreditation Board. The Council will be strengthened and it will function in a decentralised manner with greater involvement of State governments and technical institutions of good quality.*

6.19 (NPE, 1986) The All India Council for Technical Education will be vested with statutory authority for planning, formulation and the maintenance of norms and standards, accreditation, funding of priority areas, monitoring and evaluation, maintaining parity of certification and awards and ensuring the coordinated and integrated development of technical and management education. Mandatory periodic evaluation will be carried out by a duly constituted Accreditation Board.

6.20 In the interests of maintaining standards and for several other valid reasons, the commercialisation of technical and professional education will be curbed. An alternative system will be devised to involve private and voluntary effort in this sector of education, in conformity with accepted norms and goals.

Part VII
MAKING THE SYSTEM WORK

7.1 It is obvious that these and many other new tasks of education cannot be performed in a state of disorder. Education needs to be managed in an atmosphere of utmost intellectual rigour, seriousness of purpose and, at the same time, of freedom essential for innovation and creativity. While far-reaching changes will have to be incorporated in the quality and range of education, the process of introducing discipline into the system will have to be started, here and now, in what exists.

7.2 The country has placed a boundless trust in the educational system. The people have a right to expect concrete results. The first task is to make it work. *All teachers should teach and all students study.*

7.3 The strategy in this behalf will consist of :

(a) a better deal to teachers with greater accountability;

(b) provision of improved student's services and insistence on observance of acceptable norms of behaviour;

(c) provision of better facilities to institutions; and

(d) creation of a system of performance appraisals of institutions according to standards and norms set at the National or State levels.

Part VIII
REORIENTING THE CONTENT AND PROCESS OF EDUCATION

The Cultural Perspective

8.1 The existing schism between the formal system of education and the country's rich and varied cultural traditions needs to be bridged. The preoccupation with modern technologies cannot be allowed to sever new generations from the roots in India's history and culture. De-culturisation, de-humanisation and alienation must be avoided at all costs. Education can and must bring about the fine synthesis between change-oriented technologies and the country's continuity of cultural traditions.

8.2 The curricula and processes of education will be enriched by cultural content in as many manifestations as possible. Children will be enabled to develop sensitivity to beauty, harmony and refinement. Resource persons in the community, irrespective of their formal educational qualifications, will be invited to contribute to the cultural enrichment of education, employing both the literate and oral traditions of communication. To sustain and carry forward the cultural tradition, the role of old masters, who train pupils through traditional modes will be supported and recognised.

8.3 Linkages will be established between the university system and institutions of higher learning in art, archaeology, oriental studies etc. Due attention will also be paid to the specialised disciplines of Fine Arts, Museology, Folklore etc. Teaching, training and research in these disciplines will be strengthened so as to replenish specialised manpower in them.

Value Education

8.4 The growing concern over the erosion of essential values and an increasing cynicism in society has brought to focus the need for readjustments in the curriculum in order to make education a forceful tool for the cultivation of social and moral values.

8.5 In our culturally plural society education should foster universal and eternal values, oriented towards the unity and integration of our people. Such value education should help eliminate obscurantism, religious fanticism, violence, superstition and fatalism.

8.6 Apart from this combative role, value education has a profound positive content, based on our heritage, national goals and universal perceptions. It should lay primary emphasis on this aspect.

Languages

8.7 The Education Policy of 1968 had examined the question of the development of languages in great details; its essential provisions can hardly be improved upon and are as relevant today as before. The implementation of this part of the 1968 Policy has, however, been uneven. The Policy will be implemented more energetically and purposefully.

Books and Libraries

8.8 The availability of books at low prices is indispensable for a people's education. Efforts will be made to secure easy accessibility to books for all segments of the population. Measures will be taken to improve the quality of books, promote the reading habit and encourage creative writing. Author's interests will be protected. Good translations of foreign books into Indian languages will be supported. Special attention will be paid to the production of quality books for children, including textbooks and workbooks.

8.9 Together with the development of books, a nationwide movement for the improvement of existing libraries and the establishment of new ones will be taken up. Provision will be made in all educational institutions for library facilities and the status of librarians improved.

Media and Educational Technology

8.10 Modern communication technologies have the potential to bypass several stages and sequences in the process of development encountered in early decades. Both the constraints of time and distance at once become manageable. In order to avoid structural dualism modern educational technology must reach out to the most distant areas and the most deprived sections of beneficiaries simultaneously with the areas of comparative affluence and ready availability.

8.11 Educational technology will be employed in the spread of useful information, the training and retraining of teachers, to improve quality, sharpen awareness of art and culture, inculcated abiding values, etc., both in the formal and non-formal sectors. Maximum use will be made of the available infrastructure. In villages without electricity, batteries or solar packs will be used to run the programme.

8.12 The generation of relevant and culturally compatible educational programmes will form an important component of educational technology, and all available resources in the country will be utilised for this purpose.

8.13 The media has profound influence on the minds of children as well as adults; some of it had encouraged consumerism.

violence etc., and thus had a deleterious effect. Radio and T.V., programmes which clearly militate against proper educational objectives will be prevented. Steps will be taken to discourage such trend in the films and other media also. An active movement will be started to promote the production of children's films of high quality and usefulness.

Work Experience

8.14 Work experience, viewed as purposive and meaningful manual work, organised as an integral part of the learning process and resulting in either goods or services useful to the community, is considered as an essential component at all stages of education, to be provided through well-structured and graded programmes. It would comprise activities in accord with the interests, abilities and needs of students, the level of skills and knowledge to be upgraded with the stages of education. This experience would be helpful on his entry into the workforce. Pre-vocational programmes provided at the lower secondary stage will also facilitate the choice of the vocational courses at the higher secondary stage.

Education and Environment

8.15 There is a paramount need to create a consciousness of the environment. It must permeate all ages and all sections of society, beginning with the child. Environmental consciousness should inform teaching in schools and colleges. This aspect will be integrated in the entire educational process.

Population Education

8.16 *(Reviced Para) Population education must be viewed as an important part of the nation's strategy to contain the growth of population. Starting at the primary and secondary levels with inculcation of consciousness about the looming crisis due to expansion of population, educational programmes should actively motivate and inform youth and adults about family planning and responsible parenthood.*

8.17 *(Reviced Para) Mathematics should be visualised as the vehicle to train a child to think, reason, analyse and to articulate logically. Apart from being a specific subject, it should be created as a concomitant to any subject involving analysis and reasoning. With the recent introduction of computers in schools, educational computing and the emergence of learning through the understanding of cause-effect relationships and the interplay of variables, the teaching of mathematics will be suitably redesigned to bring it in line with modern technological devices.*

Mathematical Teaching

8.16 (NPE, 1986) Mathematics should be visualised as the vehicle to train a child to think, reason, analyse and to articulate logically. Apart from being a specific subject, it should be treated as a concomitant to any subject involving analysis and reasoning.

8.17 (NPE, 1986) With the recent introduction of computers in schools, educational computing and the emergence of learning through the understanding of cause-effect relationships and the interplay of variables, the teaching of mathematics will be suitably redesigned to bring it in line with modern technological devices.

Science Education

8.18 Science education will be strengthened so as to develop in the child well defined abilities and values such as the spirit of inquiry, creativity, objectivity, the courage to question, and an aesthetic sensibility.

8.19 Science education programmes will be designed to enable the learner to acquire problem solving and decision making skills and to discover the relationship of science with health, agriculture, industry and other aspects of daily life. Every effort will be made to extend science education to the vast numbers who have remained outside the pale of formal education.

Sports and Physical Education

8.20 ***(Revised Para)*** *Sports and physical education are an integral part of the learning process, and will be included in the evaluation of performance. A nationwide infrastructure for physical education, sports and games will be built into the educational edifice. The infrastructure will consist of playfields, equipment, coaches and teachers of physical education as part of the School Improvement Programme. Available open spaces in urban areas will be reserved for playgrounds, if necessary by legislation. Efforts will be made to establish sports institutions and hostels where specialised attention will be given to sports activities and sports-related studies, along with normal education. Appropriate encouragement will be given to those talented in sports and games. Due stress will be laid on indigenous traditional games.*

8.20 (NPE, 1986) Sports and physical education are an integral part of the learning process, and will be included in the evaluation of performance. A nation-wide infrastructure for physical education, sports and games will be built into the educational edifice.

Yoga

8.21 ***(Reviced Para)*** *As a system which promotes an integrated development of body and mind, Yoga will receive special attention.*

Efforts will be made to introduce Yoga in all schools. To this end, it will be introduced in teacher training courses.

8.21 (NPE, 1986) The infrastructure will consist of playfields, equipment, coaches and teachers of physical education as part of the School Improvement Programme. Available open spaces in urban areas will be reserved for playgrounds, if necessary by legislation. Efforts will be made to establish sports institutions and hostels where specialised attention will be given to sports activities and sports-related studies, along with normal education. Appropriate encouragement will be given to those talented in sports and games. Due stress will be laid on indigenous traditional games. As a system, which promotes integrated development of body and mind, Yoga will receive special attention. Efforts will be made to introduce Yoga in all schools; to this end, it will be introduced in teacher training courses.

The Role of Youth

8.22 Opportunities will be provided for the youth to involve themselves in national and social development through educational institutions and outside them. Students will be required to participate in one or the other of existing schemes, namely, the National Service Scheme, National Cadet Corps, etc. Outside the institutions, the youth will be encouraged to take up programmes of development, reform and extension. The National Service Volunteer Scheme will be strengthened.

The Evaluation Process and Examination Reform

8.23 Assessment of performance is an integral part of any process of learning and teaching. As part of sound educational strategy, examinations should be employed to bring about qualitative improvement in education.

8.24 The objective will be to re-cast the examination system so as to ensure a method of assessment that is a valid and reliable measure of student development and a powerful instrument for improving teaching and learning. In functional terms, this would mean:

(i) The elimination of excessive element of chance and subjectivity;

(ii) The de-emphasis of memorisation;

(iii) Continuous and comprehensive evaluation that incorporates both scholastic and non-scholastic apsects of education, spread over the total span of instructional times;

(iv) Effective use of evaluation process by teachers, students and parents;

(v) Improvement in the conduct of examinations;

(vi) The introduction of concomitant changes in introductional material and methodology;

(vii) The introduction of the semester system from the secondary stage in a phased manner, and

(viii) The use of grades in place of marks.

8.25 *(Revised Para) The above goals are relevant both for external examinations and evaluations within educational institutions. Evaluation at the institutional level will be streamlined and the predominance of external examinations reduced. A National Examination Reform Framework would be prepared to serve as a set of guidelines to the examining bodies which would have the freedom to innovate and adapt the framework to suit the specific situations.*

8.25 (NPE, 1986) The above goals are relevant both for external examinations and evaluations within educational institutions. Evaluation at the institutional level will be streamlined and the predominance of external examinations reduced

Part IX
THE TEACHER

9.1 The status of the teacher reflects the socio-cultural ethos of a society; it is said that no people can rise above the level of its teachers. The Government and the community should endeavour to create conditions which will help motivate and inspire teachers on constructive and creative lines. Teacher should have the freedom to innovate, to devise appropriate methods of communication and activities relevant to the needs and capabilities of and the concerns of the community.

9.2 The methods of recruiting teachers will be reorganised to ensure merit, objectivity and conformity with spatial and functional requirements. The pay and service conditions of teachers have to be commensurate with their social and professional responsibilities and with the need to attract talent to the profession. Efforts will be made to reach the desirable objective of uniform emoluments, service conditions and grievance-removal mechanisms for teachers throughout the country. Guidelines will be formulated to ensure objectivity in the postings and transfers of teachers. A system of teacher evaluation–open, participative and data-based–will be created and reasonable opportunities of promotion to higher grades provided. Norms of accountability will be laid down with incentives for good performance and disincentives for non-performance. Teachers will continue to play a crucial role in the formulation and implementation of educational programmes.

9.3 Teachers' associations must play a significant role in upholding professional integrity and enhancing the dignity of teachers in curbing professional misconduct. National level associations of teachers could prepare a National Code of Professional Ethics for Teachers and see to its observance.

Teacher Education

9.4 Teacher education is a continuous process and its

pre-service and in-service components are inseparable. As the first step, the system of teacher education will be overhauled.

9.5 The new programmes of teacher-education will emphasise continuing education and the need for teachers to meet the thrusts envisaged in this Policy.

9.6 District Institutes of Education and Training (DIET) will be established with the capability to organise pre-service and in-service courses for elementary school teachers and for the personnel working in non-formal and adult education. As DIETs get established, sub-standard institutions will be phased out. Selected Secondary Teacher Training Colleges will be upgraded to complement the work of State Council of Educational Research and Training. The National Council of Teacher Education will be provided the necessary resources and capability to acredit institutions of teacher-education and provide guidance regarding curricula and methods. Networking arrangements will be created between institutons of teacher education and university departments of education.

Part X
THE MANAGEMENT OF EDUCATION

10.1 An overhaul of the system of planning and the management of education will receive high priority. The guiding considerations will be:

(a) Evolving a long-term planning and management perspective of education and its integration with the country's developmental and manpower needs;

(b) Decentralisation and the creation of a spirit of autonomy for educational institutions;

(c) Giving pre-eminence to people's involvement, including association of non-government agencies and voluntary effort;

(d) Inducting more women in the planning and management of education;

(e) Establishing the principle of accountability in relation to given objectives and norms.

National Level

10.2 The Central Advisory Board of Education will play a pivotal role in reviewing educational development, determining the changes required to improve the system and monitoring implementation. It will function through appropriate Committees and other mechanisms created to ensure contact with, and coordination among the areas of Human Resource Development. The Departments of Education at the Centre and in the States will be strengthened through the involvement of professionals.

Indian Education Service

10.3 A proper management structure in education will entail the establishment of the Indian Education Service as an All-India Service. It will bring a national perspective to this vital sector. The basic principles, functions and procedures of recruitment to this service will be decided in consultation with the State Governments.

State Level

10.4 State Governments may establish State Advisory Boards of Education on the lines of CABE. Effective measures should be taken to integrate mechanisms in the various State departments concerned with Human Resource Development.

10.5 Special attention will be paid to the training of educational planners, administrators and heads of institutions. Institutional arrangements for this purpose should be set up.

District and Local Level

10.6 District Boards of Education will be created to manage education up to the higher secondary level. State Governments will attend to this aspect with all possible expedition. Within a multi-level framework of educational development, Central, State, District and Local level agencies will participate in planning, coordination, monitoring and evaluation.

10.7 A very important role must be assigned to the head of an educational institution. Heads will be specially selected and trained. School complexes will be promoted on a flexible pattern so as to serve as networks of institutions and synergic alliances to encourage professionalism among teachers, to ensure observance of norms of conduct and to enable the sharing of experiences and facilities. It is expected that a developed system of school complexes will take over much of the inspection functions in due course.

10.8 Local communities, through appropriate bodies, will be assinged a major role in programmes of school improvement.

Voluntary Agencies and Aided Institutions

10.9 Non-Government and voluntary effort including social activist groups will be encouraged, subject to proper management, and financial assistance provided. At the same time, steps will be taken to prevent the establishment of institutions set up to commercialise education.

Redress Of Grievances

10.10 *Educational tribunals, fashioned after Administrative Tribunals, will be established at the national and state levels.*

Part XI
RESOURCES AND REVIEW

11.1 The Education Commission of 1964-66, the National Education Policy of 1968 and practically all others concerned with education have stressed that the egalitarian goals and the practical, development-oriented objectives of Indian society can only be realised by making investments in education of an order commensurate with the nature and dimensions of the task.

11.2 Resources, to the extent possible, will be raised by mobilising donation, asking the beneficiary communities to maintain school building and supplies of some consumables, raising fees at the higher levels of education and effecting some savings by the efficient use of facilities. Institutions involved with research and the development of technical and scientific manpower should also mobilize some funds by levying a cess or charge on the user agencies, including Government departments, and entrepreneurs. All these measures will be taken not only to reduce the burden on State resources but also for creating a greater sense of responsibility with the educational system. However such measures will contribute only marginally to the total funding. The Government and the community in general will find funds for such programes as: the universalisation of elementary education; liquidating illiteracy; equality of access to educational opportunities to all sections throughout the country; enhancing the social relevance, quality and functional effectiveness of educational progrmames; generating knowledge and developing technologies in scientific fields crucial to self-sustaining economic development; and creating a critical consciousness of the values and imperatives of national survival.

11.3 The deleterious consequences of non-investment or inadequate investment in education are indeed very serious. Similarly, the cost of neglecting vocational and technical education and of research is also unaccceptable. Sub-optimal performance in these fields could cause irreparable damage to the Indian economy. The network of institutions set up from time to time since Independence to facilitate the application of science and technology would need to be substantially and expeditiously updated, since they are fast becoming obsolete.

11.4 ***(Revised Para)*** *In view of these imperatives, education will be treated as a crucial area of investment for national development and survival. The National Policy on Education, 1968, had laid down that the investment on education be gradually increased to reach a level of 6 per cent of the national income as early as possible. Since the actual level of investment has remained far short of that target, it is important that greater determination is shown now to find the funds for the programmes laid down in this Policy. While the actual requirements will be computed from time to time on the basis of monitoring and review, the outlay on education will be stepped up* *to ensure that during the Eighth Five Year Plan and onwards it will uniformly exceed 6 per cent of the national income.*

11.4 (NPE, 1986) In view of these imperatives, education will be treated as a crucial area of investment for national development and survival. The National Policy on Education, 1968, had laid down that the investment on education be gradually increased to reach a level of expenditure of 6 per cent of the national income as early as possible. Since the actual level of investment has remained far short of that target, it is important that greater determination be shown now to find the funds for the programmes laid down in this Policy. While the actual requirements will be computed from time to time on the basis of monitoring and review, the outlay on education will be stepped up to the extent essential for policy implementation in the Seventh Plan. It will be ensured that from the Eighth Five Year Plan onwards it will uniformly exceed 6 per cent of the National Income.

Review

11.5 The implementation and parameters of the New Policy must be reviewed every five years. Appraisals of short intervals will also be made to ascertain the progress of implementation and the trends emerging from time to time.

Part XII
THE FUTURE

12.1 The future shape of education in India is too complex to envision with precision. Yet, given our tradition which has almost always put a high premium on intellectual and spiritual attainment, we are bound to succeed in achieving our objectives.

12.2 The main task is to strengthen the base of the pyramid, which might touch a billion people at the turn of the century. Equally, it is important to ensure that those at the top of the pyramid are among the best in the world. Our cultural well-springs had taken good care of both ends in the past; the skew set in with foreign domination and influence. It should now be possible to further intensify the nationwide effort in Human Resource Development, with education playing its multi-faceted role.

3
Ramamurti Committee, 1990
Reviewing NPE, 1986

Introduction

In pursuance of its election manifesto, the National Front Government headed by Shri V.P. Singh, appointed on May 7, 1990, a Committee with Acharya Ramamurti as its Chairman, to review the National Policy on Education (NPE), 1986. The Committee submitted its report to the Minister of State in the Ministry of Human Resource Development on December 26, 1990. The report was tabled in the Parliament on January 9, 1991.

The report is entitled *Towards an Enlightened and Humane Society.*

Terms of Reference of the Committee for Review

(a) To review the National Policy on Education, 1986 and its implementation;

(b) To make recommendations regarding revision of the Policy;

(c) To recommend action necessary for implementation of the revised policy within a time frame

Text of Government of India Resolution No. F.1-6/90-PN (D.I) dated 7th May, 1990

Despite efforts at social and economic development since attainment of Independence; a majority of our people continue to remain deprived of education, which is one of the basic needs for human development. It is also a matter of grave concern that our people comprise 50 per cent of the world's illiterate and large sections of children have to go without acceptable level of primary education. Government accords the highest priority to education–both as a human right and as the means for bringing about a transformation towards a more humane and enlightened society. There is need to make education an effective instrument for securing a status of equality for women, and persons belonging to the backward classes and minorities. However, it is essential to give a work and employment orientation to education and to exclude from it the elitist aberrations which have become the glaring characteristic of the educational scene. Educational institutions are increasingly being influenced by casteism, communalism and obscurantism and it is necessary to lay special emphasis on struggle against this phenomenon and to move towards a genuinely egalitarian and secular social order. The National Policy on Education, 1986 (NPE), needs to be reviewed to evolve a framework which would enable the country to move towards this perspective of education.

2. Government have, therefore, decided to set up NPE Review Committee.

Members of the NPE Review Committee

Acharya Ramamurti, *Chairman*, NPE Review Committee, P.O. Khadigram-811313, Dist. Munger, Bihar.

Members: Dr. C.N. Rao, Director, Indian Institute of Science, Bangalore-560011; Dr. Sukhdev Singh, 5, Sector 11-A, Chandigarh-160001; Dr. M. Santappa, Scientific Adviser, Tamil Nadu Pollution Control Board, 25, Dr. Radhakrishnan Salai, Madras-600004; Dr. Obaid Siddiqi, Molecular, Biology Unit, Tata Institute of Fundamental Research, Homi Bhabha Road, Bombay-400005; Dr. Bhaskar Ray Chaudhuri, Vice-Chancellor, Univeristy of Calcutta, Calcutta-700001; Dr. M.G. Bhatawdekar, 41, Sangram Colony, Jaipur-302001; Prof. Usha Mehta, Mani Bhavan, Gandhi Museum, 19, Laburnum Road, Gamdevi, Bombay-400007; Prof. K. Satchidananda Murty, 'Aparajita' Sangam, Jagarlamudi-522213, Guntur Distric, Andhra Pradesh; Prof. Mrinal Miri, Deptt. of Philosophy, North-Eastern Hill Univeristy (NEHU), Shillong-793003 (Meghalaya); Shri Veda Vyasa, 64, Golf Links, New Delhi - 110003; Dr. Vidya Niwas Misra, Vice-Chancellor, Sampurnanand Sanskrit University, Varanasi - 221002; Dr. S.Z. Qasim, Vice-Chancellor, Jamia Milia Islamia, Jamia Nagar, New Delhi - 110025; Father T.V. Kunnunkal, Chairman, National Open School, 39, Community Centre, Wazirpur Industrial Area, Ring Road, Ashok Vihar Turn, Delhi - 110052; Dr. Anil Sadgopal, Kishore Bharati, P.O. Bankhedi, Distt. Hoshangabad - 461990, Madhya Pradesh; Shri Manubhai Pancholi, Lok Bharati, Sanosara - 364230, Distt. Bhavanagar, Gujarat.

Member Secretary: Shri S. Gopalan, Additional Secretary, Department of Education, Ministry of H.R.D., Shastri Bhawan, New Delhi.

MAJOR OBSERVATIONS AND RECOMMENDATIONS

1. Principal Concerns and Approach of the Committee in Reviewing NPE

The approach of the Committee in reviewing the National Policy on Education, 1986 and its implementation has been guided by the following principal concerns:

- Equity and social justice.
- Dencentralisation of educational management at all levels.
- Establishment of a participative educational order.
- Inculcation of values indispensable for creation of an enlightened and humane society.
- Empowerment for work. (2.1.1)

2. Roles, Goals and Values in Education

The Committee specified the following roles, goals and values in education:

(a) Education must provide a techno-informative or a sound *knowledge* base, empowering the person through knowledge and on which one can build later on.

(b) Education must also provide opportunities to acquire *skills,* through engaging the students in a variety of processes and situations. These skills would be basic life skills, such as foundational skills in communication, computation, social skills and manual skills, which would enable the student to develop specific job oriented skills later.

(c) Education must further provide a *climate for the nurture of values,* both as a personalised set of values forming one's character and including necessarily social, cultural and national values, so as to have a *context of meaning* for actions and decisions, and in order to enable the persons to act with conviction and commitment.

(d) Education must play an *interventionist and catalytic* role too for promoting national cohesion and unity by empowering the students to become agents of social change. (3.3.0)

The NPE was clear on the essential role of education as an acculturating process. It also saw and emphasised the role of development of human resource through education and training. The Committee views man as more than a mere resource, an economic commodity and have stressed the human and have put the accent on the cultural and spiritual, as on science and technology for the total education of the total person. The Committee is in basic agreement with the 1986 Policy perspective and thrust but have elaborated on certain *key result areas,* which have not received adequate ground level priority, such as a re-design of curriculum and methodologies and a machinery for effective implementation. (3.15.0)

This, the Committee feels, remains the *great unfinished task.* (3.16.0)

3. Education in the Overall Context

In order to achieve equity and social justice and thereby remove elitist aberrations, education has been viewed by the

Committee in the overall context of social, economic, regional and gender based disparities. For example, any effort at vocationalising education will carry no meaning unless, concurrently, the Government lays down an appropriate Income and Wages Policy. Likewise, national policies concerning removal of economic disparities such as for land reforms–employment, health and nutrition etc., have to be concurrently established/reviewed. (2.2.1)

4. Development of Common School System

A very vital component of the overall strategy for securing equity and social justice in education is the development of the Common School System. Concrete steps for translating this concept into action have to be taken. In order to achieve this objective, the existing Government, Local Body and Government-aided schools have to be transformed through quality improvement into genuine neighbourhood schools. Private schools also should be similarly transformed in course of time by making them freely accessible. (2.2.2)

5. Removing Disparities in Education

The rural areas in general, and the tribal areas in particular, have suffered in terms of resources, personnel and infrastructure facilities. This phenomenon of regional disparities in educational development has acquired a major political dimension in the current Indian scene. It is reflected in the regional and sub-regional movements. Therefore, the need of the hour is planning for, and implementation of, educational development programmes in terms of disaggregated targets and, area, community and gender specific activities. This would mean concrete programmes being established on ground for the disadvantaged groups–SCs and Tribes, women, the educationally backward minorities and the handicapped with appropriate budgeting for the same. (2.2.4)

6. Promotion of Women Education

In order to promote participation of the girls and women in education at all levels, there is need for an integrated approach in designing and implementing the schemes that would address all the factors that inhibit their education. Mere implementation of disaggregated schemes such as Opening of Non-formal Education Centres for Girls, Adult Education Centres for Women etc., by themselves are not adequate. In this context special mention may be made of inter-action of Early Childhood Care and Education (ECE) with primary education. Education of women is not to be construed of a question of mere access but of empowering them through education of all on equality of sexes. (2.2.5)

Numbers in parenthesis refer to paras of the Report.

7. Vocationalisation of Education: A Single Stream

The modifications suggested in the case of vocationalisation of school education have been construed in the context of equity and social justice as well. The scheme, as it is now implemented, though unintendedly, has come to be viewed by the students as well as the parents, as one meant for the less fortunate. It is also on account of this that a single stream of school education with vocational as well as non-vocational components of different mixes becomes relevant and important. (2.2.6)

8. Examination Reforms

Examination reforms also have their justification from the point of view of equity and social justice. The examination system tilts heavily in favour of the privileged who have access to certain facilities such as special teaching learning material, special coaching etc. It is inter alia, to rectify this inequitable tilt that examination reforms have been suggested. (2.2.7)

9. Regional Language as the Media of Education

One of the factors seriously inhibiting access for the rural students to higher education is the continuing sway of English. Hence, equity demands that education in the media of regional languages is encouraged at all levels. This would call not merely for political and academic commitment for the switch over to the regional languages media but a package of other measures including conscious efforts at organising tests for recruitments in the public and private service in the regional languages, at least options for taking university examinations in these languages and incentives for the same apart from production of appropriate teaching learning materials, reference literature etc. (2.2.8)

10. Decentralised Planning and Management of Education

The fundamental justification for decentralised planning and management of education is the sheer size and diversity of the country. There is need for decentralisation of educational planning and management all the way down at all levels, from the Centre to the States, from the State to the districts, from the districts to the blocks, from the blocks to the panchayats/villages and habitations. (2.3.1)

11. University Autonomy

Decentralisation in the university system would mean autonomy for the universities and colleges as well as for the respective facilities and individual teachers. Examination reforms including establishment of continuous, comprehenisve internal evaluation cannot come about unless delegation of authority and decentralisation of functions becomes real down to the level of teachers. Educational complexes recommended by the Committee are construed as an instrument of bringing about decentralisation. (2.3.2)

12. Participative Education Order

The Committee has envisaged the concept of participative educational order as being relevant to every stage of education as only involvement through participation can bring about the environment for genuine reform. (2.4.0)

13. Human Being to be Valued as More than a Human Resource

NPE, 1986 as a whole reflects that educational development was construed in the backward of human resource development. In fact, the Policy called for new designs of human resource development for availing of the unprecedented opportunities that would be thrown up by the ensuring decades. In the view of the Committee, the human being is to be valued as more than a resource. Mere emphasis on the resource aspect has overtones of utilitarian connotations. While utilitarian aspects are important, the human being has to be developed with accent on character building, dignity of labour and value to the society at the national and international levels. (2.5.1)

In order to de-emphasise the utilitarian overtones of the expression *Human Resource Development,* the Committee is of the opinion that the nomenclature of the Ministry, namely, Ministry of Human Resource Development should be changed into Ministry of Education. The Term Education is broad enough to encompass the aspects of Culture and Arts, Youth Affairs and Sports and Women and Child Development

14. Value Education

In the view of the Committee value education is to be construed as a continuous process which is to be sustained throughout the process of growth of the individual from childhood to adolescence, then to adulthood and so on. It is also the role of value education to bring about integration of the hand, head and heart to ensure that education does not alienate the students from the family, community and life. One of the key roles of education should be creation of a work culture at all stages of education so that the individual develops into a socially and economically useful human being with respect for the welfare of all living beings (*Sarva bhootha hitha*). Above all else, critical appreciation and concern for the cultural and artistic heritage of the country has to be instilled amongst the students. It is this package of values what will help the creation and sustenance of an enlightened and humane society in the country. (2.5.2)

15. Resources

(1) The first step, therefore, should be to provide for at least 6% of the GNP for education which has not so far been provided, though this has been repeatedly urged for over quarter of a century.

(2) All technical and professional education should be made self-financing, education being viewed as involving the use of resources (inputs) that should be necessarily paid for by the beneficiaries as it confers on them greater employability (output).

(3) In the circumstances, a justifiable strategy is bringing about an appropriate increase in the fees payable by students going in for higher education. This increase should be appropriately linked to at least the cost of recurring expenditure and levels of income of the parents of the beneficiaries. The richest quartile of the people can bear 75% of the cost of the education, the next richest quartile 50% of the cost and the next richest quartile 25%. The last quartile of the economically weak (to be appropriately defined) need not bear any part of the cost.

(4) Besides tuition fees, charged for specific purposes in the Higher Educational Institutions like laboratory fees, library fees, building fees, magazine fees, games fees etc. also have to be increased on a rational basis with reference to the costs of providing the relevant facilities/services.

(5) With the ever increasing number of examinees, examination fees can also be an important means of raising internal resources to meet the cost of higher education.

(6) However, institutional loans as a strategy for releasing the pressure on government resources and as a means of putting resources in possession of those aspiring for higher education is indispensable. Problems in administration of loans should not result in the easy solution of opting out of them.

(7) Therefore, there is need for a committed programme of the nationalised banks for providing loans for recipients of higher education.

(8) Terms lending institutions like the Industrial Development Bank of India (IDBI), Industrial Finance Corporation of India (IFCI) and Industrial Credit and Investment Corporation of India (ICICI) should launch programmes for promoting research in universities.

(9) Institutional finance for infrastructure needs to be raised in the circumstances. Housing Finance Institutions, therefore, could take up programmes for creation of capital assets in the educational sector, i.e., for buildings for schools, colleges, universities as also hostels for the students, staff and teachers. Repayment of loans

may have to be guaranteed by the appropriate Governments.

(10) There is a strong case for LIC's investment in the area of housing going for hostel facilities for the students, staff and teachers in the educational institutions. However, diversion of these resources for the education sector would mean doing so at the expense of other development schemes, 90% of the accretions of the LIC already being committed to socially oriented sectors. Therefore, this is a matter on which the Government as well as Planning Commission will have to take a conscious decision regarding the reallocation: of the LIC's investible resources with substantive priority for the education sector.

(11) Economically weaker sections of the people going for higher education who cannot afford the enhanced fees or loans from financial institutions could be provided appropriate scholarships.

(12) Funds provided in the Central sector for scholarships during the Seventh Plan period was of the order of Rs 22.26 crores. This would have to be considerably enhanced for the benefit of the economically weaker sections in the interest of equity and providing access to higher education for them. There is also need for rationalisation of the whole programme of awarding scholarships.

(13) The Government of India scheme of scholarships in approved residential secondary schools could as well as be discontinued and the number of scholarship enhanced for meaningful programmes like for upgradation of merit of SC/ST students.

(14) One of the modalities for securing better implementation of scholarships schemes with more direct and responsible involvement on the part of the States no doubt, would be for the administration of the scholarships being left totally to the States themselves necessary outlays being provided to the States as part of the State Plan Outlays on an earmarked basis.

(15) Other measures for raising resources for education:

(a) A sustained programme to be implemented every year right down to the Panchayat levels for raising community contribution.

(b) Institution of innovative programmes like the Savatribhai Public Foster Parent Scheme of Maharashtra for promoting primary education of girls under which registered foster parents pay Rs 25/- p.m. in cash or kind to the needy girls from weaker sections.

(c) Collection of educational cess related to revenue sources such as land revenue, excise duties, charges on cash crops, charges on buildings in urban areas etc.

(d) Introduction of shift scheme in school so that the existing infrastructure can be utilised better.

(e) Identification of surplus teacher in schools and colleges and their deployment otherwise.

(Summary of pages 361 to 368)

4
The CABE Committee Report 1992[1]

Introduction

The National Policy on Education (NPE) and the Programme of Action (POA) for its implementation were formulated in 1986. Several measures have been taken by the Central and the State Governments for the implementation of NPE and POA. NPE envisages a review of the implementation of the various parameters of the policy every five years.

The Central Government had, in May, 1990, appointed a Committee under the Chairmanship of Acharya Ramamurti to review NPE. The Committee submitted its report in December, 1990. The Central Advisory Board of Education, in its meeting held on 8-9 March, 1991, examined the procedure to be adopted for consideration of the report of the NPE Review Committee and decided that a CABE Committee be constituted by the Chairman, viz., Union Minister of Human Resource Development, to consider the recommendations of the NPE Review Committee.

The Minister of Human Resource Development therefore set up a Committee of CABE to review the implementation of the various parameters of NPE, taking into consideration the report of the Committee for Review of the NPE and other relevant developments since the Policy was formulated and to make recommendations regarding modifications to be made in NPE.

Composition of the Committee

The Committee consists of the following:

Shri Janardhana Reddy, Chief Minister & Minister of Education, Andhra Pradesh—*Chairman*

Shri Vikram Verma, Minister of Education, M.P.; Shri Gegong Apang , C.M. and Minister of Education, Arunachal Pradesh; Dr. Ram Chandra Purve, Minister (SE & PE), Bihar; Shri R.M. Veerappan, Minister of Education, Tamil Nadu; Shri S.S. Chakraborty, Minister (Higher Education), West Bengal; Shri E.T. Mohammad Basheer, Minister of Education, Kerala; Member (Education), Planning Commission; Chairman, University Grants Commission; Dr. M.S. Adiseshiah, Chairman, Madras Institute of Development Studies, 79-II, Main Road, Gandhi Nagar, Adayar,

Madras 600020; Dr. Radhika Herzberger, Director, Rishi Valley School, P.O. Madanapalli, District Chittoor; Dr. A.P. Mitra, Formerly Director General CSIR, 30, Kailash Kunj, Greater Kailash I, New Delhi; Smt. Jagannathan Krishnammal, Secretary, Land for Tiller's Freedom (LAFTI), Kilvelur-61104, Tanjore District, Tamil Nadu; Dr. Ram Dayal Munda, Professor of Regional Language, Ranchi University, Ranchi; Shri Habib Tanvir, Director, Naya Theatre, L-15, Bar Sarai, New Delhi-110016; Dr. R.V. Vaidyanatha Ayyar, Joint Secretary (Planning), *Member-Secretary*.

Union Education Secretary, Director, NCERT and Director, NIEPA were permanent invitees to the meetings of the Committee.

The Committee was asked to submit its report within two months from the date of its first meeting.

Terms of Reference

The Committee was free to lay down its own procedures and methodology of work.

Gist of Recommendations of CABE Committee on Policy[2]

1. Only a few of the recommendations of the National Policy on Education Review Committee (NPERC) have policy implications. While very little of policy requires reformulation the Programme of Action (POA) needs to be revised considerably, taking into account the recommendations of the NPERC.

2. A standing Central Advisory Board of Education (CABE) Committee on education of SCs, STs and other educationally backward sections should be constituted to monitor educational programmes for these disadvantaged groups; educationalists from these groups should have representation in that Committee. Further at the State level, a single focal agency should be identified in each State for the purpose of monitoring the programmes and reporting to the Central Government.

3. Effective measures need to be taken to implement the provision of National Policy on Education, 1968 and National Policy on Education, 1986 (NPE) in regard to Common School System. To this end disparities between schools should be ended as early as possible by upgrading the quality of ordinary schools and providing amenities for achieving minimum levels of learning. Both the Centre and the States should take determined action in this regard. The privileged schools should accept social accountability by sharing their facilities and resources with other institutions, taking up community activities, and facilitating access to children of the disadvantaged groups.

4. The scheme of Navodaya Vidyalayas (NVs) should continue and a NV should be set up in each district as originally envisaged. Further, the following measures are suggested:

i) constant review to keep the scheme as cost effective as possible;

ii) ensuring the continued validity and reliability of the admission tests by periodic evaluation and appropriate modification of admission procedure; and

iii) more particular attention to the pace-setting role of these institutions.

5. It is also necessary to begin thinking about the future course of the scheme after NVs have been established in all districts with the requisite facilities in the existing institutions. Planning has also to begin for catering to the higher educational needs of students who pass out of NVs. A scheme needs to be formulated for central financial support to residential schools. In this scheme priority should be given to ST areas and areas predominantly inhabited by SCs.

6. The NPERC had suggested enlarging the scope of Article 45 of the Constitution to include early childhood care and education. It is not necessary.

7. Every effort should be made to ensure that the constitutional obligation of providing free and compulsory education up to the age of 14 years becomes reality before we enter the twenty-first century. Para 5.12 of NPE, which laid the targets for achievement of Universalisation of Primary Education (UPE) and Universalisation of Elementary Education (UEE) needs to be revised.

8. The following points deserve priority during the Eighth Five Year Plan in the area of UEE:

i) Universal enrolment of all children, including girls and persons belonging to SCs and STs;

ii) Provision of primary school for all children within one kilometre of walking distance and of facility of non-formal education for school drop-outs, working children and girls who cannot attend schools;

iii) Improvement of ratio of primary school to upper primary schools from the existing 1:4 to 1:2, this being a precondition for larger opportunity for widening girl's participation at upper primary stage;

iv) Reduction of drop out rates between Classes I to V and I to VIII from the existing 45 per cent and 60 per cent to 20 per cent and 40 per cent respectively;

v) Improvement of school facilities by revamped Operation Blackboard, to be extended to upper primary level also;

vi) Achievement of minimum levels of learning by approximately all children at the primary level, and introduction of this concept at the upper primary stage on a larger scale;

vii) Local level committee, with due representation to women and teachers, to assist in the working of primary education and to oversee its functioning;

viii) Improvement of the monitoring system for universalisation of elementary education to see to the achievement of above mentioned goals.

NPE and POA may be revised accordingly.

9. The 'dual-track approach' of promoting simultaneously

UEE and adult literacy should continue to inform educational planning; the special needs of women and of disadvantaged groups like SCs and STs should be specially attended to.

10. The NPERC's perception of Mahila Samakhya (MS) as an alternative model is not valid.

11. Events since December, 1990, when the NPERC submitted its report have established that NPERC had underestimated the significance of the 'Ernakulam Experiment'. The Total Literacy Campaign (TLC) approach is a potent and viable model which could help achieve a significant breakthrough in the literacy scene in the Eighth Five Year Plan.

12. Programmes of post-literacy and continuing education should be planned for neo-literates and youth passing out of primary education system (through the school system or non-formal education programme) and these programmes should be planned simultaneously with literacy campaigns and be made effective as soon as large numbers of persons complete literacy courses.

13. The policy should be reformulated to bring about the new initiatives that are required in secondary education.

14. Teacher training in secondary education needs to be given more importance.

15. The ongoing programme of Computer Literacy and Studies in Schools (CLASS) needs to be revamped.

16. Open learning should be given utmost encouragement and the National Open School should play the same lead role within the open school system as Indira Gandhi National Open University with open universities.

17. The existing vocational stream at the +2 level may be suitably strengthened and, wherever possible, the vocational courses may be started from Class IX also.

18. The idea of a core vocational course, mooted by the NPERC, is attractive. Generic vocational courses may be introduced on a selective basis; to begin with generic vocational courses may be tried out in about ten per cent of the schools.

19. The work Experience programme may be systematically implemented by allocating from 12.5 per cent to 20 per cent of the school time for these activities; the activities should have a practical orientation in relation to various subjects under this programme. The vocational 'core' would find place at the secondary and higher secondary stages; Work Experience/Socially Useful Productive Work (SUPW) would relate to elementary education.

20. It is not advisable to set up a national level statutory mechanism to regulate the opening of non-standard and substandard universities and colleges. The proliferation of colleges without adequate facilities can be curbed to a large extent if the universities exercise rigorous control and insist on creation of necessary infrastructure and educational facilities before granting affiliation and if the State Governments respect the decision of the universities in these matters. The establishment of operationalisation of State Councils of Higher Education will go a long way in the

planned development of higher education.

21. Efforts should be made to secure involvement of teachers and students in extension work such as literacy. Adequate facilities should be provided to ensure that all students participate in one or the other existing schemes, particularly National Service Scheme (NSS) and National Cadet Corps (NCC). Specific schemes should be formulated to encourage out of school youth to participate in national service and development. The feasibility and financial implications of a two-year composite programme for students who complete the +2 stage, comprising paramilitary service, development of vocational and professional skills, and extension work in rural areas be worked out. An important feature of the programme would be that the students would be required to participate in these programmes outside their home state with a view to promoting national integration.

22. National Testing Service (NTS) should undertake the conduct of tests so that it acquires the required expertise and develops into a competent resource centre.

23. A Central Council of Rural Institutes is necessary to provide the much needed fillip to rural education on Gandhian lines; it should be set up immediately.

24. The recommendation of the NPERC on National Council of Higher Education (that it need not be set up) is sound and Para 5.34 of NPE should be reformulated.

25. Regional offices of University Grants Commission (UGC) should be set up at the earliest, with adequate authority and functions.

26. The All India Council of Technical Education (AICTE) Act should be amended and Para 6.19 of NPE should be reformulated. The Regional Committees of AICTE should be adequately staffed and the Chairman of the Regional Committee should be an Education Minister of a State from the region, by rotation. The Regional Committee should have the power to make recommendations on the opening of new institutions, starting of new courses and enhancing the intake within the framework of the guidelines laid down by the AICTE. The State Governments and the universities should issue the necessary approvals based on the recommendations of the Regional Committees only.

27. Rather than leaving examination reforms to the individual initiatives and inclinations of the examining bodies, strong and coordinated effort should be made by the Centre and the State Government in this area. *Inter alia* the following measures are suggested:

i) Preparation of a status report of examination Reform measures undertaken by the examining bodies.
ii) Preparation of a National Examination Reform Framework to serve as a set of guidelines to the examining bodies which would have the freedom to innovate and adapt the framework to suit the specific situation.
iii) Developing an effective mechanism for coordination, monitoring and evaluation of the implementation of the

examination reforms by the different examining bodies.

iv) Documentation and dissemination of innovations and measures for examination reforms.

28. While the load of the school bag is a valid concern, one cannot afford to ignore the requirements of modernisation and relevance.

29. The NPE provision and the National Curricular Framework should be followed faithfully so that the problem of the 'load of the school bag' will be mitigated. The teachers of the expensive private schools in urban areas should be reoriented so that they give up the habit of prescribing unnecessarily a large number of books.

30. Licensing of teachers as suggested by the NPERC is not desirable.

31. First degree in teacher education should not be given through correspondence courses.

32. The idea of education complex, as suggested by the NPERC, may be tried on an experimental basis in selected areas.

33. It would be necessary to hasten the process of consultation with States and to give concrete shape to the idea of Indian Education Service (IES) with due regard to the views and concerns of the States.

34. Constitution of specialised State Level Educational Tribunals is desirable. The details of setting up of these tribunals may be worked out in consultation with the State Governments.

35. In Part VII the NPE had suggested strategies for 'Making the System Work'. This concept has to be treated as non-negotiable. Formulation and implementation of an Action Plan to put into practice the strategy outlined in Para 7.3 of NPE is strongly recommended.

36. The practice of treating education as a residual sector in the matter of allocation of resources should be reversed; para 11.4 of NPE which lays down that it would be ensured that from the Eighth Five Year Plan onwards the outlay on education would uniformly exceed six per cent of the national income, should be implemented forthwith. Need-based financing requires to be provided for priority areas like UEE, Adult Literacy and Vocationalisation.

37. Higher budgetary allocation for education should be complemented by other measures such as:

i) Prioritisation within the Education Sector in the matter of allocation of Government resources.

ii) Progressively making higher education and technical and management education largely self-financing by revising the fee structure with appropriate support to the needy students by way of student loans.

iii) Institutional finances for development of educational infrastructure.

iv) Incentives to academic institutions to augment income by way of consultancy and other studies.

v) Encouraging Community and the cooperative sectors to

financially support education. The time and effort given by thousands of unpaid volunteers in the Total Literacy Campaigns is a concrete demonstration of the possibility of raising social capital without any opportunity cost.

vi) Efficiency and effectiveness of expenditure which would imply that programmes should be judged not only with reference to the financial expenditure or coverage in terms of geographical area or number of beneficiaries but also in terms of outcome.

Notes

1. Government of India, Ministry of Human Resource Development, Department of Education, New Delhi, January, 1992.
2. Statement of the Minister of Human Resource Development, Government of India, attached in reply to Question No. 625 for 28.2.92 in Rajya Sabha.

5
Committee on Committee*

Overall Observations on Ramamurti Committee

After a careful consideration of the recommendations of NPERC as well as developments since NPE, we have come to the conclusion that while very little of policy requires reformulation the POA needs to be revised considerably. In the body of the report we have indicated which of the recommendations of the NPERC need to be taken into account for the realisation of POA (2.3).

In this chapter an attempt has been made to give observations of the CABE Committee on those recommendations of the NPERC which involve policy implications.

Major Observations and Recommendations of NPERC are given in Chapter 3.

Chapter 4 provides a gist of Recommendations of CABE Committee on Policy.

Thus Chapters 3, 4 and 5 are complementary and supplementary. All possible efforts have been made to avoid repetition.

---

* *Source*

1. *Report of the CABE Committee on Policy.* Government of India, Ministry of Human Resource Development, Department of Education, New Delhi, January, 1992.
2. *Towards an Enlightened and Human Society: NPE, 1986–A Review* (NPERC). Committee for Review of National Policy on Education, Ministry of Human Resource Development, New Delhi, December, 1990.
3. *Report of the Committee for Review of National Policy on Education–1986: Recommendations.* Manager, Government of India Press, Faridabad, 1991.

Note: S. No. 3 contains a summary of S. No. 2.

RAMAMURTI COMMITTEE

APPROACH (Chapter 2)

2.4.0 The Committee has envisaged the concept of participative educational order as being relevant to every stage of education as only involvement through participation can bring about the environment for genuine reform. Important modalities contemplated in this regard are involvement of the colleges and universities in issues of regional development and improvement of school education; creation of school complexes, bringing about mutual coordination between primary schools, middle schools, high schools, colleges and universities

2.2.6 The modifications suggested in the case of vocationalisation of School Education have been construed in the context of equity and social justice as well. The Scheme, as it is now implemented, though unintendedly, has come to be viewed by the students as well as the parents, as one meant for the less fortunate. It is also on account of this that a single stream of School education with vocational as well as non-vocational components of different mixes becomes relevant and important.

2.6.0 It has been clearly within the perception of the Committee that much of what is contained in its report has already been dealt with by different Commissions and Committees which were called upon to go into educational policy from

JANARDHANA COMMITTEE

OVERVIEW (Chapter 2)

2.2 We feel that the concept of participative educational order as outlined by the NPERC was rather restrictive. The NPERC had rightly underlined the importance of involving educationists, teachers and educational institutions not only in educational improvement but also in the overall process of development. However, the concept of participatory educational order should go beyond involvement of educational institutions and should extend to the community itself.

2.5 While we do favour retention of the present policy formulation in regard to a distinct stream for vocational education at the +2 stage, we find the idea of a core vocational course attractive. Generic vocational courses which cut across various occupational fields and which are primarily non-occupation specific have many potential benefits.

2.3 The NPER (has) made it explicit.

time to time from the 19th century onwards. However, it is a fact that many of the ideas and concepts have remained as such without being translated into action and much impact has not been brought to bear upon the educational development of the country in the desired lines. The Committee's effort has, therefore, largely been one of advising on possible alternative modalities of implementation.

WOMEN'S EDUCATION

EQUITY, SOCIAL JUSTICE AND EDUCATION (Chapter 4)

4.1.1 The evaluation of policy in relation to education needs necessarily to be made in the larger context of the socio-cultural reality in which women live; and the educational situation that is sought to be addressed and subsequently redressed.

EDUCATION AND WOMEN'S EQUALITY (Chapter 3)

3.1 It rightly addressed the issue of women's education with reference to the special existential problems of women – such as the prevailing cultural norms of gender behaviour and the perceived domestic and reproductive roles of women which restrict the access of women to education.

In essence, the NPERC's perspective is very much in tune with what NPE envisaged in regard to women's education.

1. There is a crucial link between the easy access to water, fuel and fodder and schooling of girls. This understanding needs to be explicitly reflected in the policy of Government and be concretised in operational designs. (4.1.10)

2. 'Local Area Planning', as envisaged in the 'Approach to the

3.3 R. Nos. 1 to 5 bring out the nexus between girls' schooling and access to water, fuel and fodder. The suggestion is that this nexus should inform educational planning and that the Department of Education should co-ordinate with other departments with a view to bringing about an improvement

Eighth Five Year Plan' document, must take into account the above linkage while planning for programmes relating to forestry, drinking water and greening of common lands. (4.1.10)

3. The Department of Education should coordinate with the other concerned departments and secure adequate resource allocation for the abovementioned programmes based on parameters which indicate the status of girls education in a given habitation/village. For instance, priority needs to be given to the habitations/villages having enrolment and retention rates for girls in schools below the average rates of the States. (4.1.10)

4. To achieve the above purpose, planning for educational development of any given region would have to be necessarily conducted at the Block or sub-Block level. This task would be facilitated if it is undertaken through the proposed Educational Complexes in which there will be Block-level representatives of the various agencies/departments concerned with social welfare and development, along with teachers, Anganwadi workers and representatives of poor women's groups and Panchayati Raj institutions. (4.1.10)

5. Teachers, Anganwadi workers, village-level functionaries of other departments, and representatives of women's groups and community-level organisations should play an important role in making micro-level information available to the Educational Complex for prioritisation of action in this regard. (4.1.10)

Note: The number given in brackets at the end of each recommendation is the paragraph number of the Report of the Review Committee under which that recommendation appears.

in the access of women to educatioon. The criticality of the nexus highlighted by the NPERC cannot be exaggerated; however, the co-ordinating role is better discharged by the Department of Women and Child Development and the Planning Commission at the Centre, the corresponding agencies at the State level, and the agencies responsible for integrated planning and development at the district and sub-district level. It would not be realistic to expect the education department alone, whether at the Centre or in the States, to play the lead role for ensuring that women's development in a holistic manner.

Empowerment of Women

53. Develop *Mahila Samakhya* in a decentralised and participative mode of management, with the decision-making powers devolved to the district or block-level, and ultimately to the poor women's groups themselves. (4.1.40)

54. Implement *Mahila Samakhya* in such a way as to establish organic linkages with the ECCE programme and the efforts towards universalisation of girls' elementary education. (4.1.40)

55. Build a component of closely working with men in the community also, as part of the process of women's empowerment. (4.1.40)

56. Along with the means for economic independence for women, the issues of women's health, including reproductive health and sexuality, should be included in the parameters for empowerment of women. (4.1.40)

R. Nos. 53. to 57 endorse the Mahila Samakhya approach which is a product of the NPE.

Adult Education

57. For imparting adult education to women and thereby empower them, the *Mahila Samakhya* model should be tried out. (4.1.41)

Resources

58. Fifty per cent of the elementary sector allocation for measures to increase girls' participation to be earmarked and this allocation be made non-divertible. (4.1.42)

59. A share of all developmental allocations for secondary,

3.4 R. Nos. 58 to 62 call for earmarking of resources for women's education not only in the allocations of elementary, secondary, vocational and higher education but also in the Special Component Plan (SCP) for SCs and the Tribal Sub-

vocational and higher education be earmarked for measures to improve girls' access thereto and the quality of education in these sectors be improved. (4.1.42)

60. There should be special earmarking for girls within the Special Component Plan for Scheduled Castes and Tribal Sub-Plan. (4.1.42)

Management

61. Continuance of all Centrally Sponsored Schemes relating, in part or in full, to women's education may be treated in terms of the detailed recommendation given by the Committee in regard to Centrally Sponsored Schemes as a whole in the chapter on Decentralisation and Participative Management (4.1.44)

62. The responsibility for planning, implementing and internal monitoring of all school-based programmes for women's education be handed over to the Educational Complexes in the Panchayati Raj framework. At the institutional level, the Head of the institution (Primary/Middle/Higher Secondary Schools) should be made fully responsible for micro-level planning and ensuring universalisation (not just enrolment) of girls' education and their access to high school or vocational education, according to disaggregated strategies and timeframes. (4.1.44).

EDUCATION FOR THE SCHEDULED CASTES SCHEDULED TRIBES AND OTHER EDUCATIONALITY BACKWARD SECTIONS (Chapter 4)

Education should not be considered autonomously outside the

Plan (TSP) for STs. However, there is a fundamental difference between SC/ST problems and the women's question. The problem of women's education cuts across caste and regional barriers. Therefore, while women's participation in education should be closely monitored and particular attention paid to remove the barriers impeding such participation, the earmarking of funds may not be administratively feasible.

3.5 To sum up, we are of the view that while the NPERC had rightly reiterated the importance of women's education, the NPE policy frame is adequate and the POA should be revised to take into account the recommendations of the NPERC.

EDUCATION OF THE SCST/STS AND OTHE EDUCATIONALLY BACKWARD SECTIONS (Chapter 4)

4.1 While the existential dilemma highlighted by the NPERC is

other basic national policies concerning equity, social justice and economic development. This is particularly relevant in regard to programmes designed for the educational development of the Scheduled Castes, Scheduled Tribes and other backward sections. For these disadvantaged sections access to, and retention in, educational systems are functions of these policies.

valid, the basic question is how to operationalise the equity package. In concrete operational terms the NPERC does not propose any departure from NPE/POA or come out with new strategies or measures different from those in operation. The NPERC had reviewed in detail the different schemes and activities and offered suggestions for improving their effectiveness.

Planning and Management

4.2 The point implied in the NPERC report that there is a two way relationship between education and socio-economic change is valid. It needs to be stressed that the District Collectors and all the agencies and personnel dealing with development in the districts need to be sensitised to the interrelationships amongst the various programmes designed for the socio-economic amelioration of weaker sections. Another dimension that is critical for the delivery of educational services is the empowerment of local communities. To a certain extent, empowerment is promoted by a strong Panchayati Raj system, particularly at the village level. However, it should be ensured that weaker sections have an effective say on the functioning of these institutions. Experience with *Mahila Samakhya* has adumbrated the possibility of organising women's groups who are articulate and demand accountability of the educational system. Such organisations, when they take root, can ensure that the various programmes and activities are really accountable to the community – a denouement which would make the delivery systems more effective.

Curriculum

69. In the curriculum of the educationally backward the following should be emphasised at all stages of education:

(a) Science and Mathematics;
(b) Expression, both oral and written, and creative writing;
(c) History and sociology of the Scheduled Castes, the Scheduled Tribes and other backward sections of society;
(d) Contribution of these communities to national life and development including the freedom struggle; and
(e) Role played by women belonging to these communities in national life and development.

(In fact, matters covering under (c), (d) and (e) should also be included in the National Core Curriculum) (4.2.7)

4.5 R. No. 69 suggests a separate curriculum for the educationally backward sections. We are of the view that all students, irrespective of caste, community and religion, should have a common curriculum. While instruction should be child-centred and cater to individual differences, it is not advisable to differentiate students in the matter of syllabus and curriculum. Even the educationally backward would not agree to be segregated through a separate curriculum. They are likely to perceive such a curriculum to be second rate. Science and Mathematics, language competencies, and contribution of different communities, regions and women to the nation's life, culture and development should be inculcated in all students.

Intensive Area Approach

77. The Ministry of Welfare, according to the Business Rules, is expected to do coordination in the implementation of programmes relating to SCs/STs. While they have given a list of blocks identified as tribal blocks they have not given, with reference to 1981 census, a list of blocks identified as those of Scheduled Caste concentration. This Ministry should, therefore, provide lists of blocks with SC concentration. With reference to such lists the Department of Education should get feedback from the States regarding their coverage under the various educational programmes. (4.2.10)

4.4 The NPERC laid strong emphasis on area-intensive approach and more vigorous monitoring, an emphasis conducive to the effectiveness of programme implementation. The recommendation of the NPERC that a single focal agency should be identified in each State for the purpose of monitoring and reporting to the Central Government is welcome. Particularly in regard to SCs, STs and minorities, there is a multiplicity of implementing agencies in State Governments because of the multiplicity of the problems. Many programmes are administered by the State Welfare Departments and some by the Education Departments. Even in Education Depart-

78. All the educational programmes should be implemented to the extent feasible conveniently in the same blocks of SC concentration/tribal blocks so that impact of educational development is felt in a demonstrable and balanced way in the respective areas. (4.2.10)

Monitoring

79. A single focal agency in each State should be identified for the purpose of reporting to the Government of India comprehensively on all the educational programmes. (4.2.11)

SECTION C: EDUCATION OF THE HANDICAPPED (Chapter 4)

4.3.4 It should be stated to the credit of NPE 1986 that revision for education of the handicapped was mentioned under the part relating to equal educational opportunities. However, the NPE, so far as it relates to education of the handicapped, is inadequate in the following respects:

- NPE had not stressed the mobilisation of the total general education system for the education of the hanidcapped. Special schools had been treated in isolation from other educational institutions from the point of view of providing the educational supervisory infrastructure, leaving it

ments activities are spread over many Directorates. There is really a need for a State-level nodal agency which can have an overview of the various programmes and can assess what the programmes all add up to. Monitoring has indeed been the Achilles' heel of programme implementation. Effective monitoring systems therefore have to be established. Representatives of beneficiaries have to be associated with the monitoring system so that they can give a fillip to programme implementation from within the system. We also suggest constitution of a standing CABE Committee on education of SCs, STs and other educationally backward sections; educationists from these groups should have representation in that Committee. The CABE Committee should review the progress of the schemes and submit reports for consideration by the CABE.

EDUCATION OF THE HANDICAPPED (Chapter 5)

5.1 The NPERC complimented the NPE for placing the education of the handicapped in the right perspective. The NPE recognizes the education of the handicapped as an integral part of the education process and as an important element of the efforts to remove disparities and equalise educational opportunities. The NPERC also appreciated the approach of NPE to the education of the handicapped, particularly in regard to involvement of voluntary agencies. The NPERC, however, felt that the NPE was inadequate

to the Ministries of Welfare and HRD to co-operatively develop the same.

89. Educational packages should be offered for hearing impaired children in a differentiated way. (4.3.6)

90. For making the boys and girls of impaired hearing economically independent, vocational training has to be specially organised.

91. Bharati Braille has been developed, thanks, inter alia, to the special effort made by the National Institute for the Visually Handicapped. Based on this, teacher training and book production programmes have also been launched. These production programmes should be intensified by their scales of operation being enlarged and diversified to cover wide range of subjects and in-school and out-of-school needs. (4.3.6)

93. For the moderately mentally retarded, special curricula should be developed and standardised – not merely for the purpose of basic education in 3 R's but for training in self-care skills like motor integration, perceptual and motor skills, language, communication and conceptual skills. It should be clearly understood that for the mentally handicapped, academic achievements are relatively unimportant in comparison to social adaptation and vocational training. (4.3.6)

101. Sustained researches should be undertaken to determine the needs of the physically handicapped and produce technological aids capable of helping in overcoming handicaps. The Indian Institute of Technology and other technological institutions in the area of higher education should be given specific responsibilities for undertaking these researches. (4.3.6)

5.2 We feel that it would not be fair to fault the NPE on these two counts.

5.3 The NPERC made very useful recommendations relating to the modalities of implementing programmes for the education of the handicapped. *Inter alia*, it had advocated the use of media in creating awareness about the problems of the handicapped, providing support to every family with a handicapped child through incentives, dialogue and training and adopting a flexible approach to the education of the physically handicapped. The NPERC examined at length the needs of different categories of the disabled such as the deaf, the blind and the mentally retarded, and made specific recommendations. The NPERC had also made important recommendations on the role of training and of technological development in the education of the physically handicapped. We suggest that these valuable recommendations be built into a revised programme of action.

Minorities

80. Government of India should establish a standing machinery to closely monitor issue of detailed guidelines by the States for the purpose of granting recognition to minority managed educational institutions; to review the pace of disposal of applications for recognition of these institutions; and thereby to secure quality of education in institutions so recognised. (4.2.12)

81. All the educational programmes that are now under implementation should be concurrently implemented, to the extent feasible, in these districts on a priority basis after conduct of bench mark surveys as envisaged in POA. (There is no evidence of implementation of education programmes in these districts based on initial bench mark surveys to assess the status of literacy therein and to build programmes thereon for further improvements). (4.2.12)

82. The twenty-five districts which have not yet been covered under the community polytechnics should also be brought under their coverage before the end of the Eighth Five-Year Plan. (4.2.12)

83. The orientation programmes for the Principals/Managers and teachers of minority managed educational institutions should be organised on a decentralised basis through SCERTs at the State level and DIETs, CTEs & IASEs at the sub-State levels. (4.2.12)

Note: The forty-one districts identified in the POA as being of minority concentration.

Recognition of Minority Institutions

4.6 Article 30 of the Constitution confers on minorities, whether based on religion or language, the right to establish and administer educational institutions of their choice. There has been a plethora of case law on these issues. The establishment of the educational institutions is regulated by the State Education Acts. Therefore, recognition of an educational institution as a minority institution falls within the competence of the State Governments. In October, 1989, the Government of India formulated policy norms and principles for recognition of minority-managed educational institutions and communicated them to various State Governments. The role of the Central Government is advisory. We feel that monitoring is better left to the State Governments, and they are deeply conscious of the need for proper monitoring. At the Central level, many organisations like the Minority Commission already exist for this purpose of monitoring.

4.7 In addition to the two recommendations dealt with in paras 4.5 and 4.6 above (Recommendations numbers 69 and 77) the NPERC made a wide range of recommendations covering incentive schemes, SC/ST habitations not served by schools, curriculum, remedial coaching, recruitment of SC/ST teachers, Special Component Plan and Tribal Sub-Plan, programmes for educationally backward minorities, and recognition of minority managed institutions.

4.8 We feel that no policy reformulation is necessary and that

84. Special coaching should be organised through reputed and progressive voluntary organisations, particularly those operating for the benefit and welfare of the minority communities. (4.2.12)
85. Open universities including the IGNOU should establish distance education programmes for imparting special coaching. (4.2.12)

COMMON METHOD SYSTEM (Chapters 2 & 4)

2.2.2 A very vital component of the overall strategy for securing equity and social justice in education is the development of the Common School System. The Committee is fully aware that this is no new innovation but has been with us for over quarter of a century since the report of the Education Commission, 1964-66 and the essential point is that this has just remained a concept and its non-implementation has only contributed to the accentuation of the existing educational disparities. Concrete steps for translating this concept into action have to be taken. In order to achieve this objective, the existing Government, Local Body and Government-aided schools have to be transformed through quality improvement into genuine neighbourhood schools. Private schools also should be similarly transformed in course of time by making them freely accessible.

all recommendations, except R. Nos. 69 and 80, be taken into account while revising the POA.

COMMON SCHOOL SYSTEM (Chapter 6)

6.1 The NPERC considered the development of Common School System to be a very vital component of the overall strategy for securing equity and social justice in education. The Common School System was originally advocated by the Education Commission (1964-66), under the chairmanship of Dr. D.S. Kothari (hereafter referred to as Kothari Commission).
The concept of national system of education would imply, according to NPE 1986, that, upto a given level, all students, irrespective of caste, creed, location, or sex, have access to education of comparable quality.

Neighbourhood Schools

6.3 The NPERC's conception of neighbourhood schools is at variance with that of the Kothari Commission as well as the normal usage.

102. The first step in securing equity and social justice in education is the building up of a Common School System. Specific actions required in this context are the following:

- Provision of significantly increased outlay for elementary (particularly primary) education. This would help in the building up of the required levels of infrastructure and quality of education, thereby transforming Government, local-body and aided schools into genuine Neighbourhood Schools.
- Provision of special allocations for improvement of school system in backward areas, urban slums, tribal areas, hilly tracts, desert and marshy areas, drought and flood-prone zones, coastal belts and islands.
- Ensuring instruction for all in the medium of mother tongue at the primary level, particularly for linguistic minorities; active encouragement of teaching in the regional languages at the secondary level; and discontinuance of State aid to the schools imparting education otherwise than in the medium of mother tongue/regional languages.
- Phased implementation of the Common School System within a ten year time frame; and essential minimum legislation, particularly to dispense with early selection process, tuition fee, capitation fee etc.
- Exploring ways of including the expensive private schools into the Common School System through a combination of incentives, disincentives and legislation. (4.4.8)

2.2.3 It is particularly in the context of the need for establishing the Common School System that some of the members of

In our view this recommendation (R. No. 102) is very appropriate. The prime objective of the Common School System is equalisation of educational opportunities; equalisation cannot be achieved without bridging the yawning gap between the few expensive private schools and the multitude of government and local body schools, at least in regard to primary education, to begin with. The NPERC advocated a ten-year time-frame to achieve the Common School System. We do appreciate the spirit underlying this recommendation. Given the magnitude of resources required, a ten-year time-frame does not appear realistic

NAVODAYA VIDYALAYAS (Chapter 7)

7.1 The members of the NPERC had, admittedly, sharp

the Committee have found it difficult to go along with the Navodaya Vidyalaya Scheme. It is, interalia, for this reason that the Committee as a whole has advocated against establishment of more Navodaya Vidyalayas, not to speak of the inequity in nurturing talent only in a few. It is on account of the unfairness in judging a scheme for the implementation of which adequate resources as originally envisaged were not provided, and of the need for a fair and total review of the scheme that the Committee has made alternative recommendations on its future. The Committee, of course, has also taken into account the practical difficulties in abruptly discontinuing a scheme which involves about 50,000 students and 3,000 teachers.

Navodaya Vidyalayas (Chapter 4)

103. The Committee, having considered the strong views expressed by the members for and against the Navodaya Vidyalaya Scheme and after taking into account all aspects of the scheme in terms of the concept, philosophy, design, its implementation and future, recommends that the Government may decide from out of the following three alternatives:

(i) *No further Navodya Vidyalya need be opened.* The existing 261 Navodaya Vidyalayas may be restructured and continued with provision of adequate resources. The scheme may also be reviewed at the end of 1992-93. The terms of reference for this review may be

– Whether the objectives for which the scheme was established have been achieved – in terms of nurturing of differences about this scheme; these are reflected in the recommendation which appeared to be hesitant and wanting in specificity. The NPERC enumerated at length the points in favour of and against the scheme and proceeded to present a recommendation (R. No. 103) with three alternatives. The NPERC did not indicate any preference among the three alternatives.

We have given very careful consideration to these different points of view.

7.5 The majority view is that the scheme should continue and that a NV should be set up in each district as originally envisaged subject to the following observations:

i) constant review to keep the scheme as cost effective as possible.

ii) ensuring the continued validity and reliability of the admission tests by periodic evaluation and appropriate modification of admission procedure, and

iii) more particular attention to the pace-setting role of these institutions.

7.6 In coming to this conclusion, we take note of the information furnished by the Navodaya Vidyalaya Samiti that 40 per cent of the NV students come from families below the poverty line, 60 per cent are first generation learners, 30 per cent are girls, 19 per cent Scheduled Castes and 11 per cent are Scheduled Tribes. The academic results of the first board examination faced by NV students, viz., class X CBSE examination, 1991, were very good. The composition of students and the class X test results adumbrate that objective of providing quality education to talented children from rural

talents, reservations for the SCs/STs, girls, representation for rural children, pace setting functions and national integration through migration of children.

If the objectives have not been achieved what are the reasons for the same?

– Restructuring, if any, of the scheme with reference to:

- redefinition of the concept of special talent or aptitude such that the selection takes into account the entire cognitive and affective domain as well as the psycho-motor skills;
- broadening the process and canvas of selection with a view to make provision for the vast potential of talent in different attributes of life that exists among rural children, but is not identifiable by conventional academic tools;
- changing the present life style and value orientation of the Navodaya Vidyalayas such that the alienation of the campuses from rural life, particularly that of the under privileged sections, is guarded against.

(ii) All the existing 261 Navodaya Vidyalayas may be transferred to the State Sector for the States to run them as residential centres on the Andhra Pradesh model.

(iii) The Navodaya Vidyalaya scheme may be transformed into a Navodaya Vidyalaya programme of broad based talent nurturing and pace-setting. (A day-school each under the Common School system can function in the premises of the Navodaya Vidyalayas). (4.5.10)

disadvantaged families is being realised. The validity and reliability of the selection procedure are central to the whole scheme; therefore, we advocate periodic evaluation of the admission tests and implementation of corrective measures.

7.7 We also find that the cost per student is reasonable in comparison with the costs of the 'public schools,' which predominantly cater to the urban children. However, a constant effort needs to be made to make the scheme as cost-effective as possible. We have reflected a great deal on the question of equity which is the main reason why some find it difficult to go along with the scheme. That talented children should be provided special facilities for quality education cannot be gainsaid. Equality cannot mean that all children are or can be equal in ability, or in merit; so long as the admission tests do not discriminate against the children from disadvantaged families and are a valid test of merit, the principal of equity cannot be considered to have been violated.

7.8 In our view, the most attractive feature of the scheme is the facility for migration of students from one region of the country to other regions. Some of us had the opportunity to personally visit NVs and meet the students who migrated from other regions of the country. We can vouch for the contribution such migration can make to promote a national outlook among the students and teachers of NVs and to spread awareness among the communities in the vicinity of NVs of the rich diversity and unity of the Indian culture and polity.

EARLY CHILDHOOD CARE AND EDUCATION
(Chapter 5)

Scope of Article 45 of the Constitution

104. The scope of the Constitutional directive (Article 45) of providing, within a specified time-frame, free and compulsory education for 'all children until they complete the age of fourteen years', should be enlarged to include ECCE. (5.1.6)

Other Models and Strategies

116. Concrete provisions should be made in financial and programmatic terms for decentralised and community-based implementation of the various models and strategies mentioned in POA, such as

(i) Strengthening and upgrading all existing models,
(ii) Promoting innovative and experimental models,
(iii) Developing special programmes for specific under-privileged or migrant communities and for remote habitations, and
(iv) Developing and promoting media support on a massive scale (as is being done at present for the adult literacy campaign) for generating public awareness and understanding regarding issue relating to care and education of children in the 0-6 age group. (5.7.4)

EARLY CHILDHOOD CARE AND EDUCATION
(Chapter 8)

8.1 The NPERC considered NPE to be a historic document in that for the first time a policy document boldly recognized the importance of the Early Childhood Care and Education (ECCE) and laid down the holistic principles on which the programme was to be developed. The NPERC strongly rearticulated the NPE's perception of ECCE as an important input in the strategy of human resource development, as a feeder and support programme for primary education and as a support service for working women from the disadvantaged sections of society.

We feel that it would not be prudent to set higher goals in policy than what is feasible. Therefore, we feel it is premature to include ECCE in Article 45 and suggest that government should instead vigorously strive for achieving the goals laid by the POA. We strongly recommend that while expanding the coverage particular attention should be paid to the under-privileged communities as suggested by the POA (Para 7, Chapter I) and reiterated by the NPERC (R.No. 116[iv]).

MNP

8.4 The NPERC's recommendation to include ECCE in MNP is in keeping with its interpretation of Article 45 of the Constitution. We expect that this recommendation would be taken into consideration by the Planning Commission when the MNP is revised.

Priority

106. ECCE should be included in the Minimum Needs Programme. (5.3.0)

Decentralisation

127. The ICDS and other related Centrally Sponsored Schemes for ECCE may be shifted to the States/UTs following the completion of the present phase. The State/UT Plans should then be proportionately augmented with additional funds with conditionality of non-divertibility and accountability. (5.103)

8.8(ii) ICDS and other CSS relating to ECCE should continue as Centrally Sponsored Schemes during the Eighth Five Year Plan. The Anganwadi workers should play an expanded role and should be the focal point for a number of activities and support services for women and children, such as child care, family welfare, nutrition and health. The recruitment and training of Anganwadi workers should be so organised as to ensure that they have the necessary skills and motivation to discharge the expanded role.

UNIVERSALISATION OF ELEMENTARY EDUCATION (Chapter 6)

The Elusive Goal

Universalisation was to have been achieved by 1960....We are still nowhere near the goal of universalisation of elementary education (i.e. upto class eighth).... The continued failure since independence to fulfil the constitutional directive of providing education to all children upto the age of 14 years is a teasing reality. (6.1.2 and 6.2.1)

UNIVERSALISATION OF ELEMENTARY EDUCATION (Chapter 9)

9.1 In the NPERC's view, the most fundamental problem of our education system is the continued failure to fulfil the Constitutional directive of providing education to all children upto the age of 14 years. The NPERC attempted a comprehensive analysis of the failure to achieve universalisation of elementary education (UEE) and came to the conclusion that urgent and sweeping changes were required in the strategy for UEE. The basic premises of the analysis were that so far there was hesitation to acknowledge the reality that more than half of the children and two-thirds of the girls were outside the ambit of education and that it was never too late to give up the

Right to Education

145. The Right to Education should be examined for inclusion amongst the fundamental rights guaranteed under the Constitution of India. All the socio-economic measures, without which realisation of this right will not be possible, should be taken. (6.1.3)

Thrust Areas

146. The Policy Statement in para 5.5 of NPE should be modified to incorporate the following three areas of concern as thrust areas:

(a) Convergence of services,
(b) Linkage between the school and the community, and
(c) Decentralised and participative mode of educational planning and management. (6.3.2)

150. Since the present enrolment data are not reliable the policy should stress a continuing concern for improving both enrolment and retention, as distinct from enrolment to retention. (6.3.7)

hesitancy and to frankly admit the facts so that an honest analysis of the causes of the problem may begin. Given these premises, it is but natural that the NPERC sought to distinguish its policy perspective and strategies from those of NPE/POA.

Constitutional Amendment

9.2 While the spirit underlining this recommendation is laudable, we feel that a legalistic approach to UEE would not be desirable. The Constitutional guarantee can be effective only if the country is in a position, financially and politically, to take all measures necessary for enforcing the guarantee; otherwise, legislation would be cosmetic. We feel that what is needed is not so much a Constitutional amendment as the manifestation of a national will to achieve UEE. We call upon the Central and State Governments to bestow overriding priority to adult literacy and UEE and to provide programmes in these two areas total support–financial, administrative and political–a support to match with the priority assigned.

Access, Enrolment and Retention

9.4 The NPERC's analysis of the problems of access and enrolment is very detailed; it rightly highlighted the deficiencies of the data on enrolment, and the disparities in enrolment–gender, regional and SC/ST–brought out even by the existing data which inflates enrolment.

152. NPE's 'Resolve' in Para 5.1 should be modified to:
(a) emphasise both enroment and retention in the school;
(b) relate fixing of targets to ground-level realities through a decentralised and participative mode of disaggregated planning, rather than fixing targets in an ad-hoc fashion; and
(c) integrate non-formal and formal education systems over a period of time such that their cadres, infrastructure and management structures would form an organic whole.
(6.4.9)

"Enrolment–Attendance–Retention–Attainment"

9.5 The NPE/POA should be credited for trying to shift the policy away from a perocccupation with provision of inputs–more schools and more teachers–towards outcomes, namely, completion by every child of five years of schooling or its equivalent. A plan reading of NPE and POA as a whole would make it clear that the concerns of the NPERC were anticipated in NPE/POA. The modalities of achieving universal enrolment and retention envisaged by NPE/POA include decentralisation, creation of a spirit of autonomy for educational institutions, a greater role for heads of institutions, community mobilisation and ensuring a voice for women and disadvantaged sections of society. Therefore, our considered view on the recommendations of the NPERC relating to access, enrolment and "concerns" is that no further refinement of the policy is required; what needs to be done is large scale operationalisation of important components of the strategy outlined by NPE/POA such as community mobilisation, school mapping and micro-planning.

Policy Agenda

9.17 Para 5.12 of NPE laid down targets for achieving the goals of universalisation of primary education and universalisation of elementary education. By 1990, it was to be ensured that all children upto the age of 11 would have had five years of schooling or its equivalent in non-formal education system and likewise, by 1995, all children upto 14

Lacunae in NPE 1986

148. The policy has certainly done well by emphasising child-centred approach to education and by pointing out that it is the best motivation for the child to attend school and learn (NPE Para 5.6). The Committee's perspective in this regard is presented below:

(i) Although implied in the warm, welcoming and encouraging approach mentioned in NPE, it would be better if the policy would explicitly refer to the elements of joy, fun, exploration and play as integral to learning in the early stages of primary education.
This explicit mention is required because the prevailing educational practice in the school system not only excludes these elements, but seems to consciously resist their introduction in the learning process.

(ii) Similarly, the policy statement should emphasise the role of singing, drawing, clay-modelling, games and particularly all forms of folk-art and folk-lore in enriching the learning process.

(iii) It is not clear why the benefit of being allowed to set their own pace and be given supplementary remedial

years of age were to be provided free and compulsory education. Para 5.12 of NPE, which laid these targets, needs to be revised. Every effort should be made to ensure that the Constitutional obligation of providing free and compulsory education upto the age of 14 years becomes a reality before we enter the twenty-first century.

Levels of Learning

9.6 We wish that NPERC had bestowed adequate attention to the important issue of levels of learning. Till recently planning for UEE tended to be pre-occupied with the extension of school facilities and enrolment targets. Little attention was paid to the standards of attainment in school. A recent study by NIEPA showed that in most schools covered by the study, children in class V could reach only mastery learning levels set for class II. UEE has, therefore, to be viewed as a composite programme comprising (i) access to education for all children upto 14 years of age, (ii) universal participation till they complete elementary education through formal or non-formal educational programmes, and (iii) universal achievement of minimum levels of learning (MLL). The endeavour has to be to delineate MLLs in terms of competencies in language, mathematics and environmental studies from class I to class V, MLLs to be determined with reference to the existing levels and corresponding over a period of time to nationally acceptable norms.

instruction is restricted only to the first generation learners. By implication, the policy would deny the other children the advantage of setting their own pace.

(iv) The policy emphasises the need to increase cognitive learning and the skill component with the growth of the child. In the same spirit, the policy should have emphasised the role of the affective domain and psychomotor skills at the earlier stages.

Non-Formal Education

153. Over a period of time non-formalise the formal school in the following ways:

(a) Shifting of the school timings to early morning hours, afternoons or late evenings, as per the convenience of the majority of children and in consultation with the Village Education Committee and the Educational Complex.

(b) Adjusting school calendar to agricultural activities, local cultural engagements and the weekly markets with a view to optimise school attendance.

(c) Introducing child-centred approach with concomitant *reduction in school hours,* but an *increase in the learning hours.* This would come about through utilisation of improved, pedagogic practices involving elements of inquiry, play-way, activity, creative writing, peer group learning, experimentation etc. Creative use of singing, drawing, story telling and particularly of folk-lores and folk-arts would enrich the pedagogic practices.

(d) Linking at least one day care centre, providing holistic

Non-Formal Edcucation (NFE)

9.13 Though some of the suggestions of the NPERC to non-formalise school are vague (e.g., reduction in school hours but increase in learning hours) and some are of doubtful validity (e.g, "ungraded classroom" and segregating written and oral tradition into "morning" and "evening classes"), many are ideas which were under articulation for the last forty years or more but have failed to take root largely because of practical problems. Making the school more flexible has very much been on the agenda of educational reforms all these years. Flexibility would necessitate decentralisation of educational administration, empowering of local communities, building up of local level capabilities for teacher support and supervision of schools and major changes in teacher recruitment policy and in teacher motivation. It is imperative to persevere with these measures; however, one should not lose sight of the fact that making the school system more flexible–not to speak of transforming, as the NPERC desired, the school into an institution with rather infinite flexibility, services for children in 0-6 age group, with the school in both physical as well as programmatic terms; the school should adopt the play-way and activity-based approach of ECCE from the day care centre; the Anganwadi workers may be viewed as associates of the school staff;

(e) Wherever required and feasible, holding of classes twice in the day–mornings for the written tradition and evenings for oral tradition, games and cultural action;

(f) Introducing 'ungraded class room' which would encourage all children at different levels of learning to set their own pace;

(g) Relating content and process of learning with environment and life of the community; and

(h) Allowing all working children, particularly the girls, to *drop-in* the school at any time of the day or the year they want; also encouraging the children of migrant families from other villages/habitations/towns to similarly *drop-in* (this flexibility becomes possible as a direct consequence of the 'ungraded class room' approach). (6.5.11)

versatility and effectiveness–is bound to be a long and arduous process; and while the process is on, one cannot ignore the educational needs of those children who cannot attend regular schools such as working children, migratory children, children pre-occupied with household chores, girls prevented by tradition-bound attitudes from attending regular schools and children who drop out due to socio-economic compulsions. The NPERC had not come forth with any suggestions to tone up the NFE system. Since it cannot be said that the NPERC was oblivious to the educational needs of 'out of school' children, the logical conclusion is that in its view the process of non-formalising the school would be smooth and rapid. Given the present condition of the schools in general, the challenges before the school system are many, e.g., enrolling and retaining children who cannot afford to attend school regularly; a harmonious interaction with the community around; improving the infrastructure, quality and the learning environment; and ensuring that every student acquires minimum level of learning. These challenges are daunting enough and it does not seem desirable to overload the school system with yet another formidable challenge of meeting the educational needs of children with severe para educational constraints. We are of the view that the NPE approach is more practical and realistic, viz., making the formal school flexible upto a point and beyond that relying on an alternative, more flexible NFE system. For a long time to come, there is no alternative but to have a large and systematic programme of first rate NFE. We cannot overstate the importance of ensuring that the quality of NFE is comparable

OPERATION BLACKBOARD (Chapter 6)

To be sure, Operation Blackboard is a laudable scheme as it has helped focus national attention on the paucity of facilities in our schools. (6.6.4)

Recommendations

Operation Blackboard

157. The question of continuance of Operation Blackboard as a centrally sponsored scheme may be treated in the light of recommendations made by the Committee in regard to Centrally Sponsored Scheme (CSS) as a whole in the Chapter of Decentralisation and Participative Management. (6.6.6)
158. The State Governments should devolve all decision-making powers concerning Operation Blackboard to the Educational Complexes which would seek consultation from DIETs on the one hand, and the concerned school and the Village Education Committee, on the other hand, for plan-

with that of the formal system in all respects. Concrete measures in this regard brook no delay. We have been informed that the Department of Education is reviewing the scheme of NFE with a view to improving the management system and the learning environment. We strongly urge (i) expeditious and effective action in this area and (ii) continuous and close monitoring by the Centre and the States in concert to ensure the effectiveness of NFE programmes.

OPERATION BLACKBOARD (Chapter 9)

9.15 It would be adequate to mention here that we are of the view that CSSs initiated after NPE should continue and a few more CSSs need to be introduced in the priority areas of education during the Eighth Five Year Plan, after due consultation with the States. Operation Blackboard admittedly being one of the priority strategies for UEE, we feel that it should continue during the Eighth Plan, in an expanded and extended form. The norms should be upgraded from the

ning and implementing the scheme. (6.6.6)

159. The schools and the Village Education Committees, made fully responsible for UEE in their respective areas, should undertake a micro-planning exercise for working out their requirements under Operation Blackboard and be accountable for its implementation. (6.6.6)

160. Operation Blackboard must be given the status of one of the priority strategies for UEE, but at the same time, it should be ensured that investment is made only on those items whose need has been established by the teachers and other related persons on the basis of micro-planning and class room requirements. (6.6.6)

161. For posting women teachers in the villages, it would be best to select them locally, wherever possible, or else make provision for their accommodation, security and other support services. (6.6.6)

STRATEGIES AND MEASURES FOR ACHIEVING UEE (Chapter 6)

169. Make each school, primary or middle, fully responsible, accountable or formulating and implementing strategies for UEE in villages/habitations/*mohallas* in the area under its coverage. For this purpose, vest the school with the necessary authority and autonomy to decide upon thier mix of strategies and measures (e.g. adult education, para-schools, Operation Blackboard). Provide each school through the avenue of the Educational Complex adequate funds and intellectual resources to implement its programme of universalisation. present level of two classrooms and two teachers for every primary school to three classrooms and three teachers and the scheme should be extended to upper primary schools. We take note of the fact that flexibility is being introduced in the scheme so that procurement of equipment is better related to local situations; we feel that this is a step in the right direction. As regards entrusting the decision making powers to the educational complex, it may be mentioned that the whole concept of educational complex was detailed by the NPERC in the chapter "Decentralisation and Participative Management" and our views have been expressed in the corresponding chapter. Suffice to say here that till operational models of an educational complex are developed, tested and tried out, it is not feasible to link the Scheme of Operation Blackboard with the educational complex.

UEE (Chapter 9)

9.18 We are of the view that the following points deserve priority during the Eighth Five Year Plan in the area of UEE:

i) Universal enrolment of all children, including girls and persons belonging to SC/ST;
ii) Provision of primary school for all children within one kilometre of walking distance and of facility of non-formal education for school drop-outs, working children and girls who cannot attend schools;
iii) Improvement of ratio of primary school to upper primary schools from the existing 1:4 to 1:2, this beiing a

(6.13.0)

170. Authorise the school Head Master/Head Mistress to recruit 'para-teachers' (*Shiksha Karmis*) for reaching out either to unserved habitations or to those children who cannot attend the school in the day hours. The issues of emoluments, rules governing their probationary period and eventual absorption in the school, and their trainiing in an 'Internship Model', have already been dealt with in this chapter. (6.13.0)

171. Encourage innovation by teachers themselves in building up diverse models of child-centred approach to education and create mechanisms for collating, integrating and disseminating the growing experience of the teaching community within and among Educational Complexes. (6.13.0)

172. In order to increase the relevance of education from the standpoint of working children, especially girls, it would be necessary to emphasise vocationalisation of the entire educational process upto Class VIII level. (6.13.0)

173. The goal of universalisation of education may be viewed in two phases the first phase of Universalisation of Primary Education (UPE) and the second phase of UEE. While the school shall be expected to undertake micro-planning for UPE in association with the Educational Complex in the first phase itself, UEE may be allowed to grow organically out of the development of Primary Education. In the second phase, after achieving the goal of UPE, micro-planning for UEE would also become necessary and viable. (6.13.0)

174. Adopt the principle of differentiated or disaggregated targets and pluralistic educational strategies for achieving UEE. This mode of decentralised and participative planning pre-condition for larger opportunity for widening girls' participation at upper primary stage;

iv) Reduction of drop out rates between Classes I to V and I to VIII from the existing 45 per cent and 60 per cent to 20 per cent and 40 per cent respectively;

v) Improvement of school facilities by revamped Operation Blackboard, to be extended to upper primary level also;

vi) Achievement of minimum levels of learning by approximately all children at the primary level, and introduction of this concept at the upper primary stage on a large scale;

vii) Local level committee, with due representation to women and teachers, to assist in the working of primary education and to oversee its functioning;

viii) Improvement of the monitoring system for universalisation of elementary education to see to the achievement of above mentioned goals.

NPE and POA may be revised accordingly.

provides scope for gender-specific, community-wise, Block-level and District-level, and regional parameters to inform the planning process. The national and State targets of UEE as well as resource allocation shall emerge from collection and integration of the disaggregated targets. (6.13.0)

175. Monitoring of the move towards UEE shall be integral to the planning process and may operate at three independent but co-ordinated levels:

(a) Within the Educational Complex, of individual schools;
(b) Within the district, of individual Educational Complexes; and
(c) Within the State, of individual District Boards of Education.

ADULT AND CONTINUING EDUCATION (Chapter 7)

Adult Literacy as a Felt Need

178. Imparting of literacy should be placed in the context of the developmental needs of the adult. Adult education programmes should be accompanied by a wide range of measures relating to health, nutrition, housing, and employment needs. They should also address themselves to issues of fundamental rights, laws, secularism and democracy. After creating awareness in respect of these essential needs and issues the adult learner himself should be expected to ask for adult literacy as a felt need. Instead of starting with adult

ADULT AND CONTINUING EDUCATION (Chapter 10)

10.3 The NPERC's recommendations (R. Nos. 178-182) leave one with a sense of hopelessness about the massive adult illiteracy problem facing the country, a problem which is in the league of transcendent problems such as population and national integration. In the NPERC's opinion, there is, as it is, no tested and tried "ready-to-use" model. The centre-based model, which dominated the adult education strategy till 1989, is too defective to be redeemed. Its successor, the TLC (Total Literacy Campaign) is not considered to be ready for universal application rightaway. Not to speak of its replicability, the NPERC is even doubtful whether lessons

literacy, the start should be in respect of creation of awareness for essential needs and from there work backward to adult literacy. (7.9.0)

Mass Campaign Strategy and Mahila Samakhya Model

179. While the mass campaign strategy may be tried out further, the alternative model being employed by the Department of Education through Mahila Samakhya may be closely monitored and its application for adult literacy examined – considering that the objective of this project is to create awareness regarding issues of survival and thereby generate felt needs. (7.9.0)

180. The mass campaign strategy as well as the Mahila Samakhya model may be objectively evaluated to look for meaningful lessons for the future. '(7.9.0)

Evaluation of NLM

182. While NLM goes ahead with its planned literacy campaign in the Eighth Five Year Plan period, an independent study group should be commissioned to evaluate the programme, particularly with a view to arrive at an understanding of what

could be drawn from the "Ernakulam experiment" for application elsewhere. However, the NPERC sees in the Mahila Samakhya (MS) an attractive alternative model, whose application to adult literacy should be examined. The NPERC did not consider it possible to come to grips with the problem of adult illiteracy during the Eighth Five Year Plan; its expectations were rather modest – no breakthrough can be expected in the adult literacy scene and the only concrete outcome that could be hoped for is the development of viable and effective models.

10.4 The NPERC's perception of Mahila Samakhya (MS) as an alternative model is not valid.

10.5 The NPERC's approach to evaluate, as brought out in R. Nos. 180 and 182, is rather narrow and restricted. Evaluation is twofold in character, namely, 'formative' and 'summative'. The formative evaluation commences right from the stage of formulation of the action plan and its implementation at various stages; while the summative evaluation deals with evaluation of learning outcome at different stages and teaching-learning process as also with the impact of the programme on acquisition of literacy and numeracy skills, and on the overall quality of life of the learner. Such evaluation, in

may be appropriate strategies to remove adult illiteracy in the quicker possible time. The evaluation may also look into the various alternative models and study their relevance with respect to diverse socio-cultural and political conditions in different parts of India. The minimum objective of this study should be to find out on objective basis what approaches do not yield results, so that, five years later, at least those models may not be encouraged. (7.9.0)

addition to being a tool of assessment and review of the status of the project, could also be a supportive tool to introduce correctives to improve the quality and content of the programme. Therefore, as suggested by the NPERC, one need not wait for the conclusion of the Eighth Five Year Plan for changing a model; if deficiencies are identified, the correctives could be introduced straightaway.

UEE and Adult Education Programmes

185. Illiterate adults are those who have either not had access to education or having had access, have been unable to complete their schooling. A person has to remain in school at least for a minimum of four years to attain a relatively irreversible level of literacy. Literacy should be a form of basic training making it possible for the adult to acquire some knowledge as may be necessary. It is imperative that Universalisation of Elementary Education is given top priority in educational planning and resource allocation. The objective should be to ensure that no child in the early nineties shall grow into an illiterate adult in the next century. (7.9.0)

10.1 The NPERC appears to have an ambivalent attitude to adult education. Therefore, R.No.185 runs contrary to the world-wide move towards a holistic view of educational needs. Further, it is based on a conceptual frame which posits a unidirectional relationship betrween adult education and UEE. This conceptual frame rightly points out that adult illiteracy arises from the failure to achieve UEE. However, it does not adequately recognize the inter-dependence of UEE and adult education. The feedback from informed observers in districts where the Total Literacy Campaigns (TLCs) have taken off successfully is that parents who were earlier apathetic towards sending their children to primary school are, after themselves becoming literate, demanding the opening of schools where they do not exist and insisting on regular attendance by the teachers so that their children receive proper education. Primary education can, so to say, ride piggyback on the advances registered in adult education. We, therefore, strongly recommend that the "dual-track ap-

EDUCATION AND RIGHT TO WORK
(Chapter 8)

Integrated Design of Vocational Education

188. An integrated design of vocational education to be operated for class IX to XII may be established as presented in the following model with a general core and vocational core and flexible mixes of academic and vocational subjects:

Clas IX to XII

Compulsory			*Core General*	
			Core Vocational	
Optional	Academic	Vocational	Academic	Academic
Groupings	Academic	Vocational	Academic	Vocational
	Academic	Vocational	Vocational	Vocational

Structural Changes in Secondary Education

189. In order to make vocationalisation a success, substantial structural changes may be introduced in secondary education

proach'' should continue to inform educational planning and that the special needs of women and of disadvantaged groups like SCs and STs should be specially attended to.

Note: Secondary Education *(Chapter 11)*

Recommendations of NPERC are dispersed in Chapter 8 'Education and Right to Work', Chapter 11 'Languages in Education' and Chapter 12 'Contents and Process of Education'.

VOCATIONALISATION OF EDUCTION
(Chapter 12)

12.4 We do note that some of the recommendations, particularly, R.Nos.188 and 189, appear to be at variance with the NPERC's vision of vocationalisation. An integrated design of vocational education was suggested for classes IX to XII, according to which the students have a compulsory general core subject, a compulsory vocational core subject and different mixes of elective academic and vocational subjects. The vocational content of one of the options suggested is more vocational-intense than the present vocational stream. R.No.189 also referred to provision for specific skill training as one of the requirements for the long term viability of vocational education. Therefore, the two recommendations seem to imply that the NPERC did not exclude, in operational terms, streaming of subjects and occupation – specific education and training.

12.5. While the NPERC did not specifically suggest any change in the 10+2 pattern, the integrated design of voca-

along the principles of modular courses and credit accumulation, at the same time providing flexibility for multiple exit and entry points for the students. In other words, students opting for any particular vocational course should have the facility of acquiring credits for specific modules of courses, go out into the world of work and come back later at their convenience for earning further credits by pursuing further modules. This would make it possible for the schools to offer vocational courses in varying combinations with subjects such as Languages, Mathematics, Sciences and Social Studies. No doubt, vocational and non-vocational subjects should be inter-woven both at the level of content and pedagogy. For those students taking up vocational courses at the secondary stage leading to direct job placements, provision should also be made for further education in those vocations or other fields and, if necessary, bridge courses may be provided. These arrangements are necessary in the expanding world of knowledge and technology, which requires continuing and updating of education for all. What is required for long term viability of vocationalised education is to make provision not merely for specific skill training but also for necessary theoretical background to enhance transferability of well planned and logically designed open learning and distance learning programmes at the school and university levels should be established as the same would be a good support system for vocationalisation of education. (8.7.0)

tional education (R. Nos. 188 and 189) would seem to imply that the four years from class IX to XII constitute a distinct four year block and that there should be a switch over to an 8+4 pattern. Each pattern has its distinct advantages and disadvantages and different countries have opted for different patterns for well considered reasons. However, it took nearly twenty years for the 10+2 pattern to be fully accepted in our country. A transition to yet another pattern would be a long-drawn-out process, and would impose further avoidable adjustment costs. The change to 8+4 pattern would necessitate re-writing the curricula and text-books not only of vocational courses but also of general education.

12.7 The idea of a core vocational course suggested by the NPERC (R.Nos. 188 and 189) is very appealing. Generic vocational courses which cut across various occupational fields and which are primarily not occupation specific have many potential benefits. The benefits would include promoting the all-round personality of students, acting as a corrective to the textbook oriented learnijng process that goes on in school, fostering right values and attitude to work and providing the students with a general skill base which would facilitate acquisition of more specific skills.

Work Experience/Socially Useful Productive Work

187. Work Experience/Socially Useful Productive Work should be integrally linked with various subjects both at the level of content and pedagogy. (8.6.0)

Vocational Programmes in NFE

190. For those who do not go in for formal secondary education in the school system, vocational programmes should be organised in non-formal stream like through TRYSEM and community polytechnics and in the formal stream through the ITIs, Rural Institutions etc. (8.7.0)

Work Benches and Practice Schools

192. In order that the process of vocational education is enriched by a meaningful combination of teaching of theory and practice and effective linkages are established with the 'world of work', 'work benches' and 'practice schools' may be identified, accredited and involved as described below:

– 'work benches' and 'practice schools' are work situations selected for the purpose of giving vocational training and direct experience to students within production units or developmental activities of the official agencies. This arrangement offers a more effective educational strategy for providing vocational experience to students than what can be arranged within the four walls of the 'classroom'.

12.9 R. No. 190 dealing with reorganization of vocational courses for those who do not go in for formal seecondary school system, R. No.192 dealing with work benches and practice schools, R. No. 193 dealing with teacher education courses, and R. Nos. 195 and 197 dealing with management of vocational education have no new policy implications. They relate to implementation modalities which are congruent with NPE/POA. We suggest that these recommendations be taken into account while revising the POA.

12.6 We have taken a holistic view of the perceptions and the recommendations of the NPERC. We appreciate the concern of the NPERC for inculcation of a positive attitude to work from class I onwards, a concern which is very much in keeping with the NPE perception. We also feel that the Work Experience/SUPW courses need to be toned up in keeping with the common perception of NPE and the NPERC on Work Experience. The National Curricular Framework brought out by the NCERT suggested compulsory Work Experience at all stages of education. However, even at middle and secondary stages, the integration of work with learning has

Here the training would revolve around real problem solving and on-the-job development of skills. Whereas 'practice school' is a more institutionalised arrangement with larger units in the organised sector, 'work benches' can be carved out of smaller units from the unorganised sector as well within the neighbourhood of the school. In both cases, the school would not be required to make any substantial investment on skilled personnel or equipment, the same being contributed by the 'world of work', with or without a mutually worked out fee.

Education at these work places would be through student involvement in work activities which would be clearly identified against different areas and levels of work. Further, information would be available to the students in regard to how, under a given work area, one could move from one level to another (vertical mobility), and skills could be transferred from one work area to another (horizontal mobility). A tested evaluation system would be identified to assess students attainment in the work activity and its inter-relationship with nature and society. Based on this assessment, certificates would be awarded by the accredited 'work benches', whether in private or public sector, government or voluntary organisations, and these should be acceptable for employment in any part of the country. Of course, this would call for devising of proper accreditation guidelines and procedures, as well as periodic review by authorised bodies, and this task will have to be done carefully, so as to ensure that this educational innovation does not degenerate into unhealthy not come about as it ought to. The time allocation for Work Experience hardly exceeds ten per cent in many States. Though the NCERT guidelines were made available to the States, there has been no planned intervention either by the Central Government or by most States.

12.8 The litmus test of any vocational programme is the eventual gainful placement of students in their chosen vocational areas. The employability of the students depends to a great extent on the relevance, quality, specificity and intensive nature of vocational education. Specifically tailored curricula have to be provided to students to develop skill proficiency for jobs. It would be necessary to improve the market orientation of the programme and to use training resources efficiently. Good vocational training costs more than general education and it is thus important to manage costs efficiently. We feel that undiffntiated teaching of vocational skills may foster the right attitudes to work but it may not facilitate the development of specific skills. The resources would be spread too thinly to provide the necessary inputs needed for preparation of employable students. We are fortified in our conclusion by the fact that countries which are making rapid progress in education and development such as South Korea, Philippines and China, are streaming their students. We, therefore, advocate retention of the present system of distinct streams of vocational education.

social and educational practices. Further, special attention should be given to identify and accredit 'work benches' in the rural sector, specially from economics built around activities such as farming, forestry, animal husbandry, dairying, fisheries, watershed management, and ecological conservation.

Personnel in the 'work benches' and 'practice schools' are not merely to engage themselves in teaching process but are also to be involved in the planning and designing vocational courses, preparation of text materials and evaluation in a sense in the entire process of education. (8.8.4)

Decentralisation of Planning and Management

194. The management, planning and implementation should be decentralised to the level of individual high schools or school complexes, as well as colleges/universities, thereby involving actively, the Heads of institutions in decision-making, along with representatives of local enterprises from both the industry and agriculture as well as those of official development agencies and voluntary organisations. This would necessitate shift from the present practice of designing vocational courses under centralised initiatives at the national level. Courses have to be designed at the institution level (school/colleges) to the extent possible, drawing upon the resources of DIETs. This would also call for greater autonomy at the institutional level in order to fully exploit local and/or regional industrial, agricultural, commercial and

12.10 R.No. 194 suggested that the management, planning and implementation of the vocational education programmes should be decentraiised and entrusted to individual high schools and school complexes. Flowing from this recommendation, R. No. 196 suggested that the concept of National and State Councils of Vocational Education should be reformulated in the framework of decentralised planning. We note that under the existing scheme, a number of functions are decentralised. These include the planning of courses, and selection of institutions and industries for collaboration. The District Vocational Surveys are expected to provide valuable inputs for the planning process. Arrangements for teaching-learning are also decentralised and are expected to be provided at the school; coordination is envisaged at the

development potential in framing courses and curriculum. This will further facilitate matching of manpower needs at different stages of development planning. The criticality of institutional autonomy for ensuring success of vocationalisation calls for redefining of roles of various central or state-level agenices under the Department of Education (NCERT, SIE, SCVE etc.), so that these agencies would play only catalytic and resource-sharing roles, rather than directing, determining, and detailing all processes. (8.9.0)

196. The concept of National and State Councils of Vocational Education should be re-formulated in the framework of decentralised planning, management, evaluation and accredition in order to involve the 'world of work', private or public, in expanding the reach of vocationalisation of education to the masses. (8.9.0)

HIGHER EDUCATION (Chapter 9)

Maintenance of Standards in Higher Education

198. Pressures for opening new colleges and universities

district level. However, a certain degree of decentralisation of the arrangement is necessary to ensure national standards of achievement. Therefore, a few functions like overall planning, monitoring and supervisory role have been envisaged at the State and Central levels. The Central Institute of Vocational Education and State Councils of Vocational Education are expected to provide the necessary resource support for the programmes at the Central and State levels. Therefore, we feel that the degree of and areas for decentralisation should be determined with reference to the monitoring and periodic evaluation of the scheme.

12.11. We take note of the fact that vocationalisation is a complex programme in which inputs of a diverse nature have to be provided in a coordinated manner. Therefore, we feel that greater rigour must be brought to bear on the planning and implementation of the programme, particularly in regard to the conduct of district surveys, the preparatory measures needed for starting a course, linkages with employers, pre-service and in-service training for teachers, preparation of good quality instructional material, adequate management strucuture and provision of vertical mobility for graduates of vocational education.

HIGHER EDUCATION (Chapter 13)

Maintenance of Standards in Higher Education

13.3 R. No. 198 is based on the following premises:

i) the unplanned proliferation of colleges and universities is being very intense, and the political system reacting to such pressures in different ways, in different states, it would only be appropriate for the Government to re-examine the feasibility of national level statutory mechanism for strongly discouraging non-standard/sub-standard colleges and universities being established. In the process of this examination, no doubt, the Central Government should have necessary prior consultations with the State Governments. (9.4.0)

the bane of higher education;

ii) the existing powers of UGC to control proliferation are inadequate.

The first premise is universally accepted. The NPE itself recognised the need to effect an all-round improvement in the institutions already established and proposed that the main emphasis will be on the consolidation of, and expansion of facilities in, the existing institutions and on protecting the system from degradation. The POA envisaged an important role for the UGC and the State Councils of Higher Education in securing a planned development of the higher education system. The UGC also is not in favour of establishment of colleges and universities established minimum prescribed facilities. We have given careful consideration to the recommendation of the NPERC. We take note of the fact that States, in general, have been averse to a Central regulatory legislation and that the UGC itself prefers to rely on persuasion than on statutory authority. It is not advisable to set up a national level statutory mechanism to regulate the opening of non-standard and sub-standard universities and colleges. We are of the view that the proliferation of colleges without adequate facilities can be curbed to a large extent if the universities exercise rigorous control and insist on creation of necessary infrastructure and educational facilities before granting affiliation and if the State Governments respect the decision of the universities in these matters. We are further of the view that the establishment and operationalisation of State Councils of Higher Education will go a long way in the planned development of higher education.

Extension in Universities

214. Universities should involve themselves in development issues in the concerned regions. They should become instruments of development in the respective regions. Consistent with this concept, curriculum, course development etc. should undergo significant changes. To be specific, for example, university teachers could involve themselves in improvement of rural schools so that they become the real 'living link' between the universities and school going population in the regions.

The school experience gained should be built into the content and pedagogy of university education. For this purpose, the universities, so to say as stated elsewhere should affilitate themselves to educational complexes engaged in the improvement of the whole system of school down to the elementary level. This way the universities would also come to contribute to enrichment of knoweldge. This would develop a cycle of overall development from content of education to competence building. In the process, students coming into the universities would also improve in quality and standards. There will be consequent overall improvement in the environment prevailing in the university system–teachers looking upon this work as of interesting social relevance and better crops of students by themselves contributing to the quality of university education. In the opinion of the Committee, the slogan of the university system should rather be "Vishwa Gyan Gaon mein Dhyan". (9.12.0)

Extension Service

13.4 In the NPERC's perspective, the higher education system should strive for a balance between regional expectations of the people and global activities in education and research. Consequently, the NPERC recommended that universities should involve themselves in developmental issues and become instruments of development for their respective regions (R. No. 214). For this purpose, it was suggested that courses in universities and colleges should be redesigned and the teachers and students should participate more actively in developmental programmes including improvement of rural schools. The spirit underlying the NPERC's recommendation is laudable; ideally extension service should be as important a funciton of the universities and colleges as teaching and research. However, considering the present state of higher education system, we feel that the first priority should be restoring intellectual vigour, seriousness of purpose and discipline into the higher education system in order to make it work. Academic Credit for extension work could be considered and in certain areas directly related to extension activities like social work and rural development. Even the courses can be redesigned. However, it would be neither feasible nor desirable to redesign all courses as suggested by the NPERC. Efforts should be made to secure involvement of teachers and students in extension work such as literary. The majority is of the view that unless the NTS undertakes the conduct of tests, the organisation cannot acquire the required expertise and develop into a competent resource centre, as

National Testing Service

215. In the view of the Committee testing of competencies is best left to the concerned user agencies–whether they be employers or educational institutions. While there is need for a National Testing Service, it need not be a body for conduct of tests in a centralised way. It need only be a development agency engaged in research and performing certain service activities including in terms of aid to building of models for tests. Model for rest development, administration scoring etc. can be built up as part of the service functions of the organisation. It can also be a clearing house of experiences in educational testing. (9.13.3)

Rural Universities

216. The Committee is in agreement with the proposal for giving suppport to rural universities and institutes. However, they should be brought under the umbrella of the State Councils of Higher Education. The State Councils, even as envisaged in the POA, are to give advice to the UGC in respect of maintenance of standards. Therefore, they can perform this function in regard to rural universities and institutes as well. As already stated, the advice of the Planning Commission on the Department's proposal is also that maintenance of the standards should be left to the UGC. If the State Councils of Higher Education and the UGC together can help in the maintenance of standards and if the present practice of routing funds to rural institutes through the UGC is continued, there envisaged by the NPERC.

Rural Universities

A proposal for setting up such a Council was formulated by the Department of Education based on a project report prepared by the Education Consultants (India) Ltd. The NPERC opined that there was no need to set up a Council and that the functions envisaged for the Council can be discharged by the UGC and the State Councils of Higher Education themselves (R.No. 216-217). However, the Department of Education felt that this was not a feasible recommendation for the following reasons:

i) Only one State has so far set up the State Council of Higher Education. Even if more Councils are set up, their main focus would remain on conventional system of higher education.

would be no need for establishment of a Central Council and the Committee recommends accordingly. (9.14.2)

217. The State Councils may peform the following specific role in handling affairs relating to rural universities/institutes:

- Ensuring autonomy of the institutions in developing their own course content, research programmes and extension activities.
- Ensuring equivalence of the diplomas awarded by rural universities/institutes with university degrees in order to facilitate horizontal and vertical mobility for its graduates.
- Coordination for involving the rural institutes with the district level rural development programmes.
- Facilitating affiliation of rural institutes with State level universities/Agricultural Universities according to their choice. (9.14.2)

Restructuring of UGC

200. The UGC has not been able to function effectively in the face of expansion of the higher education system in terms of increasing number of colleges and universities. Workload in terms of development programmes of the universities to be scrutinised by the Commission has been on the increase and their scrutiny and clearance by the Commission suffer in quality as well as on account of delays.

Therefore, restructuring of the UGC is called for. In the opinion of the Committee, the Commission should consist of at least five full time members apart from the Chairman and Vice-Chairman, with specialisation in specific areas–teaching,

ii) Because of the rapid growth of the conventional system, the UGC has not been able to give adequate attention or necessary encouragement to the development of rural universities. It will be difficult for the UGC to rearrange its priorities in favour of rural institutions.

iii) Many rural institutions provide integrated education including education at school level. These institutes are not affiliated to the university system and do not come within the purview of the UGC. Therefore, a separate body like the Central Council is required to promote their activities.

iv) The proposed Central Council will also initiate and encourage setting up of new rural institutes. The UGC cannot perform this function.

We are of the view that a Central Council of Rural Institutes is necessary to provide the much needed fillip to rural education on Gandhian lines and that it should be set up immediately.

We were informed that the question of restructuring the UGC on the lines suggested by NPERC had been considered in the past. Though the U.G.C. Act was indeed amended in 1971 to provide for three full-time Members the amendment was later repealed as it was felt that it would not be desirable to have two categories of members, viz., full-time Members and part-time Members, with the latter having, by implication, lower role and status as compared to full-time Members. We appreciate this point of view and feel that there is no need for appointment of full-time Members.

13.11 We were informed that the UGC had accepted the need

research, extension, management and finance. The Commission should also have regional offices for decentralised disposal of the problems relating to higher educational institutions in the respective regions. Structural decentralisation would be meaningless unless adequate decentralisation of authority and functions is effected and accordingly this should also be effected. (9.6.0)

for establishment of some regional offices and also received a report of the Administrative Staff College, Hyderabad. We strongly recommend that regional offices should be set up at the earliest, with adequate authority and functions.

Selectiveness in Admission

201. The universities have come under severe strain on account of the load of administering examinations at the bachelor's level. They should be relieved of the responsibility of holding these examinations so that they can concentrate on post-graduate, doctoral and post-doctoral studies, apart from research. (This matter has also been separately dealt with under the subject of Examination Reforms). (9.6.0).
202. If in a college M.A. and M.Sc. teaching is to be continued, it must be made mandatory that there are adequate facilities for research in those subjects. (9.6.0)

Undergraduate Examinations

13.12 The NPERC did not suggest any alternative arrangement for this purpose. We note that the Gnanam Committee also made a similar recommendation. However, since most of the universities are affiliating universities, this recommendation can be implemented only when most of the colleges become autonomous or when a system of internal evaluation gradually replaces a terminal examination, or when an independent State level examining body is set up to conduct common examinations for all underground courses.

New Management for Universities

204. Government, should facilitate early decisions on the report of the Gnanam Committee, the same having been received as early as January, 1990 (9.7.3)

Research Facilities in Colleges

13.13 While this is desirable, the resource constraint precludes the feasibility of implementing the recommendation in toto. The UGC may, however, consider augmenting research facilities in selected colleges within the available resources.

Curriculum Development

205. For the redesigning of courses the UGC has set up twenty-seven Curriculum Development Centres in different disciplines. The emphasis is on modernising and restructuring courses in modular form. Reportedly, twenty-two Curriculum Development Centres have given the reports and they have been circulated to universities and colleges for consideration and implementation. One important question that arises for consideration, in this context, is whether this centralised arrangement does not militate against the autonomy of the universities and colleges on which much emphasis has been laid under NPE, 1986. One view that has been expressed is that these courses are only recommended to universities and colleges which are free to adapt themselves with such modification as they deem fit. The Chairman of the UGC, in the course of interactions with the Committee, had occasion to observe that though UGC may be only issuing

Gnanam Committee Report

13.14 The NPERC recommended early decisions on the report of the Gnanam Committee (R.No. 204). We note that in accordance with the decision of the CABE, in its forty-sixth meeting held in March, 1991, a CABE Committee was appointed to examine the Gnanam Committee report in detail keeping in view the comments of the State Governments.

Curriculum Development

13.15 In 1986, the UGC initiated the Scheme of Curriculum Development Centres (CDCs) with the objective of carrying out a thorough review of existing syllabi and courses in different universities and for suggesting measures for modernising and restructuring the courses. The CDCs are located in twenty-six universities in different parts of the country. The modal curricula prepared by the CDCs were discussed in national level workshops and circulated to all universities with guidelines. The NPERC, while noting that the universities and colleges were free to adapt model curricula with such modifications as they deem fit, opined that the higher education as a whole had come to look upon the guidelines of the UGC as iron-bound mandates and that this by itself had introduced a certain rigidity. On this basis, it recommended that the work done by the CDCs should be decentralised and that it should be left to the universities and

guidelines on various subjects from time to time, the higher education system as a whole has come to look upon such guidelines as iron-bound mandates and this by itself has introduced a certain rigidity in the system. Viewed in the light of this observation, the Government and UGC should examine whether the whole process of Curriculum Development and designing of courses cannot be decentralised – the respective universities and colleges seeking the assistance of UGC and panels of experts suggested by them for the purpose of designing courses according to the locally felt needs. (9.8.0)	colleges to seek the assistance of the UGC in the area of curriculum (R. No. 205). The UGC has a legislative mandate to determine and maintain standards in higher education. Curriculum reform is, therefore, very much in the UGC's Charter. What is important is that the UGC discharges its functions in a participative and interactive manner. This is exactly how the Curriculum Development Scheme was implemented. Therefore, we feel that the scheme should be continued; however, to allay any misgivings the UGC may reiterate that the universities have full freedom to adapt model curricula. The UGC should also consider specific requests from the universities for curriculum development.
Teacher Training	**Teacher Training**
207. In order to enhance the quality of the teachers in the university system, pre-induction training for a period of one year after recruitment should be organised. This training should be organised on a decentralised basis by the respective universities themselves. (9.9.0)	We were informed that in pursuance of the NPE, the UGC had set up forty-eight Academic Staff Colleges (ASCs) in different parts of the country for organising orientation programmes for newly appointed Lecturers and re-orientation of courses for in-service teachers. We were also informed that so far nearly 20,000 teachers received training at the ASCs, that the Expert Committee appointed by the UGC found that, by and large, the ASCs had served a useful purpose and that the UGC had decided to continue to expand the Scheme. In view of the resource constraint, it may not be possible to provide training facilities in every university. We suggest that the UGC may closely monitor the implementation of the Scheme of ASCs.

National Council of Higher Eduction	National Council of Higher Education
219. The Programme of Action under NPE, 1986, envisages establishment of a National Apex Body. Action has been initiated by the Department of Education, in this context, for the establishment of a National Council of Higher Education to bring about coordination between the UGC, the All India Council for Technical Education, Indian Council of Agricultural Research, Medical Council of India and Bar Council of India. In specific terms, the objective of establishing this body, as reflected by the POA, is to deal with policy aspects of higher education and to undertake integrated planning and to reinforce programmes of post-graduate education and inter-disciplinary research. Functions envisaged are tendering of advice to Government on policy, coordination of activities of the various bodies in different fields, encouragement of inter-disciplinary and promotion of interfaces amongst different areas, allocation of resources, establishment and management of common infrastrucutre and coordination of policy concerning external academic relations. Going by these objectives and functions of the apex body, it does not seem necessary to create another institution at the national level to function as a super body, as it were. These objectives can be achieved and functions performed by an appropriate coordination mechanism that could be brought into existence by a mere Resolution of Government. This mechanism, in the opinion of the Committee, could have a two-tier structure–(i) a Council of Ministers of Higher Education, the Ministers being those holding portfolios relating	**13.7** Following NPE, the Department of Education initiated the process of consultation with Planning Commission, the UGC and other Ministries concerned like Agriculture and Health. All these organisations expressed reservations about the proposal to set up an apex body as they felt that such a body would erode the autonomy of existing institutions. Therefore, while recognising the importance of achieving coordination, we agree with the recommendation of the NPERC.

to education, agriculture, health, law and science & technology; and (ii) a Council of Secretaries dealing with these subjects and Heads of the concerned institutions apart from Finance Secretary to Government of India and Secretary, Planning Commission. Being a high powered body, the former Council may be presided over by the Prime Minister. One of the concerned Ministers may be the Vice-Chairman by rotation. The Council of Secretaries and Heads of Institutions together may basically formulate the policies and submit the same to the Council of Ministers for approval. (9.15.0)

TECHNICAL AND MANAGEMENT EDUCATION

THRUST AREA SCHEMES (Chapter 10)

221. A detailed evaluation [of the thrust area schemes should be undertaken by a national level expert committee with the following specific terms of reference:

(i) Whether funds provided for identified crucial projects have been properly spent in terms of purchase of equipment and their utilisation, civil constructions etc.

(ii) Whether the objectives of the projects have been achieved.

(iii) Whether investment in individual projects has been optimal (grants given in regard to a number of projects are small amounts and there is a seemingly thin spreading of resources).

(iv) Rearrangement of priorities, if any, that may be needed in funding projects.

(v) Advising on strengthening of monitoring system so as to

THRUST AREA SCHEMES (Chapter 14)

14.3 The NPERC had recommended a detailed evaluation of the thrust area schemes by a national level expert committee (R. No. 221). These schemes are extremely important because of their linkages with economy. Therefore, a proper system of monitoring and evaluation is extremely important. We have been informed that large scale funding has been provided for these schemes only during the last three years and that it would be premature to have the scheme evaluated by a national level expert committee. Therefore, we suggest that a detailed evaluation be taken up in 1994-95, the third year of the Eighth Plan (1992-97) by when the schemes would have operated on a large scale for about 5-6 years.

get meaningful feedbacks regarding the success of the projects. (10.4.3)	
Community Polytechnics	**Community Polytechnics**
222. The report of Kalbagh Committee estimated the financial requirements of the Community Polytechnics for the years 1988-89 and 1989-90 at Rs. 10.20 crores and Rs. 12.25 crores respectively (Non-recurring as well as recurring requirements included). Inter alia, this outlay was to include establishment of 350 Community Polytechnics and 2000 village centres during 1988-90. To the extent that three years have passed by after the report was received, the Department should update the financial requirements and take up the implementation of the recommendations of the Committee well within the first year of the Eighth Five Year Plan. (10.4.6)	**14.4** The Department of Education, GOI, should take early decision on the reports of the Kalbagh Committee.
AICTE	**AICTE**
223. Emergent steps should be taken to ensure regional offices of the AICTE are headed by senior functionaries so that they are effective in discharging their responsibilities for coordination with the state authorities. These offices should also be given adequate devolution of authority and functions so that they operate efficiently and speedily with the help of the regional offices.	**14.6** We are of the view that the Regional Committees of the AICTE should be adequately staffed and that the Chairman of the Regional Committee should be an Education Minister of a State from the region, by rotation. The Regional Committee should have the power to make recommendations on the opening of new institutions, starting of new courses. and enhancing the intake within the framework of the guidelines laid down by the AICTE. The State Governments and the universities should issue the necessary approvals based on

Future Perspective and Measures

225. *Improvement of quality and standards at all levels.*
Action:
- Introduce a broad-based flexible system through modular courses with credit system and provision for multi-point entry.
- Encourage creativity and innovation in experimental work by introducing problem/process-oriented laboratory exercises.
- Review curricula on a continuing basis.
- Improve quality of science education in schools.
- Admit students to technical education programmes based only on merit and motivation.
- Make recruitments to teaching positions strictly on merit by open competition and on all-India basis.
- Develop engineering faculty members through the effective use of study leave, summer training, consulting and research opportunities.
- Assess teachers annually through a "staff appraisal scheme".
- Introduce coordinated training programmes for non-teaching technical supporting staff.
- Grant autonomy to selected institutions and departments on the basis of the track records.
- Accredit all existing institutions and grade their quality through accreditation procedure. (10.7.0)

the recommendations of the Regional Committees only.

Future Perspective and Measures

14.7 The NPERC also made a number of recommendations regarding improvement of quality and standards, upgradation of infrastructure facilities, industry-institutions linkages, technology watch and manpower planning, promotion of R&D, special programmes for the disadvantaged, entrepreneurship development and continuing education and retraining programmes. In the revision of POA, these recommendations would have to be given due consideration.

229. *Measures to prevent brain drain.*

Action:

- Make the Scientists Pool in the CSIR more attractive by offering better remuneration according to merit and placement in the right institutions.
- Utilize all international collaboration programmes to enable Indian scientists and technologists to undertake useful collaborative projects with well established institutions abroad.
- Take concrete steps to enhance the mobility of scientists and technologists paying due attention to matters such as accommodation, financial compensation, children's education etc.
- Check migration of engineering graduates to non-engineering professions through career guidance activities.
- Make available opportunities of employment, including on part-time basis, for well trained women scienitsts/ engineers.
- Consider bringing in legislation to ensure that highly trained engineers and technologists put in at least three years of service in the country before they can go abroad as in countries like France. (10.7.0)

BRAIN DRAIN (Chapter 14)

14.2 Almost all the recommendations relate to specific modalities of implementation. The one recommendation which has policy implication is R. No. 229 relating to brain drain. The NPERC put forth the view that it should be compulsory for the graduates of IITs and RECs to serve at least three years within the country before going abroad as they receive high quality education at highly subsidised costs. The fact remains that the country has not been able to gainfully employ all the graduates passing out from technical institutions in the country, particularly in some disciplines. Further, in an age of global inter-dependence, no country can afford to insulate itself from the emerging developments in the frontiers of science and technology, for insulation entails technological and economic stagnation and even regression. Our young scientists and technologists should not be deprived of opportunities of interaction with institutions and academics outside the country and from acquiring valuable research and work experience abroad. Many of our professionals do not return to the country after study/work abroad. This trend should further increase with the modernisation and technological upgradation of the economy, the increasing availability of modern facilities in industry, universities and research institutions and the more liberalised incentives for NRI investment. If properly utilised, the Indian professionals abroad can constitute a brain bank. We are of the view that all efforts should be made to ensure that environment for science and technology in the country is attractive enough for

LANGUAGES IN EDUCATION (Chapter 11)

The Three-Language Formula

235. Whatever be the difficulties or uneveness in the implementation of the three-language formula, it has stood the test of time. It is not desirable or prudent to reopen the formula. In order to bring about uniform and rationalised implementation of the three-language formula the following measures should be taken:

(a) The Kendriya Hindi Sansthan (KHS), Central Institute of English and Foreign Languages (CIEFL), and Central Institute of Indian Languages (CIIL), the three National level institutions, charged respectively with the development of teaching of Hindi, English and modern Indian languages should come together and, in consultation with the CVSE and NCERT and each of the concerned State Governments, spell out modalities of ensuring uniformity in the matter of acquisition of language competency by the students in the school system. They should particularly bear in mind the observation of the Education Commission 1964-66 that learning of languages could be facilitated not merely in terms of years of study but in terms of hours of study and level of attainment.

(b) Unlike in the case of subordinate offices of the

talented persons. However, we do not consider regulatory legislation as advisable. One of us does not agree with the last point.

LANGUAGES IN EDUCATION (Chapter 15)

15.1 The present policy was enunciated by NPE 1968. After examining the question in great detail, the NPE came to the conclusion that the essentials of 1968 Policy on languages could hardly be improved upon and that they continue to be relevant. The NPE commended energetic and purposeful implementation of the 1968 Policy provisions. The NPERC also reiterated the 1968 Policy. It concentrated on a study of the implementation of the policy and of the measures needed to improve its implementation. Its recommendations are useful for improving the ongoing schemes and for toning up the performance of the institutions in this field, such as the Kendriya Hindi Sansthan (KHS), the Central Institute of English and Foreign Languages (CIEFL) and the Central Institute of Indian Languages (CIIL).

However, we feel that the merger of these three institutions would not be desirable. The charters of each of these institutions is different. The CHD is meant for production of bi-lingual, tri-lingual, multi-lingual dictionaries and propagation of Hindi in non-Hindi speaking areas, KHS for training of Hindi teachers and CSTT for evolution of terminology in Indian languages. Further, the body that would emerge from the merger would be unwieldy; merger is also likely to generate service litigation as the service conditions of the

Government of India exercising regualtory functions of the government, as an academic institution, the CIIL deserves to be relieved of the functional rigidities of a subordinate office. It may be converted into an autonomous body.

Development of Hindi as per Article 351 of the Constitution

239. With a view to strengthening and unifying the efforts for the promotion and spread of Hindi as envisaged in Article 351, these three organisations could be merged into a single institution.

A Fresh Linguistic Survey of India

246. The last linguistic survey of India (only one hitherto) was carried out from 1898 to 1928. Since the survey, considerable changes have come about in terms of vocabulary, diction, evolution of new dialects etc. Often, controversies also do arise regarding the identity of the languages. Therefore, a fresh linguistic survey of India based on rational principles should be undertaken. This new Survey would be of immense help in use of languages in the educational system particularly in the North-East and other areas where education is not taking place necessarily in the mother tongue. (11.4.6)

employees of these three organisations would be affected.

15.5 We notice that many agencies including the Registrar General of India, Anthropological Survey of India and some institutions of educational research are already engaged on the collection of data on languages. In view of this as well as sharp differences of opinion on the issue of languages, and the possibility of controversies arising out of a linguistic survey, we feel that a fresh linguistic survey is not desirable.

CONTENT AND PROCESS OF EDUCATION
(Chapter 12)

While Central Coordination would be useful, the process of preparation of curriculum should be decentralised through the involvement of State Agencies. (12.2.2)

Cultural Content

248. The cultural content of education should include not merely the common cultural heritage of India as a whole but also diversities of cultural traditions of all parts of India, particularly those symbolised by the oral and folk traditions. (12.3.2)

249. In conveying to the student community, through the content of education, the cultural traditions of the country, the needs for acceptance/rejection of the same based on critical analysis should also be inculcated. (12.3.2)

Value Education

251. Democracy, secularism, socialism, scientific temper, equality of sexes, honesty, integrity, courage and justice (fairness), respect for all life forms, different cultures and languages (including tribal) etc. constitute the mosaic of values which is vital to the unity and integrity of the country. The content and process of education should be all pervasively informed by these basic values. (12.4.0)

CONTENT AND PROCESS OF EDUCATION
(Chapter 16)

16.2 We note that even now the national curricular framework prepared by the NCERT merely provided guidelines and that the actual preparation of the curriculum is done by the State agencies for their schools. Therefore, NCERT's role in curriculum is one of coordination only.

Rich cultural identity of the tribal people. Implicit in R. No. 249 is a static view of culture. In the process of historical and cultural development, many elements become obsolete and are given up while some others undergo change and modifications. Therefore, culture should be viewed as a process and not as something which was created at any fixed time in the past in its final form which is either to be revered or denigrated.

These suggestions (R. No. 251-253) should be taken into account while revising the POA.

Educational Technology

255. The Educational Technology Programme as a whole should be reviewed by the Government in the light of the past experience. Specifically –

(i) Status of utilisation of the RCCPs and TVs already provided to the various States should be quickly studied in detail, closely involving the States themselves so that their proper utilisation is ensured.

(ii) Teacher training in the use of these equipment should be organised. The emphasis in teacher training should be on instructional designs suitable to local needs. Techno aids should be made available to the teachers only if and when needed.

(iii) Already, infrastructure and capability are available in existing institutions in the country for the production of educational software. The UGC, NCERT, the Central Institute of 'English and Foreign Languages, Central Institute of Indian Languages, and the Kendriya Hindi Sansthan' are the organisations. These Institutions themselves could tap talents from the open market for production of educational software.

We suggest that this recommendation should be followed up by the Central and State Governments and that it be taken into account while revising the POA.

Sports, Physical Education and Youth Activities

259. As in the case of implementing programmes relating to synthesis of culture and education, in the matter of provision of opportunities for the youth to involve themselves in national and social development through educational institutions and outside them, the primary responsibility should lie

Youth

16.7 R.Nos. 259-266 contain the suggestions of the NPERC on the schemes for involvement of youth in national and social developmental programmes. We urge that these suggestions be taken into account while revising the POA. We are strongly of the opinion that students should be required to

with the Department of Education. (12.9.0)

266. National Integration camps should be so organised that opportunities are offered for the mixing of the youth with the underprivileged tribal population. This will also bring about national integration in the true sense of the terms. (12.9.0)

Examination Reforms

267. The question of examination reform should be construed as a package of all the following factors:

- Introduction of semester system.
- Continuous internal evaluation; and maintenance of integrity of such evaluation (and examinations in whatever form and scale they may be conducted); within the same classes, in primary stage, disaggregated evaluation of groups of students to cater to individual differences.
- Teachers, playing the key role, the principal being "He or she who teaches shall lay down the syllabus and also evaluate."
- Facilities for students to move from one stage of education to another by appearing in entrance tests.
- Facilities for students to have the freedom of choice of modules rather than whose course packages.
- Provisions for credit accumulation by students and facilities for transfer of grade from one institution to another; facilities of multiple entry and exit for students which in effect facilitates opening up and non-formalising the school system. (12.10.7)

It is this package as a whole which should be brought under

participate in one of the other existing schemes, such as NSS and NCC, as envisaged in para 8.22 of NPE.

Examination Reforms

16.10 The reading of the recommendations as a whole would make it appear that the NPERC was itself undecided about the immediate feasibility or acceptability of the package suggested by it. Given the diversity of the educational institutions, it would not be realistic to prescribe a single package of reforms across the board. Some of the reforms like introduction of semester system may be relevant for higher education rather than for school stage. Facilities for multiple entry and exit, and transfer of grade from one institution to another are not immediately feasible, at least in the school stage, and call for a degree of uniformity in curriculum and medium of instruction, which are difficult to achieve in a continental nation like ours. Therefore, the endeavour should be to strive for the best achievable results rather than plan for the best unobtainable package. Examination reforms have necessarily to be contextual and evolutionary.

16.11 The essentiality of examination reforms cannot be overstated. We do feel that rather than leaving examination reforms to the individual initiatives and inclinations of the examining bodies, a strong and coordinated effort should be made by the Centre and the State Governments in this area.

implementation and not merely individual elements, that too in a piecemeal or ad-hoc fashion.

268. Implementation of this package, however, bristles with several practical problems, diversities in the educational system in the country being vast. Therefore, there is need for an Examination Reforms Commission. This should also be a permanent body which will facilitate monitoring of progress in examination reforms from time to time until the task is fulfilled in stages. The terms of reference for this Commission may be:

(i) Review of the status of examination reforms from time to time.
(ii) Phasing of examination reforms, indicating time-frame within which and levels at which, the reforms are to be effected.
(iii) Introduction of fair and objective systems of grading/ scaling.
(iv) Laying down norms for continuous comprehensive internal evaluation and suggesting safeguards against abuse of this evaluation system.
(v) Advising on minimum levels of learning to go with internal evaluation system.
(vi) Laying down modalities for semesterisation and modularisation.
(vii) Advising on inter-institutional linkages to secure comparable standards.
(viii) Teacher orientation for successful implementation of examination reforms.

It is obvious that the Examination Reforms Commission The idea underlying the constitution of an Examination Reforms Commission is appealing. However, rather than creating yet another institution, we suggest that the NCERT and the UGC should play a lead role in promoting and guiding examination reforms in school and higher education systems respectively. Inter alia, the following measures are suggested:

i) Preparation of a status report of examination reform measures undertaken by the examining bodies.
ii) Preparation of a National Examination Reform Framework to serve as a set of guidelines to the examining bodies which would have the freedom to innovate and adapt the framework to suit the specific situation.
iii) Developing an effective mechanism for coordination, monitoring and evaluation of the implementation of the examination reforms by the different examining bodies.
iv) Documentation and dissemination of innovations and measures for examination reforms.

will have to go into problems relating to the reforms in each State, fully involving the State level authorities such that problems at the State as well as the sub-State levels are fully taken into consideration. Functionaries of UGC, AIU, AICTE, NCERT, NIPEA, State resource institutions, State Boards of Education, and other expert bodies at the national and other levels, apart from teacher and student organisations will also have to be consulted from time to time by the Commission. The Commission may be headed by an eminent educationist with the rank of Minister of State, Government of India. The Commission may be a compact body consisting, apart from the Chairman, of experts in the areas of school, university and technical education. The Chairman and members may be full time functionaries. (12.10.7)

Load of the School Bag

269. The knowledge in different disciplines needs to be viewed in an integrated manner, rather than in water-tight compartments. By doing this it would be possible to avoid unnecessary repetition of facts. (12.11.0)

270. Emphasis on supplementary reading material and library work as important elements in school education can help in reducing exclusive dependence on textbooks, without losing the quality of education. (12.11.0)

271. There is need to stress the scientific method of acquiring knowledge, rather than knowledge itself. Equipped with the tool of the method of acquiring knowledge, the students would be in a position to learn throughout life according to his/

Load of School Bag

16.12 The NPERC expressed concern about the "load of the school bag" and made a number of recommendations (R. No. 269 to 276). The whole question of curriculum is complex and there are no simple solutions. The concern about curriculum load is universal. There is invariable tension between the knowledgeable explosion, particularly in the fields of science and technology, and the limitations of time during which the curriculum is to be transacted. While the load of the school bag is a valid concern, one cannot afford to ignore the requirements of modernisation and relevance. The NPERC questioned the value of preparing science material to catch up with the exponential growth of knowledge and emphasised

hcrneeds. (12.11.0)

272. A shift in the emphasis from mere information to concepts and principles would make it possible to eliminate the irrelevant material from the textbooks. (12.11.0)

273. At present the curriculum at the +2 level is used to put pressure on the designing of curriculum in the middle and primary schools. What is needed instead is to view primary and middle level curricula in a self-sufficient package of knowledge, aptitude and skills with which the child can go into the 'world of work' and continue self-learning throughout life. (12.11.0)

274. The curriculum is based on an erroneous view that learning comes to an end with the public examination. In place of this, it would be helpful if capabilities of self-learning and an aptitude to learn throughout life is emphasised. (12.11.0)

275. The entire curriculum needs to be reorganised to give due emphasis to not only all dimensions of the cognitive domain, but also to affective domain and psycho-motor skills. (12.11.0)

276. The class room learning is invariably alienated from what the child learns from home and the society. This frequently results in avoidable repetition. (12.11.0)

the need to stress upon scientific method of acquiring knowledge rather than the knowledge itself. It is no doubt important to inculcate the scientific temper and scientific method and to imbue the students with spirit of enquiry, and problem solving and conceptualisation skills. However, the distinction drawn between the scientific method and scientific knowledge is artificial. Rather than teaching the scientific method in abstract, it is better to teach it in the relation to empirical facts and knowledge. Such an approach is all the more important in the initial stages of science education.

TEACHERS AND STUDENTS (Chapter 13)

Teacher Education

277. Selection of students (for teacher training courses) should be regulated through stringent aptitude and attainment

TEACHERS AND STUDENTS (Chapter 17)

17.3 In the context of teacher recruitment, NPE talked about reorganising the methods to ensure merit, objectivity and conformity with spatial and functional requirements. The selection system, whether for teachers or teacher trainees,

and not merely on University grade or mark. (13.1.4)

Correspondence Education

282. The first degree in teacher education should not be given through correspondence education. (13.4.0)

Internship Model of Teacher Training

284. The Internship Model of teacher training may be used extensively for preparing para-teachers' during their probationary period. The programme in each Educational Complex may be co-ordinated at the Complex level in close linkage with the DIET. This training would have to be sandwiched with in-service institution-based short term courses in between. (13.6.11).

285. The Internship Model may also be explored as a possible way of training other types of teachers as well. (13.6.11)

Training High School Teachers

286. The new NCTE syllabus for B.Ed. courses should be circulated to all teacher training institutions and State/UT Governments for detailed comments, before the matter is finalised. (13.7.2)

287. Encourage more institutions to open the 4 year integrated course along the lines of Regional Colleges of Education. (13.7.2)

should be objective and immune from undue inducements, thereby fostering the credibility of the selection process.

Correspondence Courses

17.5 This recommendation is very sound and needs to be followed up vigorously by the Central and State Governments and the universities.

Internership Model

17.6 There are at the moment no well-documented experiences on the internership model and the practical aspects for its adoption on a large scale and its comparative advantages need to be examined further. An expert body like the NCTE should study the model in-depth and guide the SCERTs and teacher education institutions.

B.Ed. Syllabus

17.7 R. Nos. 286-287 deal with details of syllabus for B.Ed. course and the types of courses to be opened. NCTE may take necessary action in consultation with States/UTs.

Preparing Teacher Educators for Leadership Role

288. Give the teacher educator a leadership role in all aspects of the educational system, including policy making, strategy formulation, implementation and monitoring. (13.8.4).

289. For the above purpose, organise a specially designed training programme such that all the desired attributes of a teacher educator would be inculcated in the trainee. (13.8.4).

Attributes of Teacher Educator

17.8 In R.Nos. 288-289, the NPERC had identified the attributes which a teacher educator should possess. The NPERC also suggested that the programmes should be designed for teacher educators and that such programmes should inculcate all the desired attributes in the trainee (R. No. 288-289). We understand that the NCERT is preparing a special programme for teacher educators. Recommendations of the NPERC may be kept in mind by the NCERT.

Continuing Teacher Education

290. The proposed Educational Complex may be given the responsibility for co-ordinating and organising in-service teacher training programmes for the teachers in the area of its coverage. In particular, the Complex can provide an effective channel of communication between the schools and DIET. (13.9.0).

In-Service Programme-Planning

17.9 It would be premature to assign to educational complexes the responsibility for planning and organising teacher training programmes before effective functional models are developed. Therefore, training and management of in-service training programmes for elementary teachers should be the responsibility of the DIETs only.

Faculty of Teacher Training Institutions

291. The practice of using teacher training institutions as a dumping ground for unwanted or troublesome persons should be stopped forthwith. Instead, competent persons may be brought into these institutions from schools and other Government institutions on a rotational basis. (13.10.3)

Teacher Education Institution: Faculty

17.10 We strongly endorse the appeal of the NPERC to the State Governments that they should give emergent attention to fill up all the posts and to frame recruitment rules. These rules should ensure that the posts are filled up by competent and motivated persons with reasonable tenure.

17.12 We do feel that every DIET should be a distinct identity with enough operational autonomy. It should have the "space"

District Institutes of Education and Training (DIETs)

294. The State Governments must ensure full autonomy to DIETs for embarking upon their programmes of research and training so that these are able to play their expected role in bringing about quality improvement and reform. (13.11.2)

295. In view of the new thrusts given by this Committee to education, DIETs would have to undertake fresh responsibilities and develop competence in the respective areas as enumerated below:

(a) Universalisation of Elementary Education (UEE);
(b) Early Childhood Care and Education (ECCE);
(c) Women's Education with emphasis on giving a gender perspective to the entire educational process;
(d) Education for promoting equity and social justice among SCs/STs and other educationally backward sections of society, including minorities;
(e) Vocationalisation of the entire educational process; and
(f) Examination reforms, modularisation, multiple entry and exitpoints. (13.11.2)

Implementation of the Scheme of Teacher Education

296. Emergent steps should be taken for getting completed all the teacher education institutions for which financial assistancce has been given by the Government of India. (13.12.0)

297. Further financial assistance to States which have had so far completed the earlier phases of project implementation

to experiment and to innovate. However, it would be more advantageous to have a networking arrangement of DIETs and the SCERT, with the SCERT providing necessary guidance and coordination. The SCERT can also act as a clearing house for sharing of experiences and information. We would recommend an independent and autonomous structure for SCERTs conducive to their emergence as genuine academic institutions. At the present, only a few DIETs have become fully operational; therefore, we do not feel that DIETs can, at this stage, take on the additional responsibilities as envisaged by the NPERC. It would be worthwhile to examine setting up separate institutions at the State level for some areas like vocationalisation; the SCERTs themselves can play a lead role in respect of some areas like ECCE and examination reforms.

Teacher Education Scheme

17.11 We also strongly endorse the recommendation of the NPERC (R. Nos. 296-297) that emergent steps should be taken for operationalising the teacher education institutions for which financial assistance was provided by the Government of India and that further financial assistance should be denied to those States in which the physical progress and

should be avoided–i.e. until physical progress is demonstrated in regard to funds given but not yet used. (13.12.0)

Powers of Heads of Schools

293. All the necessary administrative and financial powers be vested with the Head of the Institution (i.e. Primary/Middlel/High Schools), so that she/he may function with autonomy to fulfil the assigned role. (13.10.3)

Teachers' Welfare

299. Conducive working conditions and environment are necessary for improving teacher effectiveness; however, provision of various welfare facilities for them are just as necessary. These should include:

- Office-room for individual teachers with adequate provisions for interaction with students, staff lounges, departmental libraries etc.
- Residential quarters at reasonable rent.
- Facilities for community/corporate life including cultural and recreational facilities.
- Medical facilities.
- Travel facilities for visiting libraries and other advanced academic centres, industrial establishments, etc. including participation in conferences, seminars, etc. (13.14.0)

utilisation of funds are unsatisfactory.

Heads of Institutes

17.13 We are of the view that emergent action is necessary in this regard and the heads of the institutions should be vested with the necessary powers and capabilities to discharge their role.

Teacher Welfare/Participation/Mobility

17.14 The NPERC also offered suggestions regarding teacher welfare, teacher participationu and teacher mobility (R. Nos. 299-301). The NPE also called upon the government and the community to create conditions which will help motivate and inspire teachers on constructive and creative lines. It also felt that pay scales and conditions of service of teachers should be commensurate with their social and professional responsibilities, and with the need to attract talent to the profession. The NPERC's suggestions regarding office room, residential quarters, facilities for community and corporate life, cultural and recreational facilities, medical facilities, travel facilities etc. have to be considered by the State Governments in the light of their financial position and other commitments. Regarding teacher participation in management, we consider that para 9.2 of NPE put forth the most feasible proposition, namely, that teachers will continue to play crucial role in formulation and implementation of the teacher education programmes.

Teachers' Participation in Management

300. Teachers should be provided with opportunities to participate in a wide range of activities that are crucial to the growth and development of the institutions they serve.

Teacher Mobility

301. Mobility of teachers should be encouraged both within the education system as well as between the education system and other related sectors. To ensure this mobility, the conditions of service of teachers should provide for protection of their past services and provision for transfer of the beneifts of such services while moving from one institution to another and from the education sector to other sectors. (13.16.0)

Students

302. Students should play a leading role in the organisation of corporate life, cultural activities, games and sports, academic societies, hostel committees, etc.

In order to provide a direction and sense of purpose to student participation in the corporate life of institutions, State level Committees could be set up to consider the following issues: (13.17.0)

The State level committees could be constituted with student representatives elected/nominated from universities/ colleges within each State.

At the university level, Students' Councils should be set up

Students

17.15 The NPERC recommended several measures for student participation in the corporate life of the academic institutions such as setting up Students' Councils, and Departmental Student Advisory Committees. The NPERC also suggested that representation of students on these bodies be preferably by nomination. The State Governments and universities may take appropriate action on the recommendations taking into account the specific situations.

with the Vice-Chancellor as its President.

There could also be Students' Advisory Committee at the department of faculty levels. (13.17.0)

DECENTRALISATION AND PARTICPATIVE MANAGEMENT (Chapter 14)

Educational Complexes

307. On a pilot basis, at least one Educational Complex may be established in every district during the Eighth Five Year Plan so as to develop a functional model. At the pilot stage full administrative and financial support should be given to these Complexes. The features of these Complexes are described below:

- The Management model may be that of a local college, a high school or group of high school and the associated middle and primary schools coming together in a cluster. The Complex may work in coordination with Panchayati Raj institutions as well as local development and social welfare agencies, voluntary or Government. The university serving the region may affiliate itself with this Complex. The university may help in the development of the Complex through its faculty, students and technical resources. There could be a memorandum of understanding between the Complex, and the university on the one hand, and the Complex and the local body, on the other.

MANAGEMENT OF EDUCATION (Chapter 18)

The idea of school complexes was first mooted by the Kothari Commission (1964-66). The networking of schools in a school complex was expected to facilitate sharing and exchanging of resources and experiences. NPE assigned a key role to school complex and POA elaborated the NPE perception. We find that the educational complexes suggested by the NPERC is an enlargement of the idea of school complexes in that colleges and universities are also brought into the network. We find a certain measure of uncertainty in the NPERC's approach to the educational complexes. In this chapter, the NPERC had advocated experimentation with the idea of an educational complex while in other chapters the recommendations relating to educational complex proceed from the premise that educational complex is a proven institution which can be entrusted with entire responsibility of management of education and major programmes like Operation Blackboard in the area as falling in its jurisdiction. Given the present stage of higher education, it seems to be rather far-fetched to expect colleges and universities everywhere to play a leading role in educational complexes. We, therefore, suggest that the idea be tried on an experimental

- In the long run, these Educational Complexes may come under the umbrella of Panchayati Raj institutions/local bodies.
- The management of education in the Complexes should be the job of professionals, i.e. the teaching community.
- In discharging this responsibility, teachers will closely interact with the community they are serving.
- The Head of the educational institution, the Headmaster/ Headmistress/Principal shall have meaningfully delegated authority with the teachers being centre-stage.
- The Educational Complexes should be autonomous registered societies in structures. (14.5.4)

basis in selected areas.

Indian Education Service

308. Instead of creating the Indian Education Service, Cadres of Educational Advisory Service should be created in the States on the model of the Government of India. (In the Government of India, larger number of posts should be operated under the Advisory Service). (14.6.5)

18.4 We feel that it would be necessary to hasten the process of consultation with States and to give concrete shape to the idea of IES with due regard to the views and concerns of the States. Two of us do not subscribe to the idea of IES.

Centrally Sponsored Schemes

312. The on-going Centrally Sponsored Schemes started in pursuance of NPE, 1986 have been under implementation only for two years. They may continue till end of 1992-93. The status of implementation of these schemes may be reviewed well before the end of that year. In any case, no new Centrally Sponsored Schemes may be initiated unless they be

18.5 We take note of the fact that the Department of Education has undertaken a review of all the ongoing CSSs in consultation with the States. We expect that these schemes would be modified during the Eighth Plan in the light of these consultations. We would also suggest launching of new CSSs in some priority areas not so far covered, such as the advancement of education-for the purpose of securing decentralisation of education management at a grass-roots level. (14.10.4)

GRIEVANCE REDRESSAL (Chapter 9)

220. The Recommendation of the Law Commission in regard to tribulisation of justice in centres of higher education is pending decision. Early action on this may be taken by the Government. (9.17.0)

RESOURCES FOR EDUCATION (Chapter 15)

The recommendations are, in brief, as follows:
313. Public investment in education should exceed 6 per cent of GNP. (15.13.5)
314. All technical and management education may be made self-financing with appropriate support to the students by way of student loans. (15.13.5)
315 and **316.** Increase by higher education institutions of tuition fee and fees charged for specific purposes such as laboratory fee, library fee, etc. (15.13.5)
317. Mobilising institutional finance for promotion of research in universities and for creation of educational infrastructure such as buildings, hostels and staff quarters. (15.13.5)

ally backward minorities, after due process of consultations. One of us is not in agreement with the suggestion.

REDRESSAL OF GRIEVANCES

18.8 The Law Commissioin in its 123rd Report had suggested the setting up of 3-tier structure for redressal of grievances in the higher education system. This recommendation is one of the several measures suggested by the Commission to relieve the congestion and burden on the High Courts and the Supreme Court and to hasten the redressal of grievances. Constitution of specialised State Level Educational Tribunals is, therefore, desirable. The details of setting up of these tribunals may be worked out in consultation with the State Governments.

RESOURCES FOR EDUCATION (Chapter 19)

19.3 These recommendations are within the framework of the existing Education Policy; however, the Credit Policy needs to be revised to provide for a larger measure of student loans as well as developmental finances for education.
19.4 We reiterate the point which has been made by several committees and commissions earlier and which is indeed axiomatic that without adequate resources educational reconstruction would remain a slogan. The Kothari Commission had first put forth the view that public expenditure on education should be 6 per cent of the GNP. This view has been reiterated time and again and has come to acquire the characteristic of a national resolve. The NPE had proclaimed that from the Eighth Plan onwards the

323. Increase in funds provided for scholarships by the Central Government. (15.13.5)

327. Mobilisation of community countribution. (15.13.5)

328. Efforts to be made by higher, and technical and management inwstitutions to augment their income by way of consultancy and other services. (15.13.5)

outlay on education would uniformly exceed 6 per cent of the National Income (Para 11.4). The NPERC had reiterated this prescription. Though all the Five Year Plans had stressed the importance of education as crucial for national development and survival, in actuality, education has been treated as residual sector in the matter of allocation of resources. We accept this finding and feel that this practice should be reversed.

6
Current Developments in Education

Introduction

The NPE was adopted by Parliament in 1966 and its implementation commenced soon thereafter.

Universalisation of elementary education, equalisation of educational opportunities, women's education and development, vocationalisation of school education, consolidation of higher education, modernisation of technical education, improvement of quality content and process of education at all levels are themes of national endeavour in the field of education as envisaged in NPE.

Elementary Education

In elementary education, the focus shifted from enrolment, *per se*, to retention and achievement—a shift which reflects the renewed concern for improving efficiency of investment and for monitoring programmes in terms of outcomes rather than in terms of inputs such as coverage and expenditure alone. The focus also shifted from exclusive concern with schooling to a holistic perception which stressed the need of providing alternative system of education of comparable quality to working children and girls whom the schools cannot reach.

Universalisation of Elementary Education (UEE)

Universalisation of Elementary Education (UEE) is a constitutional mandate. Article 45 of the Constitution stipulates, as a Directive Principle of State Policy, that 'the State shall endeavour to provide, within a period of ten years from the commencement of this Constitution for free and compulsory education for all children until they complete the age of fourteen years.' Indeed, over the years, the Centre and the States have made considerable

---

Sources: 1. *Annual Report, 1991–92,* Part I, Ministry of Human Resource Development, Government of India, Department of Education, New Delhi, 1992,

2. *Selected Educational Statistics, 1990-91,* Department of Education, New Delhi, 1992.

investments in promoting elementary education. Facilities in elementary education have grown from about 2.34 lakh to 7.05 lakh schools, enrolment from 22.28 million to 132.4 million children (Table 6.1) and outreach of primary education facilities to over 94 per cent of the rural population within 1 km walking distance of their houses. Over the last five years in pursuant of the NPE, effort has been made to focus attention on the quality of education being provided by this vast and possibly the largest, educational network of the world. Several schemes have been launched to improve retentions and reduce disparities; provide basic minimum facilities to schools; open non-formal education centres for part-time education of school dropouts and working children; improve teacher training facilities and teacher effectiveness; lay down Minimum Levels of Learning (MLLs); decentralise educational management and involve the community in the running of schools. Most of these schemes are ambitious in target and scope, and require sustained efforts and considerable resource support to make an impact.

Table 6.1 : Expansion of Elementary Education since 1950-51

	1950–51	*1990–91*
Number of primary schools	2.20 lakh	5.59 lakh
Number of middle schools	0.14 lakh	1.46 lakh
Enrolment in classes I to V	19.15 million	99.1 million
of boys	13.77 million	58.1 million
of girls	5.38 million	41.0 million
Enrolment in classes VI to VIII	3.13 million	33.3 million
of boys	2.59 million	20.9 million
of girls	0.54 million	12.4 million
Enrolment in classes I to VIII	22.28 million	132.4 million
of boys	16.36 million	79.0 million
of girls	5.92 million	53.4 million

Operation Blackboard

The Scheme of Operation Blackboard, started in 1987-88 to bring about substantial improvement in facilities in Primary schools with the aim of improving retention, has three interdependent components, namely: (i) Provision of a building comprising at least two reasonably large all-weather rooms with a deep verandah and separate toilet facilities for boys and girls; (ii) at least two teachers in every school, as far as possible one of them a woman; and (iii) provision of essential teaching learning material including blackboards, maps, charts, toys and equipment for work experience. Funds for construction of school buildings are provided mainly from rural development schemes. Funds for the other two components are provided by Department of Education, Ministry of Human Resource Development. The scheme envisages coverage of primary schools in all the blocks/municipal areas in the country in a phased manner.

In the period 1987-88 to 1990-91, the scheme was implemented in 69 per cent of the blocks in the country comprising 64 per cent primary schools. An assistance of Rs 523.41 crore was released by the Department of Education. Of this Rs 150.09 crore was released in 1990-91. There was a provision of Rs 100 crore for Operation Blackboard during 1991-92. The scheme would continue during the Eighth Plan till completion.

In order to move towards a position where every class has a class room and a teacher, it has been proposed to expand Operation Blackboard during the Eighth Plan to provide a third teacher and a third class room to every primary school where enrolment warrants it. Central assistance will be provided for the third teacher, while State Government will be expected to find resources for the construction of class rooms from the Jawahar Rozgar Yojna and State Plan budgets.

Data on achievements under Operation Blackboard till 1991-92 is presented in Table 6.2.

Table 6.2: Operation Blackboard : Achievements

	1987-88	*1988-89*	*1989-90*	*1990-91*	*1991-92 anticipated*
(1)	(2)	(3)	(4)	(5)	(6)
Amount spent (Rs in crores)	110.61	135.73	126.98	150.09	168.44
Amount committed by States for school buildings (Rs in crores)	300.00	340.00	64.60	140.00	140.00
No. of States/UTs covered	27	22	22	25	15
No. of blocks covered	1703	1795	578	343	1000
No. of schools covered (in lakhs)	1.13	1.40	0.52	0.39	0.76
Percentage of primary schools covered	21.00%	26.40%	9.90%	7.35%	9.22%
Post of primary teachers sanctioned	36891	36327	5274	14379	22032

Non-Formal Education

The role of non-formal part-time education in providing education to working children, and children in habitations without schools has been recognized since the Education Commission of 1964-66. During 1979-80, the scheme of Non-Formal Education (NFE) was introduced as an alternative strategy to impart education to children, who for various reasons cannot attend formal schools. The NPE envisaged a large and systematic programme of NFE to achieve UEE. The scheme was revised in its content and emphasis in 1987-88. Although its focus is on the ten educationally backward States, namely, Andhra Pradesh, Arunachal Pradesh, Assam, Bihar, Jammu & Kashmir, Madhya Pradesh, Orissa, Rajasthan, Uttar Pradesh and West Bengal, it has been extended to cover urban slums, hilly, tribal & desert areas and areas with concentration of working children in the other States as well. Financial responsibility is borne by the Central and State Governments in the ratio of 50:50 for general (co-educational) and 90:10 for girls NFE centres. Assistance to the extent of 100 per cent is provided to voluntary agencies for running NFE centres and for experimental and innovative projects.

The (revised) NFE scheme has been visualized as child-centred, environment-oriented, flexible system to meet the educational needs of the comparatively deprived geographical areas and socio-economic sections of society. Other features of the scheme are its organisational flexibility, relevance of curriculum, diversity in learning activities to relate them to the learner's needs and decentralized management. The programme is being implemented on a project basis, generally co-terminus with the community development Block comprising about 100 NFE Centres.

Particulars of achievements under the programme during the year 1991-92 (anticipated by 31.3.1992) are given in Table 6.3.

Table 6.3 Non-Formal Education : Achievements

		1991–92 (anticipated by 31-3-1992)
1.	Amount spent (Rs. in crores)	50.00
2.	NFE Centres brought to function (in lakhs) cumulative.	2.72
3.	No. of exclusive girl centres sanctioned (cumulative).	81,607
4.	No. of voluntary organisations approved for NFE programme (cumulative).	419
5.	NFE Centres brought to function by voluntary agencies (cumulative).	27,342
	Estimated enrolment (in lakhs)	68.00
	No. of experimental innovative projects approved (cumulative).	49
	No. of District Resource Units	19
	No. of States/UTs. covered.	18

During the year 1991-92, action was initiated to improve the technical aspect of the scheme. The NCERT and voluntary agencies have been involved in the development of teaching and learning materials of a standard quality in conformity with MLLs designed to suit learner's needs.

A project has been sanctioned to the NCERT for the development of training module and is being implemented in the States. Multi-level training personnel have been made available to provide technical and administrative support to NFE field functionaries.

Mahila Samakhya

In pursuance of para 4.2 of the NPE, Mahila Samakhya was

launched in April, 1989. This programme seeks to mobilise rural women for education through Mahila Sanghas in each of the villages concerned. This is a Central Sector scheme where 100 per cent financial assistance is provided to Mahila Samakhya Societies in Karnataka, Uttar Pradesh and Gujarat, set up under the Chairmanship of the concerned State Education Secretary. As an Indo-Dutch programme it receives 100 per cent assistance from the Government of the Netherlands.

Essentially, the programme revolves around Mahila Sanghas where women are mobilised around issues like access to health, education, water, information about development programmes, general information about their immediate environment, and above all, issues related to their personality and self-image in society.

Mahila Samakhya is currently operational in 1,500 villages in 10 districts. It is proposed to expand the programme to 20 districts in the three States and 3 districts of Andhra Pradesh in a phased manner in Eighth Plan period.

Bihar Education Project

The Bihar Education Project (BEP) has been conceived as a societal mission for bringing about fundamental change in the basic education system and through it the overall socio-cultural situation.

The BEP will cover all components of basic education and will be expanded in a phased manner to cover 20 districts over a period of five years. The outlay will be Rs 360 crore of which the UNICEF will contribute Rs. 180 crore, Government of India Rs 120 crore and Government of Bihar Rs 60 crore. A simultaneous process of mobilisation and micro-planning characterizes the project. The most important characteristic of the BEP management is a mission mode which pre-supposes a time-bound scheme of things in which specific responsibility is attached to institutions, agencies, or individuals. Accordingly, the management of the project has been vested in a state-level autonomous registered body namely 'Bihar Shiksha Pariyojana Parishad' (BSPP) which has been constituted having two bodies–a Council with the Chief Minister as Chairman, and an Executive Committee with State Education Secretary as its Chairman. Representation of teachers, NGOs, Government of India and institutions of national stature has been secured in the deliberative bodies of BSPP.

Shiksha Karmi Project

The Shiksha Karmi Project is being implemented since 1987 in Rajasthan with assistance from the Swedish International Development Authority (SIDA). Its aim is UPE in selected remote and socio-economically backward villages of the State.

The project identifies teacher absenteeism as a major obstacle in achieving the objective of universalisation. It accordingly, envisages substitution of the primary school teacher in single teacher schools by a team of two locally resident educational workers called 'Shiksha Karmis'. To ensure appointment of local persons, educational qualifications prescribed for teachers are not insisted upon in the selection of Shiksha Karmis. But they are provided training and academic support on a sustained and intensive basis to enable them to function efficiently as teachers. The existing primary school when run by Shiksha Karmis is called a 'Day Centre'. Besides, each Shiksha Karmi also runs a 'Prehar Pathshala' (Night Centre) for children who cannot attend the Day Centre. The project also lays emphasis on recruitment of female Shiksha Karmis and establishment of Mahila Shiksha Karmi Training Centres in order to prepare local women to function as Shiksha Karmis.

As of 31st December, 1991, the project was being implemented in 359 villages of 33 block units in 30 blocks of 17 districts in the State. The number of Shiksha Karmis was 750 and amongst them, they were looking after 359 Day Centres and 706 Prehar Pathshalas with a total enrolment of 35,795.

An independent study of the Shiksha Karmi Project was done in the second half of 1990. The study revealed that the achievement levels of the children in Shiksha Karmi Schools compared favourably with the children in the Panchayat Samiti schools.

Teacher Education

A Centrally Sponsored Scheme of Restructuring and Reorganisation of Teacher Education is being implemented since 1987-88. It aims at strengthening the teacher education system in the country so as to provide effective training and academic support to schools and adult and non-formal education systems. The scheme has the following five components.

- Mass Orientation of about five lakh School Teachers (MOST) to familiarise them with the major thrusts envisaged in the NPE and to improve their professional competence;
- Setting up of about 400 District Institutes of Education and Training (DIETs) either by upgrading suitable existing Elementary Teacher Education Institutions or, where necessary, by establishing new ones so as to provide total academic and training support to the elementary and adult education systems at the district level;
- Strengthening of about 250 Secondary Teacher Education Institutions (STEIs), development of about 50 of them as Institutions of Advanced Study in Education (IASEs) and the rest as Colleges of Teacher Education (CTEs);
- Strengthening of SCERTs; and
- Establishment and strengthening of Departments of Education in Universities by the UGC.

Achievements under the scheme since 1987-88 have been given in Table 6.4.

Table 6.4: Teacher Education: Achievements

	Total for 1987-88 to 1991-*92(as on 22-2-92)*
1. Amount spent (Rs. in crore)	Rs.187.29
2. No. of persons oriented under MOST (in lakh)	12.96 (In addition, 4.66 lakh teachers were covered in 1986)
3. No of DIETs sanctioned.	287*
4. No. of CTEs sanctioned.	25
5. No. of IASEs sanctioned.	12
6. No. of States/UTs covered	24

* DIETs where Principals have been posted and/or training programmes are being organised and/or in whose case the States/UTs have sought recurring assistance are considered Operational.

Minimum Levels of Learning (MLLs)

The strategy of MLLs seeks to improve learning acquisition in schools by focusing attention on what is happening in the classroom, and bringing the principles of equity to bear upon it.

Secondary Education

Growth of Recognised Educational Institutions and Enrolment since 1951.

Year	*High/Hr. Secondary Schools, Inter/Pre Degree Jr. Colleges*	*Enrolment in Lakhs*		
		Boys	*Girls*	*Total*
1950–51	7416	13	2	15
1960–61	17329	27	7	34
1970–71	37051	57	19	76
1980–81	51624	84	35	119
1990–91	78619	140	69	209

Vocationalisation of Secondary Education

Keeping in view the priorities accorded to vocationalisation of education in the NPE-86, the Centrally Sponsored Scheme of Vocationalisation of Secondary Education was started in February, 1988. The main objectives of the scheme are to provide diversification of educational opportunities so as to enhance individual's employability, reduce the mismatch between demand and supply of skilled manpower, and provide an alternative avenue for those pursuing higher education.

The selection of vocational courses is made on the basis of area vocational surveys, registration in the Employment Exchanges, and a general assessment of manpower needs made under District Developmental Plans. This ensures, to some extent, that students are trained in those occupational areas wherein self or wage employment opportunities are assured. On-the-job training is an integral part of the curricula. The remaining time is allocated to the study of languages and general foundation course.

Under the scheme, a Joint Council of Vocational Education (JCVE) has been set up at the national level, with counterpart bodies at the State level, for laying down policy guidelines, planning and coordination of vocational programmes conducted by different agencies/organisations. The JCVE has as its members representatives from various Ministries/Departments, members of Parliament, State Governments, voluntary organisations, experts in vocational education and all-India professional bodies. Union Education Minister is its Chairman. A Standing Committee of the JCVE has also been set up under the Chairmanship of the Union Education Secretary to ensure that the tasks laid down by JCVE are effectively performed.

The scheme is presently being implemented in 27 States/UTs. Up to the end of the Seventh Plan 7888 vocational sections had been approved with an enrolment capacity of 3.9 lakh students in classes XI and XII together. During 1990-91 an additional 1128 sections were approved. During 1991-92 it was proposed to sanction another 1400 vocational sections. Thus by the end of 1991-92 facilities would have been created for 5.85 lakh students in the vocational stream. The estimated enrolment during 1991-92 at +2 level was 66.05 lakh. This would mean a diversion of about 8.7 per cent to the vocational stream. The actual enrolment is however likely to be less as optimum utilisation of facilities created may not be achieved.

Educational Technology Programme

An Educational Technology Programme was started in the Central sector in the year 1972 during the Fourth Plan period for widening access to and bringing about qualitative improvement in education. Under the scheme, a Centre for Educational Technology was set up in the NCERT and 100 per cent assistance was provided to twenty-one States for setting up Educational Technology (ET) Cells. A Central Institute of Educational Technology (CIET) in the NCERT and State Institutes of Educational Technology (SIETs) in six States, viz., Andhra Pradesh, Bihar, Gujarat, Maharashtra, Orissa and Uttar Pradesh have been set up.

To meet the objectives of NPE, the Educational Technology Scheme was revised in 1987 with the broad objectives of strengthening of both ETV and audio programme production capabilities and providing wider access to the same by supplying one lakh Colour Television (CTV) sets and five lakh Radio-cum-Cassette Players (RCCPs) to primary schools during the Seventh Plan.

Programme production has commenced in CIET and all the six SIETs. The satellite based ETV service presently provides telecast of educational programmes for the children and their teachers at the primary level in the morning for 45 minutes duration in each of the five regional languages, namely, Gujarati, Hindi, Marathi, Oriya and Telugu on time sharing basis. The programmes for children are telecast from Monday to Friday and for primary level teachers on every Saturday. There are separate programmes for the children in the age groups of 5-8 and 9-11 years on each day.

The ETV programmes are relayed by all high and low power transmitters in the six INSAT States. The programmes in Hindi are relayed by the other five Hindi speaking States also, namely, Haryana, Himachal Pradesh, Madhya Pradesh, Punjab and Rajasthan and the Union Territory of Chandigarh.

With the availability of uplinking facilities from Bombay and Hyderabad, the telecast timings have been rescheduled from November, 1991.

The CIET has produced 646 ETV programmes up to October, 1991 and 914 language versions. It has also produced 450 capsules for the programme of MOST during the summers of 1986, 1987, 1988 and 1989. The number of programmes produced by SIETs is given in Table 6.5.

Table 6.5 Number of Programmes Produced by SIETs as on July, 1991

1. Andhra Pradesh	562
2. Bihar	105
3. Gujarat	805
4. Maharashtra	1058
5.. Orissa	107
6. Uttar Pradesh	604

The summary of achievements under the ET programme is given in Table 6.6.

Improvement of Science Education in Schools

In order to improve the quality of science education and promote scientific temper, as envisaged in NPE, a Centrally Sponsored Scheme of Improvement of Science Education in Schools was started during the last quarter of 1987-88. Under this Scheme, financial assistance is provided to States/Union Territories for provision of science kits to upper primary schools; upgradation and strengthening of science laboratories in secondary and higher secondary schools up to a desired standard; upgradation of libraries in secondary and higher secondary schools; setting up of District Resource Centres for science education, development of instructional materials; and training of Science and Mathematics teachers. The scheme also provides for assistance to voluntary organizations active in the field of science education for undertaking innovative projects and resource support activities in science education.

Table 6.6: Educational Technology : Achievements

	1987 -88	*1988 -89*	*1989 -90*	*1990 -91*	*1991 -92*	*Total (as on 12.12.91)*
Amount Spent (Rs in crore)	14.14	16.20	16.50	14.57	3.15	64.56
No. of States covered (cumulative)	13	29	31	32		32
No. of TV sets distributed	10049	12049	2799	6232	–	31129
No. of Radio cum Cassette Players distributed	37562	67735	49963	72883	3115	231228
Continuing Schemes						
1. Amount released to CIET (Rs in crores)	5.28	3.10	3.146	2.37	2.00	15.89
2. Amount released to SIETs (Rs. in crores) (6 INSAT States A.P., Bihar, Gujarat, Maharashtra, Orissa and U.P.)	1.40	1.53	2.20	0.44 Plan 0.45 Non-Plan	0.63	6.65
3. Amount released to ET Cells (Rs in crores)	0.22	0.26	0.54	–	–	1.02
4. Amount released to States/UTs for TVs/RCCPs (Rs in crores)	7.15	11.19	10.60	11.66	0.33	40.93
5. Development of software for RCCPs (Rs in crores)	–	–	–	0.10	0.19	0.29

The actual achievements up to 1990-91 and the anticipated achievements during 1991-92 are given in Table 6.7.

International Mathematical Olympiad in School Education

With a view to identifying and nurturing talent in Mathematics at school level, the International Mathematical Olympiad (IMO) is held every year. India has been participating in this Olympiad since 1989. Each participating country is required to send a team comprising not more than six secondary school student contestants, a team leader and a deputy team leader.

Environmental Orientation to School Education

In order to promote integration of educational programmes in the schools with local environmental conditions, as envisaged in the NPE, a Centrally Sponsored Scheme of Environmental Orientation to School Education was started in 1988-89.

Table 6.7: Science Education : Achievements

	1987-88	*1988-89*	*1989-90*	*1990-91*	*1991-92 (anti-cipated*	Total
Amount spent (Rs. in crores)	29.27	29.16	21.60	20.59	23.99	124.61
No. of States/UTs covered	19	15	21	24	25	
No. of schools covered						
i) Upper Primary (science kits)	20,719	14,037	8,463	5,791	6,000	55,010
ii) Sec./Higher Sec. Library assistance	8,899	5,784	1,699	3,843	3,000	23,225
iii) Sec./ Higher Sec. (laboratory assistance)	6,920	5,392	2,761	3,981	4,200	23,254
iv) No. of Vol. orgns. covered (for innorative programmes) (Cumulative)		8	11	7	6(new)	20
No. of institutions assisted for setting up of District Resource Centres	80	13	22	60	60	235

Under the Scheme, 100 per cent assistance is provided to the States/Union Territories and voluntary agencies. The State/Union Territories are provided assistance for taking up the various programme/activities aimed at creating environmental consciousness among the students on project basis. Each project area should consist of a few blocks/districts having homogeneous ecological conditions. In order to plan, co-ordinate and monitor the activities proposed to be taken up by a State/Union Territory, assistance is provided for creation of a State level cell. Similarly, in order to design and organize various educational programmes in schools keeping in view the local environmental conditions and concerns, assistance is provided for setting up of project cells for each project area. The project activities include review and development of curriculum to make it local specific; preparation of textbooks, instructional material, informative books, booklets, brochures, posters, slides, audio tapes, and films on environment; organisation of seminars for creating environmental consciousness; orientation of teachers; adoption of monuments for their upkeep and maintenance; study of ecological problems; etc. One of the preferred activities under the project is setting up of school nurseries. Voluntary organisations are assisted for taking up of various kinds of experimental and innovative programmes in the field of environmental orientation to school education.

A summary of actual achievements during 1987-88 to 1990-91 and the anticipated achievements during 1991-92 under the

Scheme is presented in Table 6.8.

Table 6.8: Environmental Orientation to School Education: Achievements

	1987-88	*1988-89*	*1989-90*	*1990-91*	*1991-92 (antici-pated)*	*Total*
Amount spent (Rs in crores)	Nil	1.92	1.65	2.00	3.00	8.57
No. of States/UTs covered	Nil	15	10	8	11	32
No. of projects sanctioned	Nil	25	7	6	12	50
No. of schools covered	Nil	7,298	4,512	4,876	6,000	22,686
No.of voluntary bodies assisted (cumulative)	Nil	6	9	7	5 (new)	17

Computer Education in Schools

A pilot project on Computer Literacy and Studies in Schools (CLASS) was initiated in 1984-85 in 248 selected secondary/higher secondary schools jointly by the Department of Electronics and the Department of Education to acquaint students and teachers with the range of computer applications and its potential as a learning medium. In pursuance of the objectives laid down in the NPE, an expanded programme was prepared in 1987-88 to cover 13,000 higher secondary schools all over the country. However, due to paucity of funds and other administrative reasons, the proposal to cover 13,000 schools was not finalised.

In Table 6.9, a summary of achievements under CLASS Project is presented.

Table 6.9 : Class Project : Achievements

	1987-88	1988-89	1989-90	1990-91	*1991-92 (antici-pated)*	Total
Amount spent Rs. in crore	5.39	5.98	6.00	5.86	6.00	29.23
No. of States assisted	30	31	32	–	–	32
No. of schools covered (Cumulative)	1949	2327	2598	–	–	2598

National Population Education Project
(School and Non-Formal Education)

The National Population Education Project (NPEP) was launched in April 1980 with the main objective of institutionalising population education into the formal and non-formal education system. The programme activities have been developed in collaboration with the United Nations Population Fund (UNPFA) and UNESCO and also with the active involvement of the Ministry of Health and Family Welfare. The NCERT provides technical assistance. The Ministry of Human Resource Development has decided to extend the NPEP into the Eighth Five Year Plan. Population Education aims at making young students aware of the inter-relationship between population, development and the quality of life. It further seeks to develop in them a rational attitude and responsible behaviour towards population issues and to foster in them positive value orientation so that they may take informed decisions which, in turn, would promote the small family norm. The project is currently being implemented in twenty-nine States and Union Territories.

Integrated Education for the Disabled Children

It has been established scientifically that children with mild handicaps make better progress academically and psychologically if they study in common schools alongside normal children. The Scheme of Integrated Education for Disabled Children provides 100 per cent financial assistance to State Governments, Union Territory Administrations and voluntary organisations for creating necessary facilities in the schools. Admissible items of expenditure are books and stationery allowance, transport allowance, uniform allowance, readers allowance (for blind children), escort allowance for orthopaedically handicapped children with lower extremity disabilities, equipment allowance and wherever necessary, hostel charges. Besides, the scheme also provides for meeting the cost of salary and incentives for teachers, setting up of resource rooms, carrying out assessment of disabled children, training of teachers, removal of architectural barriers in schools, development and production of special instructional materials for disabled children, etc. Assistance is also given, through the UGC, to selected universities and institutions for running training courses in special education for teachers of the handicapped children. Training facilities are also provided by the NCERT and the four Regional Colleges of Education.

The scheme is at present being implemented in Andhra Pradesh, Bihar, Goa, Gujarat, Haryana, Himachal Pradesh, Jammu & Kashmir, Karnataka, Kerala, Madhya Pradesh, Maharashtra, Mizoram, Nagaland, Orissa, Punjab, Rajasthan, Sikkim, Tamil Nadu, Uttar Pradesh, Daman & Diu, Delhi and A & N Islands.

There is one UNICEF assisted Project of Integrated Education for Disabled (PIED) which envisages development of context-specific strategies for education of children with disabilities in general schools. Assistance is given to the States/Union Territories implementing this project also for meeting the expenditure on account of various facilities provided to disabled children. One block each in the States of Haryana, Madhya Pradesh, Maharashtra, Mizoram, Nagaland, Orissa, Rajasthan and Tamil Nadu and the

Municipal Corporations of Delhi and Baroda are covered under this project.

About 28,000 children spread over 6000 schools are presently receiving benefits under this scheme. A much larger number are receiving indirect benefit through special teachers and other learning material.

Promotion of Yoga

The Ministry of Human Resource Development has been implementing a scheme for promotion of yoga as part of its overall programme for development of physical education in the country taking into consideration the potential usefulness of yoga in promoting physical fitness. Under the scheme financial assistance is given to yoga institutions of an all-India character, towards maintenance and also developmental expenditure on basic research, teacher training and programmes in other aspects of yoga except therapeutic. Financial assistance to yoga institutions for promotion of therapeutical aspect is being extended by the Ministry of Health & Family Welfare.

A new Centrally Sponsored Scheme was started in 1989-90 under which yoga institutions are assisted for training yoga teachers and for building infrastructural facilities for the purpose.

Assistance to Agencies for Strengthening Culture/Art/Values in Education and for Assistance to Educational Institutions Implementing Innovative Programmes

It has been envisaged by the Central Government that India's cultural heritage should be strengthened and creative activities like art, education, etc. should be emphasised. Within these overall objectives, a Central Scheme for Assistance to Agencies for Strengthening Culture/Art/Values in Education and for Assistance to Educational Institutions Implementing Innovative Programmes was formulated in 1987 for providing assistance to Government agencies, educational institutions, Panchayati Raj institutions, registered societies, public trusts and non-profit making companies.

Break-up of the students selected so far in 275 Navodaya Vidyalayas is as follows:

Boys	*Girls*	*Rural*	*Urban*	*SC*	*ST*	*Gen*	*Total*
55927	22222	60528	17621	15900	8405	53844	78149
72%	28%	77%	23%	20%	11%	69%	

Navodaya Vidyalayas are co-educational and primarily for children from rural areas. Hence admission of children from urban areas is restricted to a maximum of one-fourth. Efforts are made to ensure that at least one-third of the students in each Navodaya Vidyalaya are girls.

Reservation of seats in favour of children belonging to the

Scheduled Castes and Scheduled Tribes is provided in proportion to their population in the concerned district, provided that in no district such reservation is less than the national average.

Navodaya Vidyalaya Samiti

In order to provide good quality modern education to the talented children predominantly from the rural areas, Government of India launched in 1985-86 a scheme to establish Navodaya Vidyalayas on an average one in each district. Two hundred and seventy-five Navodaya Vidyalayas covering 22 States and 7 Union Territories have so far been established in the country.

HIGHER EDUCATION AND RESEARCH

Growth of the Higher Education System

At the beginning of the year 1991-92, the total student enrolment in Universities and Colleges was 44.25 lakh. This was 1.78 lakh more than the enrolment in the previous year. The enrolment in the University Departments was 7.32 lakh and that in the affiliated Colleges was 36.93 lakh. Enrolment in the Faculty of Arts constituted 40.4% of the total enrolment. In the faculties of Science and Commerce the percentage was 19.6 and 21.9 respectively. Enrolment at the first degree level was 38.99 lakh (88.1%), at the postgraduate level 4.20 lakh (9.5%); at the research level 0.49 lakh (1.1%); and at the diploma and certificate level 0.57 lakh (1.3%).

The number of teachers increased to 2.63 lakh during the year. Of these, 0.59 lakh were in the University Departments/University colleges and the rest in the affiliated colleges. Of 58,661 teachers in the Universities, 7,509 were Professors, 15,369 were Readers, 33,437 were Lecturers and 2,346 were Tutors/Demonstrators. In the affiliated colleges, the number of senior teachers was 28,421, the number of Lecturers was 1,67,047 and that of Tutors/Demonstrators was 8,996.

Higher Education among Women

The enrolment of women students at the beginning of 1991-92 was 14.37 lakh as against 13.67 lakh in the previous year. At the postgraduate level, the enrolment of women was 34.2 per cent of the total enrolment. The enrolment of women students was the highest in Kerala (53.0%) followed by Punjab (48.2%), Delhi (46.3%), Haryana (42.2%) Meghalaya/Nagaland/Mizoram (39.0%), Tamil Nadu (38.5%) and West Bengal/Tripura/Sikkim (38.4%). The enrolment of women was the lowest in Bihar (16.4%).

Programmes and Activities of the U.G.C.

Some of the major thrust areas pursued were: Autonomous Colleges, Redesigning of Courses, Academic Staff College for Orientation of Teachers, Eligibility Test for recruitment of lecturers, Inter-University Centres and Consortiums, Distance Education. Fellowships/Scholarships, Special Assistance Programme, Committee on Strengthening of Infrastructure in Science and Technology (COSIST) programme, Adult Education and National Literacy Mission, Education for the Minorities, Scheduled Castes/ Scheduled Tribes, Handicapped and Women, Spread of Mass Communication and Educational Technology Network and Alternative models of management focusing on accountability, planning, funds and inter-relationship between University, State Government and UGC.

Autonomous Colleges

The total number of such colleges was 106 up to December, 1991.

Re-designing of Courses

The scheme of restructuring under-graduate courses in general education was introduced by the UGC with a view to making the first degree courses more relevant to environment and developmental needs of the community and linking education with work/field/practical experience and productivity. Several universities and colleges have introduced these courses. Further, in order to provide an impetus to the programme of redesigning of courses, the UGC has set up 30 Curriculum Development Centres (CDCs)–11 in Sciences and 18 in Humanities and Social Sciences and one in Vocational Education–up to modernising, preparing and developing new teaching and reading materials.

Indira Gandhi National Open University

The Indira Gandhi National Open University (IGNOU) was established by an Act of Parliament in September, 1985 for the Introduction and promotion of Open University and Distance Education Systems in the educational pattern of the country and for the coordination and determination of standards in such systems. The major objectives of the University include widening of access to higher education by providing opportunities to larger segments of the population, particularly the disadvantaged groups, organising programmes of continuing education and initiating special programmes of higher education for specific target groups like women, people living in backward regions, hilly areas, etc.

Academic Programmes

The IGNOU introduced its academic programmes in 1987 and has so far launched 16 programmes. These include a certificate course in Food and Nutrition, the preparatory programme for the Bachelor Degree, Diploma Programmes in Management, Distance Education, Creative Writing in English, Computer Applications, Rural Development & Higher Education and the Bachelor's Degree Programmes in Arts/Science/Commerce and Library and Information Sciences as well as the Master's Degree in Business Administration.

The total number of students registered for various programmes of study in the IGNOU during 1991-92 was 60,280. With this, aggregate enrolment of students in the University has gone beyond 1.64 lakh.

Industry -Institute Interaction

The Scheme of Industry-Institute Interaction which was launched in the middle of 1988-89 has three main components as follows:

(a) Interaction between engineering colleges and industry,
(b) Interaction between Polytechnics and industry, and
(c) Setting up of an 'Industrial Foundation' at IIT Delhi.

In the case of selected engineering colleges, the programme envisages tackling a joint project between the industry and the institution. It is also envisaged to exchange faculty with industry at the rate of two faculty members per institution. At the polytechnic level, only faculty exchange will take place at the rate of two faculty members per polytechnic.

ADULT EDUCATION

The National Literacy Mission was launched in May, 1988 with the objective of imparting functional literacy to 80.00 million adult illiterates in the 15-35 age group by 1995.

Striking Features of 1991 Census

The literacy data of the country are based on the decennial census operations conducted by the Registrar General, India. The provisional figures of the 1991 census, which was held in the earlier part of the year show that the literacy rate for the population aged 7 and above, in the country increased from 43.56 per cent in 1981 to 52.11 per cent in 1991, registering an increase by 8.55 percentage points. Whereas the male literacy rate increased from 56.37 per cent to 63.86 per cent, the female literacy rate increased from 29.75 per cent to 39.42 per cent.

The following striking features have emerged from the above data:

– The rate of growth of literacy between 1981 and 1991 is 8.55 per cent which compares well with the rate of growth in literacy between 1971-81 which was 6.97 per cent.
– The rate of growth of female literacy (9.67%) during the decade is higher than that of male literacy (7.49%).
– The number of literates (aged 7 and above) in 1991 at 352.00 million compares very well with the number of literates at 234.00 million in 1981.
– The number of illiterates (age 7 and above) in 1991 is of

the order of 324 million which is a marginal increase from the 302 million in 1981.

- The increase in the number of literates in 1991 over 1981 was 118 million whereas the corresponding increase in the number of illiterates was 22 million only.
- Kerala (90.59%) tops in the literacy rate followed by Mizoram (81.23%), Lakshadweep (79.23%) and Chandigarh (78.73%). At the bottom of the ladder are Bihar (38.54%), Rajasthan (38.81%) and Dadra and Nagar Haveli (39.45%).
- The increase in female literacy rates, has been very significant in the States/Union Territories of Sikkim (19.88%), Lakshadweep (15.56%), Nagaland (15.44%), Daman & Diu (14.87%), Haryana (14.05%), Manipur (14.03%), Andaman & Nicobar Islands (13.07%), Pondicherry (12.76%), Tripura (12.00%) and Kerala (11.28%).
- The literacy rate is above the all India level of 52.11 percentage in case of 22 States/UTs, but the eight States of Bihar, Rajasthan, Arunachal Pradesh, Madhya Pradesh, Uttar Pradesh, Andhra Pradesh, Meghalaya, Orissa and the Union Territory of Dadra and Nagar Haveli are still below the threshold level of literacy, i.e., 50 per cent. All these States/UTs except Meghalaya are also below the All India level in case of female literacy.

Total Literacy Campaign

Campaigns for total literacy constitute the major thrust and initiative in the Mission; they also constitute its principal strategy. In the heels of success of Ernakulam and Kerala experiments for achieving full literacy, these campaigns for total literacy have generated certain characteristic features which make them unique and distinguish them from other programmes. They are area-specific, time bound, volunteer-based, cost-effective and outcome-oriented.

7
Education of the SCs, STs, and OBCs

Introduction

Equality before the law is a basic Fundamental Right guaranteed under Article 14 of the Constitution. But the principle of 'equality' is a double edged weapon. It places the strong and the handicapped on the same footing in the race of life. It is a dictum of social justice that there is equality only among equals. To treat unequals as equals is to perpetuate inequality. The humaneness of a society is determined by the degree of protection it provides to its weaker, handicapped and less gifted members.

'Equality of opportunity' and 'equality of treatment' places the weak and the strong on par and to that extent, it amounts to denial of social justice. In fact, it is 'equality of results' which is the acid test of society's egalitarian pretentions. In a highly unequal society like ours, it is only by giving special protection and privileges to the under-privileged section of society that we can enable the weak to resist exploitation by the strong.

It was in view of these considerations that our Constitution makers made special provisions to protect the interests of SCs, STs and OBCs.

Article 15. *Prohibition of Discrimination on Grounds of Religion, Race, Caste, Sex or Place of Birth*

(1) The State shall not discriminate against any citizen on grounds only of religion, race, caste, sex, place of birth or any of them.

(2) No citizen shall, on grounds only of religion, race, caste, sex, place of birth or any of them, be subject to any disability, liability, restriction or condition with regard to–
   (a) access to shops, public restaurants, hotels and places of public entertainment; or
   (b) the use of wells, tanks, bathing ghats, roads and places of public resort maintained wholly or partly out of State funds or dedicated to the use of general public.

(3) Nothing in this article shall prevent the State from making any special provision for women and children.

(4) Nothing in this article or in clause (2) of article 29 shall prevent the State from making any special provision for the advancement of any socially and educationally backward classes of

citizens or for the Scheduled Castes and the Scheduled Tribes.

Article 46. *Promotion of Educational and Economic Interests of Scheduled Castes, Scheduled Tribes and Other Weaker Sections –*

The State shall promote with special care the educational and economic interests of the weaker sections of the people, and in particular, of the Scheduled Castes and the Scheduled Tribes; and shall protect them from social injustice and all forms of exploitation.

Article 338. *Special Officer for Scheduled Castes, Scheduled Tribes, etc.*

(1) There shall be a Special Officer for the Scheduled Castes and Scheduled Tribes to be appointed by the President.

(2) It shall be the duty of the Special Officer to investigate all matters relating to the safeguards provided for the Scheduled Castes and Scheduled Tribes under this Constitution and report to the President upon the working of those safeguards at such intervals as the President may direct and the President shall cause all such reports to be laid before each House of Parliament.

(3) In this article, references to the Scheduled Castes and Scheduled Tribes shall be construed as including references to such other backward classes as the President may, on receipt of the report of a Commission appointed under clause (1) of article 340, by order specify and also to the Anglo-Indian community.

Artcle 339. *Control of the Union over Administration of Scheduled Areas and the Welfare of Scheduled Tribes–*

(1) The President may at any time and shall, at the expiration of ten years from the commencement of this Constitution by order appoint a Commission to report on the administration of the Scheduled Areas and the welfare of the Scheduled Tribes in the States.

The order may define the composition, powers and procedure of the Commission and may contain such incidental or ancillary provisions as the President may consider necessary or desirable.

(2) The executive power of the Union shall extend to the giving of directions to [a State] as to the drawing up and execution of schemes specified in the direction to be essential for the welfare of the Scheduled Tribes in the State.

Article 340. *Appointment of a Commission to Investigate the Conditions of Backward Classes*

(1) The President may by order appoint a Commission consisting of such persons as he thinks fit to investigate the conditions of socially and educationally backward classes within the territory of India and the difficulties under which they labour and to make recommendations as to the steps that should be taken by the Union or any State to remove such difficulties and to improve their condition and as to the grants that should be made for the purpose by the Union or any State and the conditions subject to which such grants should be made, and the order appointing such Commission shall define the procedure to be followed by the Commission.

(2) A Commission so appointed shall investigate the matters referred

to them and present to the President a report setting out the facts as found by them and making such recommendations as they think proper.

(3) The President shall cause a copy of the report so presented together with memorandum explaining the action taken thereon to be laid before each House of Parliament.

Present State of Education of SCs and STs

Table 7.1. SCs and STs Enrolment Per Lakh Population (1990-91)

Category	*Primary*	*Middle*
General	11,745	3,944
Scheduled Castes	12,078	3,181
Scheduled Tribes	11,741	2,547

Table 7.2. Gross Enrolment Ratios of SCs and STs (1990-91)

Classes/Age-group	*Scheduled Castes*			*Scheduled Tribes*		
	Boys	*Girls*	*Total*	*Boys*	*Girls*	*Total*
I-V (6-11 years)	122.68	80.60	102.21	126.78	78.60	103.35
VI-VIII (11-14 years)	61.40	33.28	47.71	51.33	27.50	39.72

Overall gross enrolment ratios in Classes I-V are 115.29, 85.97 and 101.03 for boys, girls and combined respectively. At the middle stage these are 73.38, 46.13 and 60.11 correspondingly.

Table 7.3. Drop-Out Rates in Percentage (1986-87)

Stage/Classes	*Non-SC//ST*	*SC*	*ST*
Classes I to V	48.9	50.8	66.1
Classes VI to VIII	60.7	69.2	80.2
Classes IX to X	73.8	79.9	87.3

Table 7.4. Percentage of SCs/STs of Total Enrolment on Higher Education (1988-89)

Course Under-Graduate	SC	ST
(1) Arts	9.8	2.9
(2) Science	5.8	0.8
(3) Commerce	4.4	1.0
Post-Graduate		
(4) Arts	10.1	2.0
(5) Science	4.9	0.8
(6) Commerce	6.5	1.2

Table 7.5. Literacy Rates (In Percent)

S.No.	*Category*	*1961*	*1971*	*1981*	*1991*
1.	General	24.00	29.45	36.23	52.11
2.	SC Total	10.27	14.67	21.38	NA
3.	SCs (Women)	–	6.44	10.93	NA
4.	STs (Total)	8.54	11.29	16.35	NA
5.	STs (Women)	–	4.85	8.04	NA
6.	All Communties Excluding SCs and STs (Total)	27.91	33.80	41.30	NA
7.	All Communties Excluding SCs and STs (Women)	–	22.25	29.43	NA

Promotion of Education among SCs, STs and OBCs

Education Commission 1964-66 on Equalisation of *Educational Opportunity and Social Change* the Commission observed in Chapter VI, 'One of the important social objectives of education is to equalise opportunity, enabling the backward or under-privileged classes and individuals to use education as a lever for the improvement of their condition. Every society that values social justice and is anxious to improve the lot of the common man and cultivate all available talent, must ensure progressive equality of opportunity to all sections of the population. This is the only guarantee for the building up of an egalitarian and human society in which the exploitation of the weak will be minimized.'

The Commission, very emphatically stated that 'the education of the backward classes in general and the tribal people in particular is a major programme of equalisation and of social and national intergration. No expenditure is too great for the purpose.'

It is really very sad that we have not paid adequate heed to the words of wisdom of the Education Commission (1964-66). Non-implementation of its recommendations as outlined in Chapter VI has led to a sorry state of affairs.

National Policy on Education, 1968

Strenuous efforts should be made to equalise educational opportunity. More intensive efforts are needed to develop education among the backward classes and especially among the tribal people. (4.C)

Draft National Policy on Education, 1979

While there has been considerable expansion in all sectors of education in our country, imbalances and inequalities still persist.

Note : Figures in parentheses denote Chapter No. and Recommendation.

Girls, Scheduled Castes and Tribes, landless labourers, backward classes and urban slum poor generally continue to lag behind in education. Special effort must be made to identify the problems in these cases and to bring all such people into the fold of education. (17.1)

National Policy on Education, 1986

Part III: National System of Education

The concept of a National System of Education implies that, up to a given level, all students, irrespective of castes, creed, location or sex, have access to education of a comparative quality. To achieve this, the Government will initiate appropriately funded programmes. Effective measures will be taken in the direction of the Common School System recommended in the 1968 policy. (3.2)

To promote equality, it will be necessary to provide for equal opportunity to all not only in access, but also in the conditions for success. Besides, awareness the inherent equality of all will be created through the core curriculum. The purpose is to remove prejudices and complexes transmitted through the social environment and accident of Birth. (3.6)

Part IV: Disparities

The New Policy will lay, emphasis on the removal of disparities and to equalise educational opportunities by attending to the specific needs of those who have been denied equality so far. (4.1)

Other Educationally Backward Sections and Areas

Suitable incentive will be provided to all educationally backward sections of society, particularly in the rural areas. Hill and desert districts, remote and inaccessible areas and islands will be provided adequate institutional infrastructure.

Programme of Action, 1986

A single nodal agency for coordination of all programmes leading to the development of SC/ST and other backward sections may be developed at the Central and State levels. It is suggested that a Standing Committee of the CABE under the Chairmanship of Minister of Human Resource Development (HRD) may be constituted to monitor and review implementation of all educational programmes for SC/ST and Other Educationally Backward Sections at the Central Level. A similar committee under the State Advisory Board of Education may be constituted at the state level.

In addition to an in-built mechanism for continuous evaluation of programmes, evaluation of important schemes like scholarships, hostels and the proposed incentive scheme may be undertaken by external agencies.

Ramamurti Report, 1990

The Committee observed in Chapter 4 as 'The Committee would also give a rather broad connotation for the concepts or equality of opportunities and equity in edcuation. The concept of equality of opportunity in education started with provision for equal access. Later on equal input was considered necessary for equalising educational opportunities. Today, along with equal access and equal input, equal output is considered necessary criteria. [sic]. The last one calls for measures of protective discrimination in favour of the disadvantaged sections of the society.' (*Journal of Educational Planning and Administration :* April, 1987).

The policy, then, should be one of providing *equity package* of educational and economic measures in terms of protective discrimination in favour of the disadvantaged sections of the society.

The Ramamurti Committee the made the following recommendations for the promotion of education of the SCs, STs and Other Educationally Backward Sections.

Incentive Schemes

A series of studies should be instituted to investigate into the impact that the various incentive schemes implemented in different States have had on enrolment and retention of SC/ST children in the schools. Community profiles of educationally backward communities should also be prepared based on study of their current educational status. With reference to these profiles and the findings of the impact studies, on a disaggregated basis, appropriate and logical strategies should be established for the educational development of the backward communities. (4.2.5)

Status of Access to Education

The Fifth All India Education survey shows that a number of habitations predominantly populated by SCs and STs are not served by schools within walking distance. There should be a programme for the coverage of these unserved habitations with schools as per norms before the end of the Eighth Five-Year Plan. (4.2.6)

Improvement of Capability and Educational Environment

The scheme of remedial coaching should be re-organised such that on a phased basis, majority of the schools introduce the same. Instead of coaching being confined to two or three months of pre-examination periods, the same should be offered in a sustained way throughout the academic session in the concerned classes. (4.2.7)

A strategy to enrich learning environment and the socio-economic conditions in the tribal regions as distinct from mere remedial coaching should be evolved and brought under implementation. (4.2.7)

In the backward areas including SC, ST habitats, a network of school linked libraries should be established. For reaching out to smaller habitations without schools, a dynamic programme of bicycle-borne mobile libraries or para-school-based libraries should be brought under implementation. These libraries need to be enriched with creative children's literature. While the children's literature would be primarily in the regional languages, efforts should be made to increase the availability of children's books in the local dialects or languages spoken in educationally backward areas. (4.2.7)

In order to nurture all kinds of talents and aptitudes in children, ranging from academic subjects to co-curricular and socio-cultural spheres as may be identifiable. Educational Complexes should organise a wide-ranging programme of specific theme-based workshops/work camps, using the best available resource persons in the area. This programme should *encourage school drop-outs* as well to join and contribute in this collective endeavour towards excellence. (4.2.7)

Curriculum

In the curriculum of the educationally backward the following should be emphasied at all stages of education:

(a) Science and Mathematics;
(b) Expression, both oral and written, and creative writing ;
(c) History and sociology of the Scheduled Castes, the Scheduled Tribes and other backward sections of society;
(d) Contribution of these communities to national life and development, including the freedom struggle; and
(e) Role played by women belonging to these communities in national life and development.

(In fact, matters covering under (c), (d) and (e) should also be included in the National Core Curriculum) (4.2.7)

ECCE Centres

Above all else, in order to bring about universalisation of Elementary education among girls in backward areas, including those belonging to SC/ST communities, a network of ECCE centres should be established on a priority basis, with linkage to primary schools. (This has also been dealt with in the Chapter on ECCE). (4.2.7)

Recruitment of SC/ST Teachers

It should be ensured that in Government and Government-aided schools teachers from SC/ST communities are invariably in the order of 15% and 7.5% respectively. Recruitment to reach these levels should also be closely monitored. (4.2.8)

Curriculum and Tribal Culture

The rich diversity of the tribal cultural identities should be included in the common cultural heritage which is one of the elements of the Core Curriculum envisaged in NPE/POA. (4.2.8)

Special Component Plan and Tribal Sub-Plan

Special Component Plan and Tribal Sub-Plan should be specifically exhibited in the budget document, schemewise. (4.2.9)

To the extent feasible, schemes meant exclusively for the Scheduled Castes and Scheduled Tribes should be prepared and included under SCP/TSP. (4.2.9)

Wherever exclusive schemes cannot be formulated, specific physical targets for coverage of Scheduled Castes/Scheduled Tribes under the schemes generally applicable to all should be indicated. (4.2.9)

A more effective monitoring mechanism should be established in the Department of Education itself for the purpose of periodically following up the progress of implementation of SCP/TSP. (4.2.9)

Intensive Area Approach

The Ministry of Welfare, according to the Business Rules, is expected to do coordination in the implementation of programmes relating to SCs/STs. While they have given a list of blocks identified as trible blocks they have not given, with reference to 1981 census, a list of blocks identified as those of Scheduled Caste concentration. This Ministry should, therefore, provide lists of blocks with SC concentration. With reference to such lists the Department of Education should get feedback from the States regarding their coverage under the various educational programmes. (4.2.10)

All the educational programmes should be implemented to the extent feasible conveniently in the same blocks of SC concentration/tribal blocks so that impact of educational development is felt in a demonstrable and balanced way in the respective areas. (4.2.10)

Monitoring

A single focal agency in each State should be identified for the purpose of reporting to the Government of India comprehensively on all the educational programmes. (4.2.11)

Janardhana Committee Report (1992)

1. A single focal agency should be identified in each State for the purpose of monitoring the programmes and reporting to the Central Government. (4.4)

2. A standing CABE Committee on education of SCs, STs and other educationally backward sections should be constituted; educationists from these groups should have representation in that Committee. (4.4)
3. While instruction should be child-centred and cater to individual differences, it is not advisable to differentiate students in the matter of syllabus and curriculum. (4.5)
4. Monitoring of the implementation of the guidelines for recognition of minority-managed educational institutions is better left to the State Governments, as they are deeply conscious of the need for proper monitoring and many organisations like the Minority Commission already exist for the purpose of monitoring. (4.6)

Concluding Observations

Gross inequalities arise from differences in home environments. These inequalities are obviously the most difficult to overcome and here progress essentially depends on the general improvement in the standard of living of the population. But something can be done by arranging that special attention at school is paid to children from the under-privileged groups and by the provision of day-study centres or boarding houses.

8
Implementation and Monitoring of NPE

Education must be rescued from the tyranny of the generalist administrator, the opportunist 'jack of all trades and master of none', who uses the present structure and its resources to control power and prestige in the Education Department to subserve personal pragmatic, non-professional gains. At the same time, education needs to be saved from the stronghold of the career-minded, charlatans, over-ambitious and arm-chair academicians who with their half-backed superficial knowledge gained in foreign tours always find fault with whatever exists in the educational system of the country, trying to impose notional concepts on a real-life situation, leading to dissipation of idealism through disillusionment because of lack of success of national policy.

The main focus of the plan of action must be the determination of priorities on the basis of available funds and the rational and optimum use of resources–manpower and financial.

More Reports, More Confusion and Education Suffers

It will be of interest to note that since Independence about one hundred Committees and Commissions have been appointed by the Government of India to investigate into the malaise afflicting the education system in the country. Remedial measures have also been identified but the desired results are still elusive. In this context, an editiorial of *The Hindustan Times* dated May 25, 1992 has made very pertinent observations.

'Frequent changes in education policy do not make a sound education system. While the comprehensive educational reforms suggested by the Radhakrishnan and Kothari Commissions remain largely unimplemented, frequent review exercises continue. The National Front Government showed undue haste in rejecting the 1986 National Policy on Education (NPE) even without giving it a proper trial and appointed a committee to review the NPE. The Narasimha Rao Government was equally keen to review the review undertaken by the Ramamurti Committee. The 16-member committee headed by the Chief Minister of Andhra Pradesh, Mr N. Janardhana Reddy, has broadly endorsed the basic thrust of the NPE and recommended only minor changes. Thus it has taken full six years for the Government to realise that the 1986 policy on education is basically sound. The result of frequent changes and reviews is the inevitable drift. As a result of such tinkering with education even modest schemes like the universalisation of primary education have failed to yield the desired results. Now the target of achieving universalisation of primary education by 1995 has once again been extended by five years. The malaise afflicting the education system has been diagnosed more or less accurately. Even the corrective measures have been identified by various committees from time to time. What is indeed missing is the necessary political will to make the system viable and meaningful.'

Public Expenditure on Education

Public expenditure[1] on Education as a proportion of GNP, over the years, has been as indicated in Table 8.1 which shows that while it has increased, as of 1986-87, it fell far short of 6 %.

Table 8.1: Share of Education in GNP (%)

Year	%
1950–51	1.2
1960–61	2.5
1970–71	3.1
1984–85*	3.7
1985–86**	4.0
1986–87@	3.9

* Budget expenditure (actual).
** Budget expenditure (Revised Estimates).
@ Budget expenditure (Budget Estimates).

The Central Statistical organisation has recently released the quick estimates of National Income (GNP) for the year 1988-89 which has been placed at Rs 3,06,822 crores at current prices on the basis of which the plan and non-plan budget of Education Departments at the Centre and the States as a percentage of national income comes to 4.2 % for the year 1989-90.

India ranks 115th in the world in terms of investment in Education as a percentage of GNP. Amongst the countries with a population of 10 crores and above, India is at the very bottom, barring Bangladesh. That India's educational expenditure as a proportion of GNP compares very unfavourably vis-a-vis worldwide expenditure on Education is brought out by Table 8.2 .

The need of the hour is to implement the recommendations of the Ramamurti Committee Report on raising resouces for education. (See Chapter 3 and S.N. 15 of this book.)

World public expenditure[2] on education as a percentage of GNP increased during the mid period 1970 as the consequence of increase in both developed and developing countries, but in the 1980s it slipped back to the level of early 1970s mainly as the reslut of a decrease in developed countries.

Table 8.2 : Share of Education in Five Year Plan Outlays/ Expenditures (%) (India)

Plans	*Share of Education in Total Plan Outlays/Expenditure (%)*
First Five Year Plan	7.86
Second Five Year Plan	5.83
Third Five Year Plan	6.87
Annual Five Year Plan	4.86
Fourth Five Year Plan	5.04
Fifth Five Year Plan	3.27
Sixth Five Year Plan	2.70
Seventh Five Year Plan	3.55

In developing countries, public expenditure on education increased rapidly in relation to GNP during the early to mid-1970 and then more slowly during the 1980s.

In the early 1980s, public expenditure on education as a percentage of GNP declined in Sub-Saharan Africa and Southern Asia, but increased in Arab States, Latin America and the Caribbean, Eastern Asia and Oceania.

In the mid to late 1980s public expenditure on education as a percentage of GNP increased in Sub-Saharan Africa and Southern Asia but levelled off or declined slightly in the other regions.

(Data for the following countries are not included in the World total nor in the totals by regions: Albania, Democratic Kampuchea, Dem. People's Rep. of Korea, Lao People's Dem. Rep., Lebanon, Mongolia, Mozambique, South Africa and Vietnam).

Table-8.3 Public Expenditure on Education as a Percentage of GNP

	1970	*1975*	*1980*	*1985*	*1986*	*1987*
WORLD TOTAL	**5.5**	**5.8**	**5.5**	**5.6**	**5.6**	**5.6**
Developing Countries	***2.9***	***3.6***	***3.8***	***4.0***	***4.2***	***4.2***
Sub-Saharan Asia	3.1	3.9	4.8	4.4	4.8	4.9
Arab States	5.0	5.9	4.4	6.2	6.7	6.6
Latin America/Caribbean	3.3	3.6	3.9	4.1	4.3	4.3
Eastern Asia	1.9	2.2	2.7	3.2	3.2	3.1
Southern Asia	2.6	3.1	4.0	3.3	3.4	3.5
Oceania	7.0	7.7	6.0	6.7	6.6	6.5
Developed Countries	*6.0*	*6.3*	*6.0*	*6.0*	*5.9*	*5.9*

Table 8.4 provides a comparative data on about 170 countries in he World.

Table-8.4 Showing Duration of First Level of Education, First Level Survival and Total Public Expenditure as % GNP in Various Countries of the World.

Country	Duration of 1st level education	First level			Total public exp. as % as GNP
		% reps	Survival to grade		
			4%	Final %	
1	2	3	4	5	6
Developing Countries					
Sub-Saharan Africa					
Angola	4	36	24	24	5.2
Benin	6	26	53	36	...
Botswana	7	5	92	89	8.4
Burkina Faso	6	17	82	68	2.5
Burundi	6	18	87	87	2.6
Cameroon	6	29	78	70	3.6
Cape Verde	6	24	90	39	3.2
Central African Rep.	6	35	77	56	2.9
Chad	6	32	81	78	...
Comoros	6	37	51	31	6.5
Congo	6	31	85	71	5.1
Cote Dtvoire	6	28	78	73	...
Djibouti	6	16	94	88	...
Equatorial Guinea	6	...	...	...	...
Ethiopia	6	11	56	50	4.2
Gabon	6	31	56	44	7.0
Gambia	6	18	97	96	3.9
Ghana	6	...	...	...	3.4
Guinea	6	24	70	43	3.3
Guinea-Bissau	6	42	46	19	3.3
Kenya	8	13	65	51	7.0
Lesotho	7	23	72	52	4.6
Liberia	6	...	...	...	...
Madagascar	5	35	...	...	3.5
Malawi	8	21	51	31	3.3
Mali	6	30	61	40	2.9
Mauritania	6	19	84	78	...
Mauritius	6	10	99	98	3.5

1	2	3	4	5	6
Mozambique	4	25	34	34	...
Namibia	7	...	...	...	...
Niger	6	15	83	75	...
Nigeria	6	...	...	...	...
Rwanda	8	10	74	46	3.5
Sao Tome and Principe	4	35	77	77	...
Senegal	6	15	92	85	...
Seychelles	9	–	95	91	10.0
Sierra Leone	7	...	...	...	...
Somalia	8	...	...	..	...
Sudan	6	–	82	76	...
Swaziland	7	15	82	62	5.5
Togo	6	31	68	52	5.1
Uganda	7	14	...	...	3.9
United Rep. of Tanzania	7	5	90	71	4.1
Zaire	6	19	64	60	1.4
Zambia	7	2	91	80	5.4
Zimbabwe	7	8	82	74	8.5
Arab States					
Algeria	6	7	96	91	9.8
Bahrain	6	9	95	92	5.0
Democratic Yemen	8	...	...	...	
Djibouti	6	16	94	88	...
Egypt	6	2	99	95	5.9
Iraq	6	20	91	73	3.8
Jordan	6	6	98	96	6.9
Kuwait	4	6	90	90	5.0
Lebanon	5	...			...
Libyan Arab Jam.	6	10	...	...	10.1
Mauritania	6	19	84	78	...
Morocco	5	17	76	67	8.3
Oman	6	13	99	92	4.0
Qatar	6	8	100	96	5.6
Saudi Arabia	6	13	95	90	8.6
Somalia	8	...	...	...	...
Sudan	6	–	82	76	...
Syrian Arab Rep.	6	7	95	89	4.7
Tunisia	6	23	89	72	6.3
United Arab Emirates	6	6	94	88	2.2
Yemen	6				6.0
Latin America and the Caribbean					
Antigua and Barbuda	6				2.7
Argentina	7				4.2
Bahamas	6				...
Barbados	6				6.1

1	2	3	4	5	6
Belize	7		...	...	...
Bolivia	8	..	...	..	...
Brazil	8	20	47	22	4.5
British Virgin Islands	7	10	...	...	...
Chile	8	7	97	85	3.6
Colombia	5	17	62	57	27
Costa Rica	6	11	87	76	4.8
Cuba	6	8	96	91	6.8
Dominica	7	*5	87	79	...
Dominican Republic	8	17	49	35	1.6
Ecuador	6	6	71	63	3.5
El Salvador	9	8	57	31	...
Grenada	7	10	100	53	...
Guatemala	6	4	46	36	1.8
Guyana	6	6	97	84	10.5
Haiti	6	9	40	32	1.9
Honduras	6	15	55	43	4.8
Jamaica	6	3	97	82	5.2
Mexico	6	10	80	69	3.4
Netherlands Antilles	6	...	...	...	...
Nicaragua	6	15	51	35	6.2
Panama	6	12	87	82	5.4
Paraguay	6	9	70	50	1.5
Peru	6	14	81	70	3.3
St Kitts and Nevis	7	...	...	...	6.6
St Lucia	7	7	98	65	7.5
St Vincent & Grenadines	7	...	...	...	6.3
Suriname	6	*23	83	66	10.4
Trinidad and Tobago	7	4	...	...	5.8
Uruguay	6	10	94	86	3.1
Venezuela	6	9	85	73	5.4
Eastern Asia					
China	5		...	...	2.7
Democratic Kampuchea	6	...	...	...	...
Indonesia	6	10	89	80	...
Korea. Dem. Peo. Rep. of	4	...	...	...	...
Korea. Republic of	6	–	100	99	4.2
Lao Peo. Dem. Rep.	5	27	...	...	1.0
Malaysia	6	–	100	99	7.0
Mongolia	3	1	...	...	...
Myanmar	5	...	...	...	...
Philippines	6	2	81	75	1.7
Singapore	6	1	100	95	3.8
Thailand	6	8			3.6
Viet Nam	5	...			...

1	2	3	4	5	6
Southern Asia					
Afghanistan	8	6	89	78	...
Bangladesh	5	18	29	20	2.2
Bhutan	6	17		...	...
India	5	...	...	...	3.4
Iran. Islamic Rep. of	5	10	90	87	...
Maldives	5	...		...	...
Nepal	5			...	2.8
Pakistan	5	...	...	...	2.1
Sri Lanka	5	9	97	94	3.6
Oceania					
Cook Islands	6	...	...	...	...
Fiji	6	3	96	51	6.0
Kiribati	6	2	88	45	8.7
Papua New Guinea	6	–	...	...	...
Samoa	7	...	...	...	...
Tonga	6	6	93	92	4.2
Other Developing Countries					
Cyprus	6	–	99	99	3.6
Turkey	5	8	98	97	2.1
Yugoslavia	4	2	98	98	3.8
Developed Countries					
Albania	8	...	...		...
Australia	6	...	...		5.8
Austria	4	...	...	...	5.9
Belgium	6	16	84	78	5.1
Bulgaria	8	2	96	86	6.9
Canada	8	...	...	...	7.2
Czechoslovakia	8	1	97	93	5.3
Denmark	6	–	100	00	7.9
Finland	6	–	98	98	5.9
France	5	6	96	94	5.7
German Dem. Rep.	4	...	...	...	...
Germany. Fed. Rep. of	4	1	97	97	4.4
Greece	6	0	99	99	2.7
Hungary	8	3	97	92	5.6
Iceland	6	...	...	...	3.7
Ireland	6	...	...	...	7.1
Israel	8	13	97	93	6.8
Italy	5	1	100	100	5.1
Japan	6	–	100	100	5.0
Luxembourg	6	6	95	86	...
Malta	6	2	94	94	3.3
Monaco	5	...	...	...	...
Netherlands	8	2	95	94	6.8

1	2	3	4	5	6
New Zealand	6	3	96	96	5.5
Norway	6	–	100	100	6.8
Poland	8	13	98	93	4.4
Portugal	6				4.6
Romania	8	...			2.1
San Marino	5	1			
South Africa	7	...	...	...	...
Spain	5	6	98	98	3.2
Sweden	6	–	100	100	7.4
Swtizerland	6	2	99	99	4.8
U.S.S.R.	5	4	99	98	7.5
United Kingdom	6				5.0
United States	8	...	...	...	6.8

Explanatory Notes on Table 8.4

1*Duration, in years, of first level education*. The figures refer to the number of grades in first level education, according to the education system in force in each country.

2*% of repeaters at the first level of education.* The total number of children still enrolled in the grade that they attended the previous year is presented as a percentage of the total enrolment at the first level. Generally 1986 or 1987.

3*percentage survival to grade 4 of first level education.* The percentage shows the number of children starting primary school who eventually attain the grade specified. The estimate is based on the Reconstructed Cohort Method which uses data on enrolment and repeaters for two consecutive years. Data generally refer to a cohort starting around 1985.

4*Percentage survival to final grade of first level of education* as at serial No. 3

5*Total public expenditure as a percentage of GNP.* Total public educational expenditure expressed as a percentage of Gross National Product around 1986. For some countries with centrally planned economies the Net Material Product was used instead of GNP

Declining Share of Elementary Education[3, 4]

The share of Elementary Education has come down from the level of 56% in First Plan to 29% in the Seventh Plan. The share of Secondary Education has remained somewhat stable with marginal differences – between 13% and 18%.

High Drop-out Rates and Need for More Retention

A large percentage of children drop out in the early stages of primary education with 46.97% of them dropping out by class V. At the middle level, about 62% of the children who began education at class I drop out before reaching class VII. This percentage is 67% in the case of girls at the middle stage. Similarly, the children of SC/ST communities drop out at a faster rate than those of the non-SC/ST communities. The dimension of regional disparities is also reflected in State-wise analysis of dropout at both the primary and middle school levels.

Unfortunately in the date compiled by UNESCO (Table 8.4), figures for India are not available. Still it is quite apparent that the situation is not satisfactory if we compare Tables 8.4 and Table 8.6.

Table 8.5 Intra-Sectoral Resource Allocation for Education in the Five Year Plans (Centre and States)

(Figures in crores of rupees) – (Figures in brackets are in %)

	EXPENDITURE						*OUTLAY*	
	1st Plan	*2nd Plan*	*3rd Plan*	*Plan Holiday*	*4th Plan*	*5th Plan*	*6th Plan*	*7th Plan*
Elementary*	85 (56)	95 (35)	201 (34)	75 (24)	239 (30)	317 (50)	906 (36)	1830 (29)
Secondary**	20 (13)	51 (19)	103 (18)	53 (16)	140 (18)	156 (17)	398 (16)	1000 (16)
University	14 (9)	48 (18)	87 (15)	77 (24)	195 (25)	205 (22)	486 (19)	750 (12)
Other General	14 (9)	30 (10)	73 (12)	37 (11)	106 (14)	127 (14)	457 (18)	2121 (33)
Total General	133 (87)	224 (82)	464 (79)	241 (75)	680 (87)	805 (88)	2247 (89)	5710 (89)
Technical	20 (13)	49 (18)	125 (21)	81 (25)	106 (13)	107 (12)	278 (11)	682 (11)
Grand Total	153 (100)	273 (100)	589 (100)	322 (100)	786 (100)	912 (100)	2524 (100)	6383 (100)
% to total plan outlay	7.86	5.83	6.87	4.86	5.04	3.27	2.59	3.55

* includes pre-school education
** includes teacher education, social education (youth serv * Draft

Table 8.6 : Drop out Rates 1987-88

S. No.	*State/U.T.*	*Class I-V*			*Class I-VIII*		
		Boys	*Girls*	*Total*	*Boys*	*Girls*	*Total*
1	2	3	4	5	6	7	8
1	Andhra Pradesh	52.42	58.52	55.03	67.77	77.01	71.68
2	Arunachal Pradesh	58.75	58.43	58.63	75.20	75.91	75.44
3	Assam	51.59	59.47	55.01	70.91	74.45	72.44
4	Bihar	63.88	68.93	65.63	76.77	84.19	79.08
5	Goa	2.19	8.78	5.33	20.69	27.63	23.95
6	Gujarat	38.06	46.87	41.92	56.30	67.69	61.67
7	Haryana	24.35	31.61	27.32	33.01	48.22	38.62
8	Himachal Pradesh	28.06	29.32	28.63	16.92	34.42	24.68
9	Jammu & Kashmir	28.08	41.45	33.44	46.63	58.51	51.25
10	Karnatka	43.28	57.36	50.16	61.04	72.07	66.10

1	2	3	4	5	6	7	8
11	Kerela	−5.12	−3.62	−4.39	15.97	15.00	15.49
12	Madhya Pradesh	36.64	48.04	41.04	49.88	66.65	55.78
13	Maharashtra	34.69	45.71	39.82	53.07	68.01	59.87
14	Meghalaya	31.43	33.40	32.35	66.42	61.61	64.22
15	Mizoram	37.28	38.72	37.98	45.35	42.49	43.98
16	Nagaland	37.22	33.43	35.45	58.15	55.13	56.90
17	Orissa	40.05	37.32	38.97	60.28	71.25	64.86
18	Punjab	36.81	37.81	37.27	59.69	67.26	63.23
19	Rajasthan	53.12	60.75	52.25	62.81	76.82	66.35
20	Sikkim	60.19	58.50	59.86	63.83	60.11	62.51
21	Tamilnadu	19.44	24.46	21.78	44.08	53.14	48.22
22	Tripura	59.14	58.02	58.65	73.95	75.96	74.83
23	Uttar Pradesh	47.84	47.24	47.65	49.88	63.34	54.20
24	West Bengal	62.35	65.76	63.81	74.32	76.91	75.41
25	A&N Islands	18.60	22.74	20.54	38.35	39.59	36.31
26	Chandigarh	−21.00	24.41	4.78	5.54	13.01	8.94
27	Dadra & Nagar Haveli	29.37	45.58	36.14	63.98	70.52	66.81
28	Daman & Diu	2.24	8.82	5.34	21.03	27.97	23.95
29	Delhi	14.40	25.40	19.76	9.64	24.20	16.73
30	Lakshadweep	−2.96	11.38	4.02	40.96	56.82	48.45
31	Pondicherry	11.55	0.83	−5.59	3.11	31.52	16.29
32	Manipur	71.35	72.04	71.67	76.58	87.86	77.90
	Total	43.35	49.42	46.97	58.80	67.55	62.29

Drop-out rate is calculated as follows :

Drop-out rate from class I to V for the year 1987–88

$$= \frac{\text{(No. of students enrolled in Clas I in 1983–84)} - \text{(No. of students enrolled in Class V in 1987–88)}}{\text{No. of students enrolled in Class I in 1983–84}} \times 100$$

Drop-out rate from class I to VII for the year 1987–88

$$= \frac{\text{(No. of students enrolled in Class I in 1980-81)} - \text{(No. of students enrolled in Class I in 1987–88)}}{\text{No. of students enrolled in Class VIII in 1980–81}} \times 100$$

This ratio does not take into account :

(i) Repeaters; and (ii) Children who enter the system after Class I.

INVESTMENT IN PRIMARY EDUCATION[6]

Investing in People

It is a responsibility of governments to ensure that virtually all the members of society have adequate nutrition, primary health care, clean water, safe sanitation, family planning services, and at least a primary education. These basic investments in people are essential not only for humanitarian reasons and for the creation of civilized societies but also as the foundations for sustained economic growth. As the outgoing President of the World Bank has said, in a letter to the Secretary-General of the United Nations following the *World*

Summit for Children, 'Investment in human capital, including importantly basic health care and primary education for children, is one of the most effective means of stimulating long-term economic growth and improving general welfare.' The same conclusion was reached by the *South Commission's* review of recent development experience which included: *'satisfying basic needs should have priority both on grounds of equity and to sustain economic growth at a rapid pace.'*

In recent years, research has demonstrated the power of that investment in many different ways. World Bank studies have shown that raising the average educational level of the labour force by one year can raise GDP by as much as 9 per cent. Other studies have demonstrated that four years of education, as opposed to none, can increase agricultural productivity by 10 per cent. Research over the years in Australia, Brazil, Colombia, Ethiopia, Guatemala, India, Indonesia, Kenya, and Sierra Leone have shown that improved nutrition can increase work productivity by up to 20 per cent. Better adult and child health has been shown to save millions of lost workdays. Correcting child malnutrition and iron deficiency anaemia have been shown to reduce absenteeism, increase attention spans, and improve school results.

But for the present purpose, such studies are like striking matches in daylight. The evidence that investing in poeple lays the foundations for economic growth looms large before us in the shape of those countries which have succeeded in achieving rapid and sustained progress in the postwar world. Liberating people's potential via land reforms and universal health and education services has been fundamental to that success in countries and regions such as Japan, South Korea, and Taiwan. All of these have shown that basic education and health for all are not just social expenditures but economic investments, not just indulgences which can only be afforded after countries have become prosperous but the foundations without which widespread prosperity will not be achieved.

In other words, the lessons of the last 40 years suggest that development proceeds most steadily when it walks on the two legs of a market-friendly economic policy and a government commitment to ensuring investment in people. And as the consensus on market-friendly economic policies visibly gathers momentum, it is even more essential that the other leg of the development consensus is also exercised.

Unfortunately, 'investing in people' has been the battle hymn of the international development effort for fifteen years without battle ever really being joined.

All for Some

The governments of the developing countries spend, on average, about one quarter of their budgets on directly investing in people via health and education services (but not including government expenditures on agriculture and employment creation). Health and education together claim 17 per cent of government expenditures in Latin America, 21 per cent in the Middle East and North Africa, 23 per cent in South Asia, and 25 per cent in East and South East Asia.

In countries where high employment and reasonable wages mean that the majority are able to meet their own needs from their own earnings, such levels of social expenditure by governments might be adequate if allocated according to need. But of the sums which are allocated directly to health and education, more than half is allocated to relatively high cost services for the few, and less than half is allocated to low-cost services for the many. In other words, only about 12 per cent of all government spending in the developing world is devoted to investing in the health and education of the poor majority.

It is estimated, for example, that 80 per cent of the 12 billion dollar allocated each year to water supply system is spent on putting private taps in the homes of the relatively well-off, at a cost of approximately 600 dollar per person served, and that only 20 per cent goes to the public wells and stand-pipes which can bring clean water to the poor majority at a cost of 30 dollar to 50 dollar per person served. Reallocating even a proportion of total expenditures in favour of the poor could therefore liberate enough resources to achieve the goal of safe water supply for almost every community in almost every country by the year 2000.

A similar argument, with similar statistics, could be built around the theme of health care. For many times more money to be spent on curative than on preventive health is the norm; for 75 per cent of public spending on health to serve only the richest 25 per cent of the population is not untypical, for more to be spent on sophisticated operations than on the low-cost control of mass disease is not uncommon; for 30 per cent of health budgets to be spent on sending a privileged few for treatment abroad is not unknown.

The necessary restructuring of such expenditures may be difficult but it is not impossible. On becoming independent, for example, Bangladesh found itself with a health system which devoted only 10 per cent of its expenditure to rural health clinics serving the great majority of its population. Today, that figure has been raised to 60 per cent.

Distortions in Education

Such distortions of public spending in favour of the better-off are also evident in national education system.

Despite decades of research findings which regularly demonstrate that investment in *primary* education yields significantly higher returns in both social progress and economic growth, government spending in almost all developing countries is heavily biased towards higher education for the few rather than basic education for the many.

This is not the path that has been followed by those countries which have achieved the mutually reinforcing goals of universal education and sustained economic growth. In both Japan and South Korea, for example, universal primary education preceded economic take-off. And in both, this basic investment in people was made at a stage when their per capita incomes, in real terms, were lower than in most developing countries today. Japan moved rapidly towards universal primary education at the end of the last century. South Korea ensured that almost all its children were in primary school at a stage when its per capita GNP was little more than 100 dollar per year. Emphasis on secondary and higher education came later and was not made at the expense of primary education for the great majority. Nor did it run very far ahead of the economy's capacity to absorb increasing numbers of more highly educated people.

Many other countries have taken the opposite course, financing higher education disproportionately with the result that up to half of all children fail to complete four years in primary school while secondary and tertiary education absorbs an exaggerated share of the budget in order to produce many more graduates than the economy can usefully absorb. In India, where between 60 and 70 children could be given primary education for the cost of training one university student, approximately half of the nation's children fail to finish primary school while the country as a whole produces more graduates than it can productively employ. Inevtiably, one of the effects is a brain drain of unemployed but highly qualified people to the industrialized nations. In this way, a significant share of government spending on education is used to subsidize the rich rather than to achieve basic education for all which, as all experience suggests, is one of the cornerstones of development.

For reasons of both justice and efficiency, the overall effect of educational expenditure should be to redistribute incomes and equalize opportunities. In most developing countries today, its effect is almost the opposite. Most government spending on higher education is spending on the already advanced; in Chile, the Dominican Republic, and Uruguay, for example, more than 50 per cent of all government spending on higher education is devoted to the children of families who belong to the richest 20 per cent of the population. In India, 50 per cent of all government spending on education is used to subsidize the best-educated 10 per cent.

With these inequities lies the potential for a degree of restructuring of educational expenditures which could help to finance progress towards the goal of access to basic education for all children (and the completion of primary school by at least 80 per cent) before the year 2000.

Need for an Extraordinary Effort

If that goal is to be met, then an extraordinary effort is called for in the early 1990s. In particular, low-cost ways and means will have to be found of retraining or returning those who now drop out of school in the first year or two of formal education. Considerable progress has been made in enrolling children in school; the more difficult problem is that up to half of those who do enrol leave before becoming literate. Those children are essentially being locked out of the 21st century.

Pioneering efforts in Bangladesh, Colombia, Zimbabwe, and in many other countries in recent years, have shown that access to a basic education for all children, and completion of primary school for the great majortiy, can be achieved at an affordable cost. Using such new methods, the extra financial cost of reaching these goals can be estimated at approximately 5 billion dollar a year throughout the 1990s. The cost of not achieving that goal will be far higher. World Bank research over the last 10 years has demonstrated many times that *'productivity of an educated work force is the most reliable engine of economic growth.'* But the investment in education yields its dividends in many other forms. It confers the ability to continue learning, from a wide range of sources, throughout adult life. It modernizes attitudes and builds confidence in change. It stimulates broader participation in politicial life. It assists the process of allowing what is good in the new to replace what is bad in the old. It brings an awareness of new ideas and new choices. It raises the average age of marriage, makes family planning more likely, and reduces birth rates. As Japan's Prime Minister, Toshiki Kaifu, told the assembled heads of state at the *World Summit for Children* (Sept.1990) *'It is no exaggeration to say that the policy of promoting education constituted the very foundation of Japan's development. In developing countries the first priority should be to institute and improve basic education and raise the literacy rate among children so as to enable them to live with dignity. National development can take place only when all people have the opportunity to receive education'*

High Fees for Higher Education

The Disparity between the cost of higher education and fees is rather high. To give an example in Engineering Colleges, the annual recurring expenditure alone comes to about Rs 2500. Not only this huge expenditure, there is also the problem of brain drain

The following data compiled from the Report of the Review Committee on NPE provides relevant information related to cost of higher education in India.

There is a strong case for higher fees for higher education. The following extracts from two letters written by eminent educationists that appeared in *The Hindustan Times* dated June 2, 1992, aptly make out a case.

Dr. Suman Sahai, a member of the Central Advisory of Education writes.

'Regarding the elevation of fees for the absurdly subsidised and pampered higher education system, the debate has been going on for some time, with clear recommendations from experts that it is feasible and desirable to ask students in institutions like the IITs and IIMs to pay more for their education.

Table-8.7

Type of Higher Education Institution	*Nature of courses*	*Fee charged per annum*
Central Universities	Under-graduate level general courses	Between Rs 120/- in Banaras Hindu University and Vishwa Bharati and Rs 180/- in Delhi University.
Central Universities	Post-graduate level general courses	Between Rs 144/- in Vishwa Bharati and Rs 300/- to Rs 400/- in the North Eastern Hill University.
Central Universities	Professional courses like B.Ed., LL.B. etc.	Between Rs 120/- in Vishwa Bharati and Rs 1,440/- in Delhi University.
State Universities	Under-graduate level general courses	Between Rs 40/- to Rs 180/- in Rajasthan University and Rs 500/- to Rs 400/- in Gujarat, Bombay and Nagpur Universities.
State Universities	Post-graduate level general courses	Between Rs 100/- to Rs 200/- in Rajasthan University and Rs 500/- to Rs 600/- in Bombay University.
State Universities	Under-graduate Professional courses like B.Ed., LL.B. etc.	Between Rs 100/- to Rs 200/- in Rajasthan University and Rs 500/- inn Bombay University.
State Universities	Engineering courses.	An average of Rs 533/-

As member of the Central Advisory Board of Education, I was present at the last meeting, when the director of the IIT Kharagpur reiterated that the staff and students of IITs were of the opinion that students are both able and willing to pay more for their privileged education. It appears somewhat perverse that even though the affected group endorses higher fees, the government is dragging its feet in taking a decision. Mr Arjun Singh, who is chairman of IIT Council, would do a service to the cause of education taking a speedy decision in this matter.'

Shri Amrik Singh states

'I am not in favour of higher allocations for higher education principle. This is for the reason that higher education is by and large patronised by the middle classes. As is well known, more than 80 per cent of the Central revenue comes from indirect taxes. This means that we are robbing the ordinary people who pay taxes and using them for the benefit of those who can afford to pay but are not asked to pay.

I do not rule out the possibility of the Delhi Teachers with their exclusive line of communication with the Minister for H.R.D. to get the allocations increased. Should that happen, I would regard it as an anti-people act. In a sense it would be in line with the popular way of doing things–swear by the poor and the disadvantaged but act against them. Should the Minister bend under any such pressure, it would be totally indefensible. The teachers themselves have conceded that 'there is a case for affordable raise in fee for higher education.' Could they be a little more specific with regard to what is "affordable"? Or is it all a question of pressures and counter-pressures? My own position is as follows :

Anything less than Rs 100 at the undergraduate level would not do. Correspondingly, the fee at the honours level should be Rs 150 and at the Masters level Rs 250. Professional colleges also need to adjust accordingly.

I recognise that approximately half the students in Delhi would not be able to pay at this rate. I am particularly sympathetic to those enrolled in B.A. and B.Com (Pass) classes. A large number of them are in college not because this is the way they prefer but because the pressures of the economy propel them in that direction. That being so, a well-funded and well-oiled system of loans and scholarships should be an integral part of what is proposed to be done.

That any such move is bound to be resisted goes without saying. The question to be asked is: where do the teachers stand? Do they stand with those who pay Rs 300 or 400 per month at school but are not prepared to pay even Rs 100 at college or do they stand with those who are unable to go to school because the country is overspending on higher education? One expects the teachers to have the right values as well as a sense of social justice.'

Vocational Education

The heart of the Government's reforms was to divert a substantial portion of students at the 10+2 level to vocational courses. It is very depressing to note that even after 17 years of the introduction of the scheme, the present intake in vocational courses covers only 4% of the student population. The targets fixed have been changed frequently. The 1986 NPE envisaged 'that vocational courses cover 10 per cent of higher secondary students by 1990 and 25 per cent by 1995.' According to the modified NPE, 1992, 'It is proposed that vocational courses cover 10 per cent of higher secondary students by 1995 and 25 per cent by 2000.' Evidently targets are not fixed rationally and scientifically. A careful analysis of the factors responsible for the failure of earlier efforts, however, does not promise a significant success to the policy of vocational education even this time. NEP does not seem to have considered factors like availability and demand for different kinds of skills in the existing labour market, the amount of money involved in providing different kinds of vocational education likely to be in demand, the problem of rural unemployment, the extent of the existing infrastructure, alternative ways of raising funds and providing vocational education, and finally, enacting and enforcing legislation to implement the new vocational and employment policy.

Lack of funding may be a bottleneck but there is no conceptual problem there except in one respect. It would never be possible for the country to provide all the equipment and other resources for setting up suitable workshops and so on. To quite an extent, collaboration with industry is, therefore, indispensable.

Delinking of Degrees from Jobs

Immediate steps must be taken to delink degrees from jobs. Because of the high premium on degrees, everyone wants to join the queue for university education. By delinking degrees from jobs, more funds would be available which can be spent largely on school education.

Decline in Number of Literates: Need for Rethinking on Adult Literacy Programmes

The report of Comptroller and Auditor General of India (CAG)[7] should be an opener for all those concerned with adult literacy programme.

'Despite the infusion of substantial funds to the country's literacy mission, the average number of persons rendered literate per year has surprisingly shown a deline, the Comptroller and Auditor General of India (CAG) has observed.

In his report on the Union Government (Civil), tabled in the Lok Sabha on May 14, 1992 by Minister of State for Finance Dalbir Singh the CAG said expenditure of Rs 494 crore was incurred on adult literacy programme during 1985-90 and the average annual expenditure went up from Rs 49 crore during the years 1985-88 (pre-mission period) to Rs 89 crore during 1988-89.

But the average number of persons rendered literate per year declined from 49 lakh in 1985-88 to 44 lakh in 1989-90. The total number rendered literate (133 lakh) during 1987-90 was much below the target of 300 lakh, the CAG said.

Under rural functional literacy projects, 135 lakh persons were rendered literate out of 182 lakh enrolled during 1985-90. It said reports of attendance in several centres were not reliable.

The CAG said payment of honorarium to instructors was delayed up to 31 months in some States, while cases of non-payment of honorarium were also noticed.

On the other hand, appointment of project staff and instructors of regular scales of pay, instead of engaging them on payment of honorarium fixed emoluments envisaged in programme led to an avoidable expenditure of Rs 7.30 crore in eight States.

The report said supply of teaching and learning materials was unsatisfactory in 16 States and materials worth Rs 19.81 lakh purchased during 1985-90 had not been supplied to the centres.

It said out of Rs 18.99 crore disbursed during 1987-90 as grants to 14 States for post-literacy and continuing education through *jana shikshan nilayams*, Rs 7.23 crore remained un-utilised. The reported utilisation in five States included Rs 2.96 crore not spent but kept in banks outside Government account.

Against target for setting up of 60,000 nilayams up to 1990, only 11,691 had been established in 19 States though 16,351 were sanctioned up to March 1990. While the number of neo-literates was not made available to audit in several States, in two States no neo-literates were enrolled, the CAG said.

The CAG pointed out that utilisation certificates for grants amounting to Rs 35.34 crore paid to voluntary agencies during 1985-90 had not been received.

Out of 406 voluntary agencies evaluated by the audit, as much as 140 needed improvement, 77 were considered not capable of undertaking literacy programmes and performance of 86 agencies (grants paid Rs 1.43 crore) was categorised as wholly unsatisfactory or their bonafides were doubtful.

The report found that the number of courses organised by shramik vidyapeeths for providing education in occupational skills to urban and industrial workers and their families fell short of the target by 26 to 50 per cent during 1985-90.

It said expenditure of only Rs. 7.09 crore was incurred under the mass programme of functional literacy involving student volunteers though the budget allocation was for Rs 35 crore.

A voluntary agency in Gujarat was paid Rs. 17 lakh between March and July 1988, but its claim of rendering 5.59 lakh persons literate was not verified.

What is noteworthy, the CAG said, additional Rs 136 lakh were again paid to the same agency which did not refund unspent balance of Rs 22.96 lakh. Literacy kits costing Rs 35.10 lakh had remained unutilised.

Despite several shortcomings noticed in the implementation of the programme by the agency, including doubtful claims about the number of persons rendered literate, further grants-in-aid of Rs 503.15 lakh were sanctioned to the same agency and Rs 405 lakh were released for a third phase in June 1990.'

If past experience is any index, the entire scheme of adult education needs to be dropped and the funds utilised on elementary education. But then this requires a strong political will. Alternately it may become the responsibility of the industrial establishmentsl.

Educationists to Manage Education

Educational administration, management and planning must be professionalised. We are at the cross-roads, amidst new ideas and attitudes. The nation has already paid a heavy price by ignoring this vital reform needed in education since Independence. This reform does not involve any additional funds. It must be reiterated that the nation can ignore this only at its peril. All the educational reforms recommended by the various Education Commissions and Committees failed at the implementation stage on account of neglect of this aspect of the personnel of educational administration, management command and control. Teachers alone can provide the needed thrust for success, not bureaucrats.

Educational administration is a specialised discipline and this is accepted all over the world. It is high time we realised its importance as distinct from general administration. The illusion that there can be a generalist civil servant for all the jobs (including education), in this technological age, must be overcome and it must be ensured that the educational system is managed by experienced, competent and dedicated teachers who have commitment to the profession. To use proven educationists of high calibre to manage education should be the first priority in our educational reforms. It is very unfortunate that the words of wisdom of the Kothari Commission with regard to educational administration even now continue to be disregarded by the concerned planning and implementation authorities. The Commission observed, 'The present convention is that the post of the Secretary to the Government of India is not to be filled from the ICS or the IAS pool and that it should be given to an eminent educationist who should be designated as "Educational Adviser to the Government of India and Secretary to the Ministry of Education". This is a healthy tradition and should continue.' The Commission further emphasized the special character of educational administration, 'First, in education, administration is a service agency to teaching and research and not their master. Secondly, one cannot be a good educational administrator unless one is also a good teacher. Thirdly, there should always be possibility for an educational administrator to come back to teaching or research and for a teacher to go over to the administrative side on a tenure assignment.' These observations are equally valid at the administration of education at the state and district level.

Two factors play a major role in the effective implementation of any programme. They are identification and stability. But sadly both are wanting in the present system of educational administration, management and planning. It is common knowledge that in almost all the States and the Union Territories in India, the two key posts of the Secretary of Education and the Director of Education are conventionally entrusted to generalists belonging to the I.A.S. Cadre. The story is no different at the Ministry of Human Resource Development, Government of India and in the Planning Commission. Incumbents of these posts are not committed and change hands frequently. Their stay is usually so short that by the time they acquaint themselves with the working of the Education Department and vital to educational matters, they are transferred. Thus they are unable to make any substantial contribution. They are not in a position to provide effective professional guidance and inspiration to teachers, principals and education officers and supervisors. Nor do they have needed interest or commitment and motivation, and they are keen to move up or away before the consequences of their vague efforts come to roost, to become millstone around them or their successors' necks. It is of interest to note that in one of the Union Territories there were as many as seventeen Directors of Education in seventeen years. The framers of the National Policy on Education and the Programme of Action have completely ignored this aspect. The recommendation for the constitution of an Indian Education Service is heartening, but the Programme of Action does not hold out any hope for its early implementation. It is strongly felt that the generalists need to be immediately replaced by dedicated contractual teachers in the administration, management and planning of education, so as to provide the much needed confidence, grassroots professional competence, guidance, inspiration and motivation to the academic staff working in the field of education. The proven men and women of classroom and field experience will be able to implement the breakthrough transformation needed.

Reforms in Evaluation

In spite of the weighty recommendations of various national commissions on education the state of affairs regading examination and evaluation still remains unchanged. Though various epithets like 'an enemy' of true education, 'an incubus', 'an obstacle to learning,' 'a blood sucker,' 'a bane of educational system,' 'a necessary evil,' 'a glorification of memory,' 'a begetter of rivalry and strife,' 'a dead hand of education', 'a growing tyranny,' 'a presumptuous attempt to, gauge the depth of human ignorance,' have been used in respect to examination still they enjoy their overlordship. 'Flying squads,' 'central marking,' 'marking by a team of examiners' 'grading systems' are no answers. All these measures have resulted in the development of vested interests. As Prof. V.S. Mathur has stated, 'Boards of Education are not police or vigilance bodies meant to pounce, upon and haul up the "offender". They are academic bodies and exist to nourish the nation's children into useful maturity. If they do not seek to perform this sacred duty are not worth their salt: let there be a twist within our thinking.' (*Shikshak Sathi*, May 1988, New Delhi.) Perhaps the following measures may help:

1. There may be only one public examination to indicate the completion of the course.
2. Even this examination need not be compulsory for all.
3. Every pupil who completes the school course should get a

certificate based in school records.

4. Pupils who take the final examination should be given certificate by the Board that holds the examination.
5. Open Book System should be adopted that may make copying redundant and encourage the students to do more learning and thinking one of the basic aim of education.
6. Students be allowed the option to appear at the public examination as a whole or in parts.
7. Students be required to pass in each subject only once. They should be allowed to appear in those subjects where they fall short.

The poor implementation of the NPE in the capital of the country is clearly reflected in the June 1992 results declared by the Central Board of Secondary Education Delhi. Delhi's poor showing in the Class X and XII results has given rise to widespread concern over the state of school education in the nation's Capital. Delhi schools have scored a pass percentage of mere 59.7 for Class XII and an even more dismal 47 per cent for Class X. Though this itself represents the lowest performance for a major city across the country, the fall is nowhere near as sudden as it appears at first. Last year, for example, Delhi did only marginally better with a pass percentage of 62.5 for Class XII which stood next to Guwahati's 55 per cent, the lowest in that year. This year, Guwahati has improved its position to 64.2 per cent, pushing Delhi to the very bottom.

The greatest neglect appears to be in the sphere of human inputs such as teacher performance and lack of accountability in a highly bureaucratised Administration (including Central Board of Secondary Education).

Operation Blackboard

Observations made by *The Hindustan Times* of April 25, 1992 under the caption' In a Shambles' deserve careful consideration .

'The concern expressed by members of Parliament cutting across party affiliations over the tardy implementation of "Operation Blackboard" will be shared by all right-thinking people. The scheme was one of the biggest initiatives taken by the Government in the area of primary education with the objective of removing the glaring lacunae in the schooling system, particularly in the rural areas. The use of the term "operation" implied that there was an urgency in the programme as also a pre-determined time-frame to implement it. Despite brave claims made by political leaders and policy planners about the scheme, it is yet to take off in many parts of the country. Launched as one of the key premises of the 1986 National Policy on Education, the scheme represented the bare minimum required for sustained schooling at the elementary level. But it ran into trouble from the very beginning. While some States took unusually long time to complete detailed surveys of blocks to be covered by the Operation, the West Bengal Government wanted buildings rather than additional teachers. The scheme suffered a major setback when the financial axe fell on it in the wake of the worsening economic crisis situation in the country. But in all fairness, the resource crunch was only part of the problem. The scheme has failed to make much headway because the administrative set-up in the existing educational system is hardly geared to undertake such projects.'

Discarding the Fad of Seminars etc.

It has to be realised that there is a wide gap in our educational work between theory and practice. Most of the failures in education are due to this unfortunate gulf. Many utopian ideas are given to the teachers during full-time and even in-service training courses. There is a plethora of educational conferences, seminars, training courses and workshops. Ideas presented are too theoretical or idealistic to be translated into actual classroom situations. It is generally observed that the participants find it very difficult to spend the scheduled time fruitfully. Recently organised various programmes related to the dissemination of the information on the National Policy on Education amply demonstrate their futility. Strangely enough they were not even supplied with a copy of the National Policy on Education.

We must discard the 'fad' of bringing about reforms through speeches and sermons. Let there be down-to-earth involvement and in-service training of teachers so that they grow in stature. We must learn to determine our priorities and make the optimum use of our limited financial resources. Each available rupee must be spent in providing the essential facilities to educational institutions and not on meeting travelling and dearness allowances of government officials and self-styled experts.

Non-Creation of Departments/ Institutions/ Posts for the Implementation of NPE

Dr. U.S. Chaudhari of the Deparment of Education, Devi Ahilya Vishwavidyalay, Indore rightly sees any justification in the creation of posts. He states, 'In fact, in the name of the New Education Policy (NEP) much farce is being staged. The NEP has, so far, achieved nothing excepting the multiplication of task forces and recommendations for the establishment of top heavy institutes and councils. The new superstructure, like the 20 point committees, is being created to accommodate the power mongers and power brokers. Thus, in the implementation of the NEP greater stress has been laid on adorning the cage than on feeding the parrot within.

Surprisingly, institutions like the UGC and the Ministry for HRD are themselves contributing to the dilution of standards by starting institutes of higher education without making advance preparations.

Establishment of Academic Staff Colleges (ASCs) is a case in point. The great haste with which these colleges are coming into existence will lower the quality of teacher education and bring the idea and philosophy of training into disrepute. The borrowed model of the ASC is very expensive and does not suit the genius of our people. Could we not think of an alternative, a less expensive model? "College-based inservice training" is one such. At the most one qualified training coordinator could have been appointed in each college. This alternative approach could have saved crores of rupees. But who has the time and patience to evolve a model of education or training suited to our tradition and requirements? etc.' (*Hindustan Times,* December 12, 1987)

Rational Use of Funds and Fixing Priorities

It is apparent that it is not only the inadequacy of funds but also the lack of direction and lack of clarity in determining priorities, that has hindered educational reforms and improvement in the country. It cannot be overemphasised that it is not mere money and resources but management and execution by a better and more effective cadre and leadership that can give true content and meaning to educational programmes. A substantive improvement in the personnel of education at the highest echelons is the critical factor to-day. At the same time it must be remembered that all reforms in education are likely to become the usual, luke warm routine mixture-as-before without a 'crash programme' of making the optimal use of the available facilities and resources in the educational institutions. As Mr Manmohan Singh, in an article entitled 'Education: A Development View' in *The Hindustan Times,* dated March 22, 1986 observed, 'We have to be perhaps ruthlessly realistic about our economic and budgetary constraints. There is no point in trying to apply one cubic inch of butter to a square mile of bread. Such an attempt would imply realignment of priorities in educational investment and discarding a part of the band-wagon.' We must fix priorities and targets on the basis of actual funds available.

Consolidation of Higher Education

It is true that only 4.8 per cent of the relevant age-group is enrolled in higher education in our country and the proportion is even more adverse in some categories, particularly for women, scheduled castes and tribes. But it would be suicidal to go on absorbing scarce resources without attaining even the minimum standards laid down by the University Grants Commission. As resources are limited, proliferation of non-viable educational institutions will have to be discontinued.

The drop-outs and failures which together account for more than 59 per cent of the students enrolled, represent a colossal waste of human and material resources. This must be checked and if needed suitable directions should be issued so that results of the annual examinations are moderated appropriately. This recommendation is made as it has been found that examination results can depend on chance and environmental factors. When our tools of assessment are not fully objective and valid, why should we allow our students to suffer.

The number of effective working days and hours in a year should be increased.

In research, priority to only those programmes, should be given which will lead to the practical application of technology to the needs of villages and rural areas.

Concluding Observations

The discussion may be closed with a quote of an editorial of The Hindustan Times of April 25, 1992.

'The malaise afflicting our education system has been diagnosed more or less accurately. The various commissions have even prescribed efficacious remedies. Where we have gone wrong is in our faulty planning and sluggish administrative follow-up. We have grandiose plans but there is no proper monitoring. Whatever little feedback that is available is hardly acted upon. The project was supposed to improve school buildings. In the absence of basic infrastructure the use of audio-visual aids and other teaching materials has not been optimal. Some of the States have complained that they have virtually no initiative as everything has been handed down by the Centre. The Ramamurti Report of Education has recommended that all decision-making in this area should be delegated to the States. That will perhaps making things worse. What is perhaps most wanting in the lack of political will and commitment at the higher levels.'

For the implantation of the Policy, a 'Programme of Action' was formulated. The implementation was reviewed in 2000 and 2005. Details of these efforts are presented in the next two chapters.

NOTES

1. *Ramamurti Report* or *Committee for Review of National Policy on Education* (NPE), 1986, Department of Education, New Delhi, 1990.
2. *Basic Education and Literacy: World Statistical Indicators,* UNESCO, 1990.
3. *A Handbook of Education and Allied Statistics,* Department of Education, New Delhi, 1987.
4. *Committee for Review of National Policy on Education,* (NPE), 1986, Department of Education, New Delhi, 1990.
5. *The State of World's Children, 1992,* UNICEF, New Delhi, 1992.
6. *The Hindustan Times,* May 15, 1992.

9

Major Initiatives Taken for the Implementation of Revised National Policy on Education 1992

Programme of Action—POA (1992)

The POA for the revised NPE was evolved by constituting twenty-two Task Forces on the following dimensions of education.

1. Education for Women's Equaly.
2. Education of Scheduled Castes, Scheduled Tribes and other Backward Sections.
3. Minorities Education.
4. Education of the Handicapped.
5. Adult and Continuing Education.
6. Early Childhood Care and Education.
7. Elementary Education.
8. Secondary Education.
9. Navodaya Vidyalaya.
10. Vocational Education.
11. Higher Education.
12. Open Education.
13. Delinking Degrees from Jobs and Manpower Planning.
14. Rural Universities and Institutions.
15. Technical and Management Education.
16. Research and Development.
17. The Cultural Perspective.
18. Development of Languages.
19. Media and Education Technology.
20. Sports, Physical Education and Yoga.
21. Evaluation Process and Examination Reforms.

Universalisation of Elementary Education

Since the formulation of the NPE (1992), Following major programmes have been initiative for achieving the objectives of Universalisation of Elementary Education.

1. District Primary Education Projection (DPEP).
2. Sarva Shiksha Abhiyan
3. National Programme of Nutritional Support to Primary Education (NPNSPE) or Mid-day Meals.
4. Education Guarantee Scheme and Alternative and Innovative Education.
5. National Programme of Education of Girls at Elementary Stage (NPEGL) Scheme
6. Kasturba Gandhi Balika Vidyalaya Scheme.
7. Prathmik Shiksha Kosh.

District Primary Education Programme (DPEP)

The District Primary Education Programme (DPEP) launched in 1993 is a Centrally Sponsored Scheme for holistic development of primary education covering Classes I to V. The three major objectives of the DPEP are to (i) reduce drop-out rates to less than 10 per cent, (ii) reduce disparities among gender and social groups in the areas of enrolment, learning achievement, etc. to less than 5 per cent and (iii) improve the level of learning achievement compared to the baseline surveys.

The Programme components include construction of classrooms and new schools, opening of Alternative Schooling Centres, appointment of new teachers, setting up early childhood education centres, strengthening of State Councils of Educational Research and Training (SCERTs)/ District Institutes of Educational Training (DIETs), setting up of Block Resource Centres/Cluster Resource Centres, teacher training development of teaching-learning material, special interventions for education of girls, SC/ST, working children, etc. Initiatives for providing integrated education to disabled children and distance education for teacher training have also been incorporated in the DPEP Scheme.

Additionality Factor of DPEP—DPEP is based on the principle of 'additionality' and is structured to fill in the existing gaps by providing inputs over and above the provisions made under Central and State Sector Schemes for primary education.

District Selection Criteria—(a) Educationally backward districts with female literacy below the national average, and (b) Districts where Total Literacy Campaigns (TLCs) have been successful leading to enhanced demand for elementary education.

Funding of the Project—DPEP is an externally aided project. 85 per cent of the project cost is met by the Government of India and the remaining 15 per cent is shared by the concerned State Government. The Government of India share is resourced through external assistance. External assistance of about Rs. 6938.00 crore, comprising Rs. 5137.00 crore as credit from IDA and Rs. 1801.00 crore as grant from BC/DFID/UNICEF/Netherlands has been tied up for DPEP till date.

Coverage of DPEP—At present, DPEP is in operation in 9 states covering 129 districts. DPEP at its peak, was operational in 273 districts in 18 states. However, with the progressive closure of different phases of the programme, it now exists in 129 districts only.

Monitoring and Evaluation of DPEP—The programme is periodically reviewed through the mechanism of Joint Review Missions, Project Management Information System (PMIS), Educational Management System (EMIS), programme impact studies, etc. A mid-term in-depth review of DPEP Phase-I, II and III states have also been carried out by the Joint Review Missions in 1997-98, 1999-2000 and 2003-04. The reviews and evaluation studies of the programme have brought out that the programme has resulted in significant increase in enrolment, improvement in learning achievement, reduction in repetition rates/drop-outs with increased community involvement and improvements in classroom processes.

Allocation of Funds under DPEP—Position of Budget Estimates, Revised Estimates and Actual Expenditure for last three years is given as under:

(Rs. in crore)

Year	*BE*	*RE*	*Actual*
2000-01	969.00	820.00	856.39
2001-02	1098.00	1198.00	1198.00
2002-03	1380.00	1380.00	1285.03
2003-04	1200.00	800.00	791.19

Expenditure on DPEP—The cumulative expenditure on DPEP up to February 2004, works out to Rs. 6076.75 crore and the cumulative reimbursement to Rs. 4807.51 crore. Expenditure incurred during the financial year 2003-04 is Rs. 847.68 crore and reimbursement Rs. 609.57 crore.

Sarva Shiksha Abhiyan

The Scheme of Sarva Shiksha Abhiyan (SSA) evolved from the recommendations of the State Education Ministers' Conference held in October 1998 to pursue universal elementary education in a mission mode. The scheme of Sarva Shiksha Abhiyan was approved by the Cabinet in its meeting held on 16 November 2000. It was started in 2001.

The assistance under the programme of Sarva Shiksha Abhiyan was on a 85:15 sharing arrangement during the Ninth Plan, 75:25 sharing arrangement during the Tenth Plan, and 50:50 sharing thereafter, between the Central Government and the State Government.

The programme covers the entire country and addresses the needs of 192 million children in 11 lakh habitations. 8.5 lakh existing primary and upper primary schools and 33 lakh existing teachers would be covered under the scheme. The programme seeks to open new schools in habitations which do not have schooling facilities and strengthen existing school infrastructure through provision of additional class rooms, toilets, drinking water, maintenance grant and school improvement grant. Existing schools with inadequate teacher strength would be provided additional teachers under the programme. The capacity of existing teachers would be built by extensive training, provision of grant for developing teaching-learning material and development of academic support structure. SSA has a special focus on girls and children of weaker sections A number of initiatives, including free textbooks, target these children under the programme. SSA also seeks to provide computer education even in rural areas, to bridge the digital divide.

The approach is community-owned, and the village education plans prepared in consultation with Panchayati Raj Institutions, will form the basis of district elementary education plans. The Sarva Shiksha Abhiyan covers the entire country with a special focus on educational needs of girls, Scheduled Castes and Scheduled Tribes and other children in difficult circumstances.

Goals of Sarva Shiksha Abhiyan

- All 6-14 age children in school/EGS centre/bridge course by 2003.
- All 6-14 age children complete five year primary education by 2007.
- All 6-14 age children complete eight years of schooling by 2010.
- Focus on elementary education of satisfactory quality with emphasis on education for life;
- Bridge all gender and social category gaps at primary stage by 2007 and at elementary education level by 2010;
- Universal retention by 2010.

National Level Mission

The Ministry has also set up national-level mission under the chairmanship of Prime Minister vide Resolution dated 2-1-2001.

During Tenth Plan, an allocation of Rs. 17,000 crore has been made for SSA. For 2003-04, BE is Rs. 1951.25 crore, RE is Rs. 2732.32 crore and the final grant is Rs. 2732.32 crore. The total expenditure under SSA for the year 2003-04 was Rs. 3,650 crore.

Monitoring Under SSA

Monitoring under SSA is a three-tiered monitoring at the local community level, at the state level and the national level. The community, through its representative institutions like village education committees, has been entrusted with the primary level of ensuring that the schools are functioning effectively. Being local stakeholders, they are best placed to ensure quality education in the schools.

For assisting the various levels of management in the task of monitoring, two kinds of information systems have been developed. One is the Educational Management Information System (EMIS), also known as District Information System on Education (DISE), under which school-level data is collected every year with 30 September as the record date. This was first developed in DPEP in 1995 for capturing school-level information from primary sections. Starting from 42 districts, it grew to 273 districts during the peak of DPEP programme. With the advent of SSA, the system was expanded to the upper primary sections also and to all districts in the country. The data, as on 30 September 2002, was received from 459 districts in the 18 DPEP states. It is expected that the data from 30 September 2003 would become available for all the 600 districts in the country.

Table 9.2 : Approved Annual Plans under SSA During 2002-03 and 2003-04

	2002-2003	*2003-04*
No. of Districts	592	596
Amount Approved under SSA (Rs. in crore)	3411 crore	8547 crore
Amount Approved under DPEP (Rs. in crore)	2291 crore	1253 crore
Total Amount Approved (Rs. in crore)	5702 crore	9600 crore

The second information system developed is the Project Management Information System (PMIS), in which the emphasis is on recording the progress made, towards the implementation of the annual plans, as well as to capture the quality of the education process. The system has been developed with the assistance of NIEPA and NCERT, and is a complete monitoring framework for every tier of management. Several formats have been prescribed at various levels to assist in monitoring the implementation of the programme at those levels. Only the abstract useful at the national level is received nationally under the system.

Seeing the enormity of this task of monitoring, assistance has been taken from professional institutions, such as IIMs, departments of education of different universities and the ICSSR. These institutions have been allocated individual states, the number of institutions allocated to the states depending on the size of the State and the extent of monitoring required. They not only carry out the task of supervision and

Table 9.3 : Physical Items approved in 2002-2003 and 2003-2004

	2002-2003			*2003-2004*		
	SSA	*DPEP*	*Total*	*SSA*	*DPEP*	*Total*
No. of schools approved	18.159	1,640	19,699	67,190	57	67,247
No. of teachers sanctioned	25,782	17,108	42,890	2,98,189	5,201	4,03,390
No. of school buildings	8,095	8,849	16,944	40,960	1,586	42,546
Additional classrooms	32,028	7,485	39,523	68,779	3,950	72,729
Toilets	39,699	11,130	50,829	46,272	5,488	51,760
Drinking water	26,805	6,590	33,395	33,161	6,053	41,214
Teacher grant (No. of teachers)	21,61,514	8,52,445	30,13,959	29,67,053	3,70,798	33,37,851
School grant (No. of schools)	5,61,558	3,07,414	8,68,972	6,33,303	1,46,143	8,29,446
Repair grants (No. of schools)	5,15,700	0	5,15,700	7,33,000	42,133	7,75,133
Free text books (No. of children)	31139754	14086909	45226663	4,60 crore	1.21 crore	5.81 crore

monitoring but also act as partners of the states in the implementation of the programme. The selected institutions make field visits and send their reports every quarter. Their quarterly visits to select districts help in assessing the ground-level realities.

Apart from the above, an independent agency has also been engaged to monitor the programme from the financial management aspect. The agency selected is the Institute of Public Auditors of India (IPAI) whose patron is CAG, and which consists of personnel formerly working with the Audit and Accounts Department. They take up six states every year for monitoring the financial aspects of the programme, such as fund flow, utilisation of funds, propriety of procurement, etc. This monitoring is apart from the statutory audit of the State Societies as per law and the audit by CAG of India.

Impact of SSA

Implementation of SSA in the first two years of the Tenth Plan has seen significant developments in the field of education sector. There has been a particular emphasis in these two years to ensure that all out-of-school children are brought to school through multi-pronged strategies. The focus has been on improving the existing infrastructure of regular schools as well as on alternate strategies for mainstreaming children who are left out of the schooling process due to a number of reasons.

Towards the objective of improving the infrastructure, arrangements have been made to open more than 80,000 new schools and appointing around 4.5 lakh teachers in the last two years. Further, physical infrastructure has been sought to be improved through provision of more than 1 lakh additional classrooms, around 60,000 school buildings, 1 lakh toilets and 75,000 drinking water facilities. With the objective of improving the quality of teaching and classroom atmosphere, grants are given to all teachers for developing teaching-learning materials, 20-day training is expected to be given to all teachers and free textbooks distributed to all girls and children belonging to Scheduled Castes and Scheduled Tribes. In addition, maintenance grant for civil repairs and a school grant for replacement of equipment is given to all schools.

For children who are difficult to bring to school, SSA has relied on the Education Guarantee Scheme and Alternative and Innovative Education to bring these children to school. In the last two years approvals have been given for getting 1.42 crore children to school.

As a result of all these interventions, the number of out-of-school children has come down from 3.5 crore in 2001 to 2.3 crore in the beginning of 2003-04.

Education Guarantee Scheme and Alternative and Innovative Education

The Education Guarantee Scheme (EGS) and Alternative and Innovative Education (AIE) component of Sarva Shiksha Abhiyan (SSA) is operationally proactive and provides avenues to children in the age group of 6-14 years. This component was designed to cover those children who are habitants of remotely located inaccessible habitations, never been to school, dropouts or could not continue/complete their elementary education because of one or the other reason.

EGS & AIE is, therefore, a vital component of SSA for achieving Universalisation of Elementary Education (UEE). It has the following broad strategies:

- Setting up of EGS schools in school-less habitations.
- Interventions for mainstreaming of 'out-of-school' children through bridge courses (residential as well as non-residential), back to school camps, etc.
- Strategies for specific groups of children, who need flexible and innovative interventions to meet their requirements of elementary education.

FGS & AIE programme also envisages centres for street and slum children, remedial coaching for children enrolled in formal schools, short duration summer camps, etc.

The ratio of sharing of expenditure between the Centre and states on this component is 75:25 respectively. In case of support to voluntary agencies (VAs), Central Government bears 100 per cent cost (within the overall cost ceilings). The EGS & AIE, being a part of SSA, has no separate budget provision and expenditure on the scheme is incurred from overall budget provision of SSA.

The scheme is largely implemented and monitored by state-level societies set up for SSA by the State/UT Governments, which have powers to appraise and approve proposals running either through state agencies or voluntary sector.

The Department of Elementary Education and Literacy persuaded the State Governments to constitute state-level GIACs as per the framework of SSA and a Hand Book for EGS/AIE, in order to encourage the participation of NGOs. The GIACs have already been constituted in 22 states. The States of Bihar, Uttaranchal and Uttar Pradesh have processed 289, 272 and 425 proposals respectively from NGOs.

In order to enhance state capacities for implementation of the EGS/AIE scheme in SSA, one national and three regional-level workshops to strengthen the capacity of implementers at state as well as district-level were organised. A three-day national-level workshop was organised in Kolkata in April 2003 and 2004 and three regional workshops were organised in Pune, Allahabad and Kolkata.

The Department of Elementary Education and Literacy regularly monitors the implementation of EGS/AIE component in the States through convening quarterly meetings of Alternative Schooling Coordinators of the State SSA programmes regularly, wherein state-wise progress is reviewed, interstate experiences and good practices are shared and the issues concerning the programme are deliberated upon for better execution.

National Programme of Nutritional Support to Primary Education

A nation-wide programme of Nutritional Support to Primary Education (popularly called Mid-day Meals Scheme or MDM) was launched on 15 August 1995, with the objectives to give a boost to UPE and simultaneously impacting on the nutritional status of students in primary classes studying in government, local body and government-aided schools. During the current year, the programme has also been expanded to children of EGS centres which are being opened in the school-less habitations.

The programme aims to provide wholesome cooked/processed food through local bodies/authorities such as Panchayats and Nagar Palikas who are expected to develop institutional arrangement has not taken place, foodgrains (wheat/rice) at the rate of 3kg per student per month are distributed to the targeted children, subject to a minimum attendance of 80 percent.

The programme was expanded in a phased manner and has seen all-India coverage during 1997-98 except for Lakshadweep, which runs its own programme. The Central support under this programme is to provide foodgrains free of cost to children through the Food

Corporation of India. The cost is being reimbursed at BPL rate. The year-wise details of children targeted for coverage and quantity of foodgrains allocated and lifted by state agencies and expenditure incurred is given below.

Recently, the Hon'ble Supreme Court in its order dated 29 November 2001 directed that under the Scheme, cooked meals be provided in a time bound manner by those States/UTs that do not have such a programme. As a result, cooked meals are now being served in a number of States.

Table 9.4 : NPNSPE

Year	*No. of Children*	*Quantity of Foodgrains*		*Expenditure incurred*
		Allocated	*Lifted*	
1995-96	3.34	713223	536016	441.21
1996-97	5.57	1585388	1112489	800.00
1997-98	9.10	2567372	1810164	1017.38
1998-99	9.79	2706274	1147917	1600.15
1999-2000	9.90	2767251	1401765	1500.00
2000-01	10.54	2480692	1517816	1300.00
2001-02	10.35	2862475	2076764	1030.27
2002-03	10.26	2826248	901756 (upto Sept. 2002)	952.44

National Programme for Education of Girls at Elementary Level (NPEGEL) Scheme

In July, 2003, Government of India approved a new programme called 'National Programme for Education of Girls at Elementary Level' (NPEGEL) as an amendment to the existing scheme of Sarva Shiksha Abhiyan (SSA) for providing additional support for education of underprivileged/disadvantaged girls at the elementary level. The scheme is implemented in Educationally Backward Blocks (EBBs) where the level of female literacy is below, and the gender gap is above the national average in blocks of districts which are not covered under EBBs but have at least 5 per cent SC/ST population and where SC/St female literacy is below 10 per cent, and also in select urban slums.

Kasturba Gandhi Balika Vidyalaya Scheme

An estimated provision of Rs. 1064.80 crore has been kept for the Tenth Plan. Apart from NPEGEL, a new scheme called *Kasturba Gandhi Balika Vidyalaya (KGBV)* was approved for launching during 2004-05 for setting up 750 residential schools with boarding facilities at elementary level for girls belonging predominantly to the SC, ST, other backward castes (OBC) and minorities in difficult areas. A provision of Rs. 489 crore has been made for the Tenth Plan; and Annual Plan allocation for the year 2004-05 is Rs. 100 crore. 525 KGBVs have been approved by the Department of Elementary Education, involving an amount of Rs. 123.03 crore for 2004-05.

Prathmik Shiksha Kosh

An education cess of 2 per cent on all direct and indirect Central taxes has been imposed through the Finance (No. 2) Act, 2004. Soon after the relevant Bill was introduced in Parliament on July 8, 2004, action was initiated for the creation of a separate, dedicated, non-lapsable Fund to be named as *Prathmik Shiksha Kosh* and maintained by the Ministry of HRD, Department of Elementary Education and Literacy. The proceeds would be available on a rollover basis for the schemes of Basic Education and the Mid-Day Meal Scheme. Budget provision for the Mid-day Meal Scheme during 2004-05 was Rs. 1,675 crore. In addition Rs. 1,232 crore has been provided to the States/UTs as Additional Central Assistance (ACA) under State Sector as earmarked outlay for meeting cooking cost.

Table 9.5 : Gross Enrolment Ratios at the Elementary Stage (GER) (in per cent)

Year	*Primary (I-V)*			*Upper Primary (VI-VIII)*			*Elementary (I-VIII)*		
	Boys	*Girls*	*Total*	*Boys*	*Girls*	*Total*	*Boys*	*Girls*	*Total*
1950-51	60.6	24.8	42.6	20.6	4.6	12.7	46.4	17.7	32.1
1960-61	82.6	41.4	62.4	33.2	11.3	22.5	65.2	30.9	48.7
1970-71	95.5	60.5	78.6	46.5	20.8	33.4	75.5	44.4	61.9
1980-81	95.8	64.1	80.5	54.3	28.6	41.9	82.2	52.1	67.5
1990-91	114.0	85.5	100.1	76.6	47.0	62.1	100.0	70.8	86.0
1991-92	112.8	86.9	100.2	75.1	49.6	61.4	101.2	73.2	87.7
1993-94	90.0	73.1	81.9	62.1	45.4	54.2	80.2	63.7	72.3
1994-95	96.6	78.2	87.7	68.9	50.0	60.0	87.2	68.8	78.4
1995-96	97.1	79.4	88.6	67.8	49.8	59.3	86.9	69.4	78.5
1996-97	97.0	80.1	88.8	65.8	49.2	58.0	85.9	69.4	78.0
1997-98	99.3	82.2	91.1	66.3	49.7	58.5	87.4	70.7	79.4
1998-99*	100.9	82.9	92.1	65.3	49.1	57.6	87.6	70.6	79.4
1999-2000*	104.1	85.2	94.9	67.2	49.7	58.8	90.1	72.0	81.3
2000-01*	104.9	85.9	95.7	66.7	49.9	58.6	90.3	72.4	81.6
2001-02*	105.3	86.9	96.3	67.8	52.1	60.2	90.7	73.6	82.4
2002-03*	97.5	93.1	95.4	65.3	56.2	60.9	85.4	79.3	82.5

* Provisional

Source: *Selected Educational Statistics 2002-03*, Ministry of Human Resource Development.

Free and Universal Compulsory Elementary Education
Right to Education

After independence, the Government of India realised the significance of elementary education as it is the base of progress and accordingly incorporated article 45 in the Constitution. Since the progress in the field was not in accordance with the provisions of this Article, it was considered necessary to amend it to give more impetus.

Following amendments in the Constitution were made in 2002.

1. *Article 21A: "Right to Education"*—The State shall provide free and compulsory education to all children of the age six to fourteen years in such manner as State, may, by law determine".

2. *Article 45: "Provision for early childhood care and education to children below the age of 6 years*—The State shall endeavour to provide early childhood care and education for all children under the age of six years".

(Substituted by the Constitution (Eighty-sixth Amendment) Act, 2002.

3. *Article 51A (K) : "Fundamental Duties"*—It shall be the duty of every citizen of India who is a parent or guardian to provide opportunities for education to his child or, as the case may be, ward the age of six and fourteen years.

[Inserted by the Constitution (Eighty-sixth Amendment) Act, 2002)

Compulsory Education Acts already exist in 19 states but these have not been enforced on account of several constraints, primarily on account of lack of political will.

More than two years have passed in making amendments in the constitution regarding 'Right to Education'. However, nothing substantial has been done to fulfil this obligation. The original target for providing compulsory primary education was the year 1960.

Drop-out Rates

Of the estimated population of 205 million in the age group of 6-14 years on March 1, 2002, nearly 82.5 per cent was enrolled in schools, compared to 82.4 per cent in 2001-02. The retention rate of students at the primary school stage was about 59 per cent (1992-97).

The rates of drop out decreased from 64.5 per cent in 1960-61 to 39.0 per cent in 2001-2002 in primary classes. The rate of dropouts which was 78.3 per cent in 1960-61 came down to 54.6 per cent in 2001-2002 in the Classes I-VIII. Similarly the rate of dropouts which was 82.5 per cent in 1980-81, decreased to 66.0 per cent in 2001-2002 in the secondary classes, implying an improvement in retention rates as would be evident from Table 9.6

Table 9.6

	1960-61	*1970-71*	*1980-81*	*1990-91*	*1992-93*	*1999-2000**	*2001-2002**
			Classes I-V				
Boys	61.7	64.5	56.2	40.1	43.8	38.7	38.4
Girls	70.9	70.9	62.5	46.0	46.7	42.3	39.9
Total	64.9	67.0	58.7	42.6	45.0	40.3	39.0
			Classes I-VIII				
Boys	75.0	74.6	68.0	59.1	58.2	52.0	52.9
Girls	85.0	83.4	79.4	65.1	65.2	58.0	56.9
Total	78.3	77.9	72.7	60.9	61.1	54.5	54.6
			Classes I-X				
Boys	N.A.	N.A.	79.8	67.5	70.0	66.6	64.2
Girls	N.A.	N.A.	86.6	76.9	77.3	70.6	68.6
Total	N.A.	N.A.	82.5	71.3	72.9	68.3	66.0

* Provisional

The situation cannot be said to be satisfactory. Strenuous efforts are needed to ensure that the students once enrolled in the school do not drop out.

Teacher pupil ratio of 1.43 at the primary stage is very high. It leaves very little scope for individual attention.

Restructuring Teacher Education

The National Council for Teacher Education (NCTE) which had been in existence for the last more than two decades was given a statuary recognition by a gazette notification issued on August 17, 1995 by the Ministry of Human Resource Development (Department of Education). This was done in pursuance of the National Council for Teacher Education Act, 1973. This Act has been enacted with a view to achieving planned and coordinated development of the Teacher Education System throughout the country. However, the NCTE has not been able to check the mushroom growth of substandard hundreds of teacher education collages.

Secondary Education

A Centrally Sponsored Scheme of Pre-vocational Education at lower Secondary School was introduced in 1993-94, primarily to impart training in simple marketing skills to the students of classes IX and X.

From above, it is clear that there is a long way to reach the goal.

The Central Institute of Vocational Education was set up at Bhopal in July 1993, to provide technical and academic support to vocational education in the country.

Table 9.7: Primary and Adult Education in India vis-à-vis Select Countries

Sl. No.	*Name of the Country*	*Population (Thousands) Mid 2003*	*GNI per Capita (US $) 2003*	*Life Expectancy at Birth 2003*	*Total Adult Literacy Rate 2003*	*% of entrants primary school reaching grade 5 1998-2001*
1.	Afghanistan	24800	250	43	36	45
2.	Australia	19800	21650	79	99	99
3.	Bangladesh	146800	400	62	40	65
4.	Bhutan	2260	660	63	47	91
5.	Brazil	178500	2710	68	87	95
6.	Canada	31510	23930	79	99	99
7.	Central Africa	3860	260	40	47	24
8.	Republic of China	1304200	1100	71	85	99
9.	Ethiopia	70700	90	46	39	61
10.	Germany	82500	25250	78	79	99
11.	India	1065500	530	64	57	59
12.	Indonesia	219900	810	67	87	89
13.	Iran	68900	2000	70	76	94
14.	Iraq	25200	2170	61	39	64
15.	Japan	127800	34510	82	99	99
16.	Mexico	103500	6230	74	91	90
17.	Myanmar	49500	220	57	85	60
18.	Pakistan	153600	470	61	43	50
19.	Russian Federation	143200	2610	67	99	99
20.	Saudi Arabia	24200	8530	72	76	68
21.	Sri Lanka	19000	930	73	92	97
22.	Sweden	8800	28840	80	99	99
23.	Switzerland	7100	39880	73	99	99
24.	United Kingdom	59300	28350	78	99	99
25.	United States	294000	37610	77	99	99
(1)	Average Developing Countries	5083400	1225	62	74	78
(2)	Average Industrialised Countries	949593	28300	78	99	99
(3)	World	628628	5488	63	80	79

Notes: (1) GNI Per Capita is gross income divided y mid-year population.
(2) Life expectancy at birth: The number of years new born children survive.
(3) Adult Literacy Rate is the percentage of persons aged 15 and above who can read and write.

Source: Data compiled '*The State of World's Children 2005*', UNICEF.

The progress of vocationalisation of senior secondary education has not made much head way.

Curriculum Reforms in School Education

Curriculum reforms in school education have been taken up separately.

Expenditure on Education

The NPE 1986 and as modified in 1992 set a goal of expenditure on education at 6 percent of the GDP. As against the target, the combined total expenditure on education by Central and State Governments was 3.74 percent of GDP in 2003 (B.E.)

Higher Education

Even after the formulation of the Programme of Action, Substandard higher education has come into being in some states. In Chattisgarh State alone nearly one hundred universities were established by private enterprise. Most of these universities functioned in rented houses and had little infrastructure. The situation became so grim that the Supreme Court had to issue orders for their closure. This indicated that our mechanism of control over higher institution is very defective.

Table 9.8 depicts the expenditure on education in India during the period 1951-52 to 2000-2001. The expenditure on the education sector was slightly less than 1% of the GDP in 1951-52. The % age expenditure to GDP shows an irregular rise and fall. It rose to 2.33% in 1972-73 but in 1973-74 declined to 2.15%. It increased to 3.07% in 1979-80 and decreased to 2.83% in 1981-82. Continuing to rise and fall, it reached a level of 4.11% in 2000-2001. Similarly, the percentage of expenditure on education and training to total expenditure of all sectors during the last five decades indicates that it increased from 7.92% in 1951-52 to 13.55% in 2000-2001 i.e. by 6.37 percentage points during the last five decades. This translates to an annual growth rate of 0.13% during the period 1951-52 to 2000-2001.

Table 9.9 gives the details of expenditure by level of education in India and its percentage to GDP and total Government expenditure on all sectors during the period 1990-91 to 2001-2002. The expenditure on elementary education was 1.78% to the GDP in 1990-91. The percentage expenditure on elementary to GDP shows a gradual fall to 1.65% in 1994-95 and than shows a gradual rise to 2.02% in 2001-02. The percentage expenditure to GDP on secondary/higher secondary shows an irregular rise and fall and it has remained between 1.13 to 1.44 percent during 1997-98 to 1999-2000. The percentage expenditure to GDP on

Table 9.8: Expenditure on Education in India (1951-52 to 2001-2002) (In Crore)

Years	*Total expr. on education & trg. (Rev.)*	*Total expr. on all sectors (Rev.)*	*GDP at current prices (at factor cost) base year 1993-94*	*% of Edu. Exp. to all sectors Exp.*	*% of Edu. Exp. to GDP*
1951-51	64.46	814.13	10080	7.92	0.64
1952-53	72.26	857.67	9941	8.43	0.73
1953-54	80.06	908.20	10824	8.82	0.74
1954-55	95.82	973.74	10168	9.84	0.94
1955-56	118.39	1111.26	10332	10.65	1.15
1956-57	132.88	1158.01	12334	11.47	1.08
1957-58	150.26	1614.62	12610	10.61	1.19
1958-59	173.78	1594.36	14106	10.90	1.23
1959-60	207.59	1770.06	14816	11.73	1.40
1960-61	239.56	1997.93	16220	11.99	1.48
1961-62	260.30	2225.40	17116	11.70	1.52
1962-63	278.76	2942.67	18302	9.47	1.52
1963-64	313.93	3488.97	20916	9.00	1.50
1964-65	369.29	3844.91	24436	9.60	1.51
1965-66	432.61	4404.82	25586	9.82	1.69
1966-67	487.83	5100.24	29123	9.56	1.68
1967-68	593.14	5619.77	34225	10.55	1.73
1968-69	649.13	6922.07	36092	9.38	1.80
1969-70	960.23	7908.07	39691	9.61	1.92
1970-71	892.36	8787.12	42222	10.16	2.11
1971-72	1011.07	10610.89	44923	9.53	2.25
1972-73	1150.43	11863.56	49415	9.70	2.33
1973-74	1300.72	12884.48	60560	10.10	2.15
1974-75	1570.67	14625.03	71283	10.74	2.20
1975-76	1849.47	17958.99	75709	10.30	2.44
1976-77	2039.09	20482.83	81381	9.96	2.51
1977-78	2630.60	22666.31	92881	11.61	2.83
1978-79	2994.69	26134.84	99823	11.46	3.00
1979-80	3347.57	30915.39	108927	10.83	3.07
1980-81	3884.20	36398.39	130178	10.67	2.98
1981-82	4435.29	33667.31	152056	13.17	2.92
1982-83	5509.17	43996.18	169525	12.52	3.25
1983-84	6229.53	61889.25	198630	10.07	3.14
1984-85	7455.88	69025.45	222705	10.80	3.35
1985-86	8713.02	67091.41	249547	12.99	3.49
1986-87	9497.13	80454.66	278258	11.78	3.41
1987-88	11798.35	92518.38	315993	12.75	3.73

(*Contd.*)

(Contd.)

Years	*Total expr. on education & trg. (Rev.)*	*Total expr. on all sectors (Rev.)*	*GDP at current prices (at factor cost) base year 1993-94*	*% of Edu. Exp. to all sectors Exp.*	*% of Edu. Exp. to GDP*
1988-89	14069.82	107543.75	378491	13.08	3.72
1989-90	17192.50	126045.97	438020	13.64	3.93
1990-91	19615.85	146711.53	510954	13.37	3.84
1991-92	22393.69	170370.38	589086	13.14	3.80
1992-93	25030.30	190327.45	673221	13.15	3.72
1993-94	28279.22	218535.15	781345	12.94	3.62
1994-95	32606.22	251691.92	917058	12.95	3.56
1995-96	38178.09	286194.55	1073271	13.34	3.56
1996-97	43896.48	329389.92	1243546	13.33	3.53
1997-98	48552.14	380728.45	1390148	12.75	3.49
1998-99	61578.91	439768.11	1598127	14.00	3.85
1999-2000	74816.09	512519.33	1761932	14.60	4.25
2000-2001	82486.43	572160.14	191772P	14.42	4.30
2001-2002	84179.46 (R.E.)	639048.06	2094013Q	13.17	4.02

P-Provisional estimates, Q-quick estimates, RE-Revised estimates

Source:1. *National Accounts Statistics* published by C.S.O.

2. Expenditure on Education. Figure is taken from the publication titled '*Analysis of Budgeted Expenditure on Education*' published by D/o Secondary and Higher Education.
3. *Selected Educational Statistics* (2002-2003).

Adult Education was 0.05% during 1990-91 showing a gradual decrease of 0.01% in 2000-2001. It improved slightly to 0.02% during 2001-2002. The percentage expenditure on University and Higher Education to GDP, which was 0.77% in 1990-91 shows a gradual decrease to 0.62% during 1997-98 and rise to 0.88% in 2000-2001.

The share of expenditure on Elementary Education to total expenditure on all sectors was 6.19% during 1990-91 and which shows irregular rise and fall and finally settled at 6.61% during 2001-2002. The share of Secondary and Higher Secondary Education to total expenditure on all sectors was highest in 1999-2000 i.e. 4.97% and the lowest (4.09%) during 2001-2002. The share of adult expenditure in total expenditure on all sectors was the highest in 1990-91 (0.19%) and shows a gradual decreasing trend to 0.05% in 2001-02. The percentage share of higher education to total expenditure remained between 2.32% to 2.96% in the last decade.

Table 9.9: Expenditure by Level on Education in India

(In crore)

Year	*Total Expenditure on Education & trg. (Rev.) by Education and other Departments*														
	Elementary			*Secondary/Higher secondary*			*Adult Education*			*University & Higher Education**			*Total*		
	Expen-diture	*% age to GDP*	*% age to Total expt. on all sector*	*Expen-diture*	*% age to GDP*	*% age to Total expt. on all sector*	*Expen-diture*	*% age to GDP*	*% age to Total expt. on all sector*	*Expen-diture*	*% age to GDP*	*% age to Total expt. on all sector*	*Expen-diture*	*% age to GDP*	*% age to Total expt. on all sector*
1990-1991	9076.28	1.78	6.19	6310.33	1.24	4.30	273.15	0.05	0.19	3956.09	0.77	2.70	19615.85	3.84	13.37
1991-1992	10367.8	1.76	6.09	7400.56	1.26	4.34	228.52	0.04	0.13	4396.78	0.75	2.58	22393.69	3.80	13.14
1992-1993	11321.5	1.68	5.95	8574.97	1.27	4.51	210.97	0.03	0.11	4922.90	0.73	2.59	25030.30	3.72	13.15
1993-1994	13071.14	1.67	2.54	9371.34	1.20	4.29	280.01	0.04	0.13	5557.20	0.71	2.54	28279.69	3.62	12.94
1994-1995	15133.1	1.65	6.01	10835.33	1.18	4.30	338.31	0.04	0.13	6299.53	0.69	2.50	32606.69	3.62	12.94
1995-1996	18433.9	1.72	6.44	12530.38	1.17	4.38	259.71	0.02	0.09	6954.07	0.65	2.43	38178.09	3.56	13.33
1996-1997	21543.6	1.73	6.54	14164.00	1.14	4.30	205.74	0.02	0.06	7983.11	0.64	2.42	43894.48	3.53	13.33
1997-1998	24083.2	1 73	6.49	15663.5	1.13	4.22	209.80	0.02	0.06	8595.67	0.62	2.32	48552.14	3.49	13.09
1998-1999	30191.1	1.89	6.87	20100.97	1.26	4.57	189.45	0.01	0.04	11097.42	0.69	2.52	61578.91	3.85	14.00
1999-2000	34068.8	1.93	6.65	25447.89	1.44	4.97	186.53	0.01	0.04	15112.89	0.86	2.95	74816.09	4.25	14.60
2000-01	39274.60	2.05	6.86	26057.50	1.36	4.55	226.12	0.01	0.04	16928.21	0.88	2.96	82486.43	4.30	14.42
2001-02 (RE)	42209.81	2.02	6.61	26155.21	1.25	4.09	337.87	0.02	0.05	15476.57	0.74	2.42	84179.46	4.02	13.17

* Including expenditure on Physical education. Technical education, Language development etc.

Note: Expenditures on education by other Departments has been distributed by level on the basis of expenditure (%) by education departments.

Source: Selected Educational Statistics 2001-2002.

10

Review of NPE, National Curriculum Framework for School Education 2000 and National Curriculum Framework 2005

Introduction

In Part XI, Section 5, the NPE 1986 had observed, "The implementation and parameters of the New Policy must be reviewed every five years. Appraisal of short intervals will also be made to ascertain the progress of implementation and the trends emerging from time to time."

In this contest, it is observed that this aspect of the NPE has been, by and large, ignored. A review of almost all parameters was made only in 1992 when some amendments in the NPE 1986 were made. Thereafter no review has been attempted.

There are several dimensions of education and curriculum is one of these. Of course, it is true that it is a vital part of the system. The review of the curriculum has been politicalised. Education tends to become in 'play-thing' of the politicians.

In this chapter, a brief review of the curriculum as formulated in 2000 and 2005 is presented.

National Curriculum Framework for School Education (NCFSE) 2000

It is universally accepted that school curriculum should be so designed and implemented as it fulfills the needs of a changing society. It must take note of new concerns in the wake of revolution in information technology (IT) and other developments not only in India but also in the world. There is no doubt that the curriculum is an important devise to translate national goals into educational experiences. From time to time the National Council of Educational Research and Training has been preparing model curriculum. In pursuance of the National Policy of Education (NPE), 1986 and as revised in 1992, it prepared the National Curriculum Framework for School Education in 2000. Accordingly it brought about new school textbooks. The document was the product of a long, participatory and democratic process of wide ranging deliberations and discussions held at multilevel seminars and workshops throughout the country.

In 2005, the NCERT again formulated the National Curriculum Framework.

National Curriculum Framework (2000)

Curricular Concerns in India: The Factors Determining Curriculum

The NCERT curriculum was based on the following concerns:

1. *Education for a cohesive society*—Curriculum must create awareness among children of the inherent equality of all.

2. *Equality among sexes*—Besides making education accessible more and more to girls, gender bias in school curriculum and textbooks etc. must be removed.

3. *Education of learners with special needs*—Compensatory and remedial measures in curriculum to suit the needs of the deprived and the disadvantaged students with a view to bring them at par with other students assume central importance.

4. *Education of learners from disadvantaged groups*—Far achieving a cohesive society it would be essential to respond to specific needs of the learners of the disadvantaged sections of the society.

5. *Education of the gifted and talented*—An educational system has the dual role of promoting equality as well as excellence. Curriculum should provide for the identification and nurturing of the creative abilities of the students.

6. *Education for strengthening national identity and preserving cultural heritage*—The school curriculum must inculcate and nurture a sense of pride in being an Indian through a conscious understanding of the Indian civilisation and its contribution to the world civilisation.

7. *Integrating indigenous knowledge with India's contribution to mankind*—An indigenous Indian curriculum is envisaged to promote the ideas of the great thinkers such as Sri Aurobindo, Swami Vivekananda, Swami Dayananda Saraswati, Mahatama Phule, Mahatama Gandhi, Gurudev Tagore, Dr. Zakir Hussain, J. Krishnamurti and Gijubhai Badheka. Against this background, contributions of thinkers of other countries should also be taken note of.

8. *Responding to the impact of globalisation*—The curriculum should

be the catalyst for the desire to live together in our society on the one hand, and the global village on the other. The challenges created by globalisation for the educational processes would mean rethinking on the content of the various disciplines in the curriculum.

9. *Meeting the challenges of Information and Communication Technology (ICT)*—All innovations in the areas of media production and the interactive video and multi-media computer software shall have to be perceived as integral components of the curriculum process.

10. *Linking education with life skills*—To prepare children to face the challenges of life, curriculum must be intimately linked with the different life skills.

11. *Education for value development*—Curriculum should develop five universal values representing the five domains of the human personality—intellectual (correlated with knowledge objective of education), physical (correlated with skills), emotional (correlated with balance), psychological (correlated with vision), and spiritual (correlated with identity).

Another significant element is to provide for education about religions and not religious education.

12. *Universalisation of Elementary Education (UEE)*—UEE will have implications for curriculum in terms of the identification of basic learning needs and making provision for the minimum essential facilities.

13. *Alternative and open learning*—The scheme of studies and the academic standards in cognitive areas under alternative and open learning (Non-formal education and correspondence education etc.) should be as far as possible of a level comparable to that for the students for the formal system. However, the instructional materials and instructional strategies under the two systems have to be different.

14. *Integrating diverse curriculum concerns*—Attempts need to be made to integrate new ideas like 'environmental education', 'family system', and 'human rights education' etc. with the existing curriculum content.

15. *Relating education to world of work*—Work education and vocational education should be made an integral component of the school curriculum.

16. *Reducing the curriculum load*—Obsolete and redundant content should be taken out of the curriculum.

17. *Interface between cognition, emotion and action*—Curriculum should provide learning experiences which help describe an individual's thoughts, feelings and actions.

SCHEME OF STUDIES AT VARIOUS LEVELS

I. Elementary Education (8 years)

(1) Primary Stage (5 years)

A. Classes I-II

(i) One Language—mother tongue/regional language
(ii) Mathematics
(iii) Art of Health and Productive Living

B. Classes III-V

(i) One Language—mother tongue/regional language
(ii) Mathematics
(iii) Environmental Studies
(iv) Art of Health and Productive Living

(2) Upper Primary Stage (3 Years)

(a) Three Languages—mother tongue/regional language, modern Indian language and English
(b) Mathematics
(c) Science and Technology
(d) Social Sciences
(e) Work Education
(f) Art Education (Fine Arts: Visual and Performing)
(g) Health and Physical Education (Including games and sports, yoga, NCC, scouting and guiding)

II. Secondary Stage (2 years)

(a) Three Languages—mother tongue/regional language, modern Indian language and English.
(b) Mathematics
(c) Science and Technology
(d) Social Sciences
(e) Work Education
(f) Art Education (Fine Arts: Visual and Performing)
(g) Health and Physical Education (Including games and sports, yoga, NCC scouting and guiding).

III. Higher Secondary Stage (2 Years) Academic Stream

(1) Foundation Courses
(2) Elective Courses

(1) *Foundation Courses*—(i) Language and Literature (ii) Work Education (iii) Health and Physical Education, Games and Sports.

(2) *Elective Courses*—Three elective courses not out the subjects prescribed. Apart from well-established traditional disciplines, new subjectives of study would include computer science, technology, environmental education, etc.

Merits Claimed

Professor Rajendra K. Dixit, Head, Department of Education, NCERT claimed the following merits of the NCET Syllabi (*Hindustan Times*, February 6, 2002).

1. *Reduction in curriculum load*—Fewer, lighter books with comprehensive presentations are the hallmarks of the new syllabi. For

instance, in Social Sciences, the laborious details on the study of continents in Classes VI and VII have been done away with.

2. *New disciplines*—Subjects such as 'Art of Healthy and Productive Living' for Classes I to V and Work, Art, Health and Physical Education for Classes VI to VIII have been introduced. At the primary stage, the emphasis is on a student's mother tongue. Separate chapters on religions and sects at the upper primary level (Classes VI to VIII) have been introduced.

3. *Integration of related disciplines*—While Social Sciences have been integrated at the Secondary level in classes VI to VII, the introduction of Technology integrated with Science aims at motivating children to design experiments and understand the processes of Science.

4. *No more mechanical learning*—The need to memorise tedious tables on square cube roots in Mathematics has been done away with. In fact, the syllabus proposes the setting up Maths Laboratories in schools emphasising the practical nature of the subject.

5. *India-Centric flavour*—The new syllabus focuses on India and her relation with the World, Nurturing a sense of equality, the syllabi have freed themselves from Euro-Centric approach while including India's traditional wisdom.

6. *Tutorial*—The curriculum envisages tutorials for classes IX to XII.

National Curriculum Framework (NCF), 2005

Formation of the National Curriculum—The United Progressive Alliance (UPA) Government was formed in May 2004. It decided to follow the Common Minimum Programme (CMP) which was released on May 27, 2004. The Common Minimum Programme included the following programme on education.

"The UPA Government pledges to raise public spending in education to at least 6% of the GDP with at least half this amount being spent on primary and secondary schools. This will be done in a phased manner.

The UPA Government will introduce a cess on all Central taxes to finance the commitment to universalise access to quality basic education. A National Commission on Education will be set up to allocate resources and monitor programmes.

The UPA government will take immediate steps to reverse the trend to communalisation of education that had set in the past five years. It will also ensure that all institutions of higher learning and professional education retain their autonomy. The UPA will ensure that nobody is denied professional education because he or she is poor.

Academic excellence and professional competence will be the sole criteria for all appointments to bodies like the ICHR, ICSSR, UGC and NCERT. Steps will be taken to remove the communalisation of the school syllabus that has taken place in the past five years. A review committee of experts will be set up for this purpose.

A national cooked nutritious mid-day meal scheme, funded mainly by the Central Government, will be introduced in primary and secondary schools. An appropriate mechanism for quality checks will also be set up. The UPA will also universalise the Integrated Child Development Services (ICDS) scheme to provide a functional anganwadi in every settlement and ensure full coverage for all children. The UPA Government will fully back and support all NGO efforts in the area of primary education.

Proper infrastructure will be created in schools for NCC, NSS, physical development, sports and cultural development of all students."

The Minister of Human Resource Development made a statement in the Lok Sabha that the NCERT should take up the revision of the curriculum. Accordingly Executive Committee of the NCERT took the decision at its meeting held on 14 and 19 July 2004 to revise the National Curriculum Framework. It may be recalled that the National Curriculum Framework which was being implemented was prepared by the National Democratic Alliance (NDA). Subsequently, the Education Secretary, Ministry of HRD communicated to the Director of NCERT the need to review the NCFSE-2000 in the light of the Report '*Learning without Burden*' (1993). In the context of these decisions, a National Steering Committee, chaired by Prof. Yash Pal, and 21 National Forum groups were set up.

Approval of the Central Advisory Board of Education

The draft NCP prepared by the NCERT was placed before the Central Advisory Board of Education in the month of June 2005. The Education Ministers of the BJP led states did not approve of the curriculum. Nevertheless the CABE put its seals of approval.

Extracts from the Executive Summary of the Curriculum (*Captions inserted by the author of the book*)

Curricular Reforms Since Independence: Brief History

The revised National Curriculum Framework (NCF) opens with a quotation from Rabindranath Tagore's essay *Civilisation and Progress*, in which the poet reminds us that 'creative spirit' and 'generous joy' are key in childhood, both of which can distorted by an unthinking adult world. The opening chapter discusses curricular reform efforts made since independence. The National Policy on Education—(NPE, 1986) proposed National Curriculum Framework as a means to evolve a national system of education, recommending a crore component derived from the vision of national development enshrined in the Constitution. The Programme of Action (POA, 1992) elaborated this focus by emphasizing relevance, flexibility and quality.

Constitutional Vision as the Source of Guidance

Seeking guidance from the Constitutional vision of India as a secular, egalitarian and pluralistic society, founded on the values of social justice and equality, certain broad aims of education have been identified in this document. These include independence of thought and action, sensitivity to others' well being and feelings, learning to respond to new situations in a flexible and creative manner, pre-disposition towards participation in democratic processes, and the ability to work towards and contribute to economic processes and social change. For teaching to serve as a means to strengthen our democratic way of life, it must respond to the presence of first generation school goers, whose retention is imperative owing to the Constitutional amendment which has made elementary education a fundamental right of every child. Ensuring health, nutrition and an inclusive school environment support all children in their learning, irrespective of caste, gender, disability, is enjoined upon us by the Constitutional amendment.

Guiding Principles for Curriculum Development

The fact that learning has become a source of burden and stress on children is an evidence of a deep distortion in educational aims and quality. To correct this distortion, the present NCF proposes four guiding principles for curriculum development: (i) connecting knowledge to life outside the school; (ii) ensuring that learning shifts away from rote methods; (iii) enriching the curriculum so that it goes beyond textbooks; and (iv) making examinations more flexible and integrating them with classroom life.

Child's Nature and Environment

All our pedagogic efforts during the primary classes greatly depend on professional planning and significant expansion of Early Childhood Care and Education (ECCE). Indeed, the revision of primary school syllabi and textbooks needs to be undertaken in the light of the well known principles of ECCE. The nature of knowledge and children's own strategies of learning are discussed in Chapter 2 which formulates a theoretical basis for the recommendations made in Chapter 3 in the different curricular areas. The fact that knowledge is constructed by the child implies that curriculum, syllabi and textbooks should enable the teacher to organize classroom experiences in consonance with the child's nature and environment, and providing opportunities for all children. Teaching should aim at enhancing children's natural desire and strategies to learn. Knowledge needs to be distinguished from information, and teaching needs to be seen as a professional activity, not as coaching for memorization or as transmission of facts. Activity is the heart of the child's attempt to make sense of the world, therefore every resource must be deployed to enable children to express, handle objects, explore their natural and social milieu, and to grow up healthy. If children's classroom experiences are to be organised in a manner that permits the child to construct knowledge, then our school system requires substantial systematic reforms [Chapter 5] and reconceptualisation of curricular areas or school subjects [Chapter 3] and resources to improve the quality of the school ethos (Chapter 4).

Languages, Mathematics, Sciences and Social Science, New Approach

In all the four familiar areas of school curriculum, i.e., language, mathematics, science and social sciences, significant changes are recommended with a view to making education more relevant to the present day and future needs and in order to alleviate the stress children are coping with today. This NCF recommends the softening of subject boundaries so that children can get a taste of integrated knowledge and joy of understanding. In addition, plurality of textbooks and other material, which could incorporate local knowledge and traditional skills, and a stimulating school environment which responds to the child's home and community environment, are also suggested.

Language Teaching

In language, a renewed attempt to implement the three language formula is suggested, along with an emphasis on recognition of children's mother tongues, including tribal languages, as the best medium of instruction. The multilingual character of Indian society should be seen as a resource to promote multilingual proficiency in every child, which includes proficiency in English. This is possible only if learning builds on a sound language pedagogy in the mother tongue. Reading and writing, listening and speech contribute to the child's progress in all curricular areas and must be the basis for curriculum planning. Emphasis on reading throughout the primary classes is necessary to give every child a solid foundation for school learning.

Teaching of Mathematics

The teaching of mathematics should enhance the child's resources to think and reason, visualize and handle abstractions, to formulate and solve problems. This broad spectrum of aims can be covered by teaching relevant and important mathematics, embedded in the child's experience. Succeeding in mathematics should be seen as the right of every child. For this widening in its scope and relating it to other subjects is right of every child. For this widening in its scope and relating it to other subjects is essential. The infrastructural challenge involved in making computer hardware, software, and connectivity to every school should be pursued.

The Teaching of Science

The teaching of science should be recast so that it enables children to examine and analyse everyday experiences. Concern for the environment should be emphasized in every subject and through a wide range of activities, involving outdoor project work. A social movement along the lines of Children's Science Congress should be visualized in order to promote discovery learning across the nation, and eventually throughout South Asia.

Teaching of Social Sciences

In social sciences, the approach proposed in the NCF recognizes disciplinary markers while emphasizing integration on significant themes, such as water. A paradigm shift is recommended, proposing the study of social sciences from the perspective of marginalized groups. Gender justice and sensitivity towards tribal and dalit issues and minority sensibilities must inform all sectors of the social science. Civics should be recast as political science, and the significance of history as a shaping influence on the child's conception of the past and civic identity should be recognized.

Other Curricular Areas

This NCF draws attention to four other curricular areas: work, the arts and heritage crafts, health and physical education, and peace. In the context of work, certain radical steps to link learning from the primary stage upwards with work are suggested on the ground that work transforms knowledge into experience and generates important personal and social values, such as self-reliance, creativity and cooperation. It also inspires new forms of knowledge and creativity. At the senior level, a strategy to formally recognize out-of-school resources for work is recommended, to benefit children who opt for livelihood-related education. Such out-of-school agencies need accreditation so that they can provide 'work benches' where children can work with tools and other resources. Craft mapping is recommended to identify zones where vocational training in craft forms, involving local craft persons, can be made available to children.

Teaching of Art and Craft

Art as a subject at all stages is recommended, covering all four major spheres, i.e. music, dance, visual arts and theatre. Emphasis should be on interactive approaches, not instruction, because the goal of art education is to promote aesthetic and personal awareness and the ability to express oneself in different forms. The importance of India's heritage crafts, both in terms of their economic and aesthetic values, should be recognized as being relevant to school education.

Health and Physical Education

The child's success at school depends on nutrition and a well-planned physical activity programmes, hence resources and school time must be deployed for the strengthening of the mid-day meal programme. Special efforts are needed to ensure that girls receive as much attention in health and physical programmes from the pre-school stage upwards as boys.

Peace Education

peace as a pre-condition for national development and as a social temper is proposed as a comprehensive value framework which has immense relevance today, in view of the growing tendency across the world towards intolerance and violence as a way to resolve conflicts. The potential of peace education for socializing children into a democratic and just culture can be actualised through appropriate activities and judicious choice of topics in all subjects and at all stages. Peace education as an area of study is recommended for inclusion in the curriculum for teacher education.

School Ethos and Flexible School Calendars

The school ethos is discussed as a dimension of curriculum, as it predisposes the child towards the aims of education and strategies of learning necessary for success at school. As a resource, school time needs to be planned in a flexible manner. Locally planned, flexible school calendars and time tables which permit time slots of different lengths required for different kinds of activities, such as project work and outdoor excursions to natural and heritage sites, are recommended. Efforts are required to prepare more learning resources for children, especially books and reference materials in regional languages, for school and teacher reference libraries, and access to interactive rather than disseminative technologies. The NCF emphasizes the importance of multiplicity and fluidity of options at the senior secondary level, discouraging the entrenched tendency to place children in fixed streams, and limiting opportunities of children especially from the rural areas.

Other Recommendations

1. *Panchayati Raj Institutions*—In the context of systemic reforms, this document emphasises strengthening the Panchayati Raj Institutions by the adoption of a more streamlined approach to encourage community participation as a means of enhancing of quality and accountability.

2. *Leadership at the School Level*—Academic planning and leadership at the school level is essential to improve quality; strategic differentiation of roles is necessary at block and cluster levels.

3. *Teacher Education*—In teacher education, radical steps are required to reverse the recent trend towards the dilution of the professional norms recommended by the Chattopadhyaya Commission (1984). Pre-service training programmes need to be more-comprehensive and lengthy, incorporating sufficient opportunities for observation of children and integration of pedagogic theory with practice through school internship.

4. *Examination Reform*—Examination reforms constitute the most important systemic measure to be taken for curricular renewal and to

find a remedy for the growing problem of psychological pressure that children and their parents feel, especially in Classes X and XII. Specific measures include changing the typology of the question paper so that reasoning and creative abilities replace memorization as the basis of evaluation, and integration of examinations with classroom life by encouraging transparency and internal assessment. The stress on pre-board examinations must be reversed and strategies to enable children to opt for different levels of attainment should be encouraged to overcome the present system of generalized classification into 'pass' and 'fail' categories.

5. *Partnership between the School System and Other Civil Society*—Finally, the document recommends partnerships between the school system and other civil society groups, including non-governmental organizations, and teacher organizations. The innovative experiences already available should be mainstreamed, and awareness of the challenges implied in the Universalisation of Elementary Education (UEE) should become a subject of wide ranging cooperation between the state and all agencies concerned about children.

Organisation of School Experiences (Chapter 2)

A. *General Activities*
1. Assembly
2. Celebrations and Special Activities
3. Games
4. Free Play Time
5. Dialogue, Debates and discussions.
6. Participation in Management and Organisational Work

B. *Subject Area Language:* Medium of Instruction, English, Third Language.

7. Mathematics
8. Sciences
9. Social Sciences and History
10. Arts
11. Crafts and Work

Principles Regarding Approach to Knowledge in the Curriculum (Chapter 2)

1. Acquiring a critical perspective on social reality and the natural environment, through the lenses provided by the subject matter.

2. Connecting with the local, and conceptualised in order to 'situate' knowledge and realizing its relevance and meaningfulness, to reaffirm one's experiences outside school; to draw ones learning from observing, interacting with, classifying; categorizing, to question, reason and argue in relation to these experiences.

3. Making connections across disciplines and bringing out the interrelatedness of knowledge.

4. Realising the 'fruitfulness' and 'openness' of enquiry, and the provisional nature of truths.

5. Engaging with 'local knowledge'/indigenous and practices in the local area, and relating this to school knowledge wherever possible.

6. Encouraging questions and leaving space open for the pursuit of new questions.

7. Being sensitive to the issues of 'equality' to classroom transaction as well as established stereotypes and discrimination, regarding learnability of the knowledge area by different groups (e.g. girls not given field based projects, blind excluded from the option of learning mathematics, etc.)

8. Developing the imagination, and keeping imagination and fantasy alive.

Chapter-wise Summary of Recommendations

Chapter 1 : Perspective

- Strengthening a national system of education in a pluralistic society.
- Reducing the curriculum load based on insights provided in '*Learning Without Burden*'.
- Systemic changes in tune with curricular reforms.
- Curricular practices based on the values enshrined in the Constitution, such as social justice, and equality, and secularism.
- Ensuring quality education for all.
- Building a citizenry committed to democratic practices, values, sensitivity towards gender justice, problems faced by the Scheduled Castes and the Scheduled Tribes, needs of the disabled, and capabilities to participate in economic and political processes.

Chapter 2 : Learning and Knowledge

- Reorientation in our perception of learners and learning.
- Holistic approach in the treatment of learners' development and learning.
- Meeting learning disability needs through data based and need specific programmes.
- Learner engagement for construction of knowledge and fostering creativity.
- Active learning through experimental mode.
- Adequate room for voicing children's thinking, curiosity and questions in curricular practices.
- Connecting knowledge across disciplinary boundaries to provide a broader frame for insightful construction of knowledge.
- Forms of learner engagement-observing, exploring, discovering,

analysing, critical reflection, etc. are as important as the content of knowledge.

- Activities for developing critical perspectives on socio-cultural realities need to find space in curricular practices.
- Local knowledge and children's experiences are essential components of textbooks and pedagogic practices.
- School years are a period of rapid development with changes and shifts in capabilities, attitudes and interests that have implications for choosing and organizing the content and process of knowledge.

Chapter 3 : Curriculum Areas : School Stages and Assessment

Language

- Language skills-speech and listening, reading and writing-cut across school subjects and disciplines. Their foundational role in children's construction of knowledge right from elementary classes through senior secondary classes needs to be recognised.
- A renewed effort should be made to implement the three-language formula, emphasizing recognition of children's mother tongue(s) as the best medium of instruction. These include tribal languages.
- Success in learning English is possible only if it builds on sound language pedagogy in the mother tongue.
- The multilingual character of Indian society should be seen as a resource for enrichment of school life.

Mathematics

- Mathematization (ability to think logically, formulate and handle abstractions) rather than 'knowledge' of mathematics (formals and mechanical procedures) is the main goal of teaching mathematics.
- The teaching of mathematics should enhance the child's ability to think and reason, to visualize and handle abstractions, to formulate and solve problems. Access to quality mathematics education is the right of every child.

Science

- Content, process and language of science teaching must be commensurate with learner's age-range and cognitive reach.
- Science teaching should engage the learner in acquiring methods and processes that will nurture their curiosity and creativity, particularly in relation to the environment.
- Science teaching should be placed in the wider context of children's environment to equip them with the requisite knowledge and skills to enter the world of work.
- Awareness of environmental concerns must permeate the entire school curriculum.

Social Sciences

- Social science teaching should aim at equipping children with moral and mental energy so as to provide them the ability to think independently and reflect critically on social issues.
- Interdisciplinary approaches, promoting key national concerns such as gender justice, human rights and sensitivity to marginalized groups and minorities.
- Civics should be recast as political science, and significance of history as a shaping influence on the child's conception of the past and civic identity should be recognized.

Work

- Work should be infused in all subjects from the primary stage upwards.
- Agencies and settings offering work opportunities outside the school be formally recognized.
- Design of Vocational Education and Training (VET) programme is based on the perspective of 10-12 years of work centre education with in-built features of:
  - — flexible and modular course of varying durations
  - — multiple entry and exit points
  - — accessibility from the level of village clusters to district levels.
  - — decentralized accreditation and equivalence mechanism for agencies located outside the school system.

Art

- Arts (folk and classical forms of music and dance, visual arts, puppetry, clay work, theatre, etc.) and heritage crafts should be recognized as integral components of the school curriculum.
- Awareness of their relevance to personal, social, economic and aesthetic needs should be built among parents, school authorities and administrators.
- The arts should comprise a subject at every stage of school education.

Peace

- Peace-oriented values should be promoted in all subjects throughout school years with the help of relevant activities.
- Peace education should form a component of teacher education.

Health and Physical Education

- Health and physical education are necessary for the overall development of learners. Through health and physical education programmes (including yoga), it may be possible to handle successfully the issues of enrolment, retention and completion of school.

Chapter 4 : School and Classroom Environment

- Availability of minimum infrastructure and material facilities, and support for planning a flexible daily schedule are critical for improved teacher performance.
- A school culture that nurtures children's identities as 'learners' enhances the potential and interests of each child.
- Specific activities ensuring participation of all children—able and disabled—are essential conditions for learning by all.
- The value of self-discipline among learners through democratic functioning is as relevant as ever.
- Participation of community members in sharing knowledge and experience in a subject area helps in forging a partnership between school and community.
- Reconceptualization of learning resources in terms of:
  - Textbooks focused on elaboration of concepts, activities, problems and exercises encouraging reflective thinking and group work.
  - Supplementary books, workbooks, teachers' handbooks, etc. based on fresh thinking and new perspectives.
  - Multimedia and ICT as sources for two-way interaction rather than one-way reception.
  - School library as an intellectual space for teachers, learners and members of the community to deepen their knowledge and connect with the wider world.
- Decentralized planning of school calendar and daily schedule and autonomy for teacher professionalism practices are basic to creating a learning environment.

Chapter 5 : Systemic Reforms

- Quality concern, a key feature of systemic reform, implies the system's capacity to reform itself by enhancing its ability to remedy its own weaknesses and to develop new capabilities.
- A broad framework for planning upwards, beginning with schools for identifying focus areas and subsequent consolidation at the cluster and block levels could form a decentralized planning strategy at the district level.
- Meaningful academic planning has to be done in a participatory manner by headmasters and teachers.
- Monitoring quality must be seen as a process of sustaining interaction with individual schools in terms of teaching-learning processes.
- Professional training of teachers can be strengthened by linking it to:
  - post-graduate studies in different subjects.
  - provisions for integrated undergraduate studies in teacher education.

  - inclusion of a course on language proficiency as an integral component.
  - engaging the trainees with the larger context of education, interacting with children in real contexts and critically questioning their own beliefs about knowledge and learning, gender, caste, equity and justice, shifting the focus from pure disciplinary knowledge to the learner and his/her context.
- In service education needs to become a catalyst for change in school practices.
- Panchayati Raj system should be strengthened by evolving a mechanism to regulate the functioning of parallel bodies at the village level so that democratic participation in development can be realized.

Examination Reforms

- Reducing stress and enhancing success in examination necessitate:
  - shift from content-based testing to problem-solving and understanding. For this to happen the present typology of the question paper must change.
  - shift toward shorter examinations.
  - Setting up of a single nodal agency for coordinating the design and conduct of entrance examinations.
- Availability of multiple textbooks to widen teachers' choices and provide for the diversity in children's needs and interests.
- Sharing of teaching experiences and diverse classroom practices to generate new ideas and facilitate innovation and experimentation.
- Development of syllabi, textbooks and teaching learning resources could be carried out in a decentralized and participatory manner involving teachers, experts from universities, NGOs and teachers' organizations.

11

Overview of Implementation of National Policy of Education

Introduction

In this chapter an attempt is made to provide an overview of the efforts made in India for the implementation of NPE (National Policy of Education). A brief description is given here for the achievements made in the implementation of various educational schemes launched at various levels. The facts and figures are taken freely from '*INDIA 2008: A Reference Manual*, published by the Government of India.

I. Expenditure on Education

In line with the commitment of augmenting resources for education, the allocation for education has over the years, increased significantly. The Plan outlay on education increased from Rs. 151.20 crore in the First Five-Year Plan to Rs. 43,825 crore in the Tenth Five-Year Plan (2002-2007).

The outlay for Education in the Tenth Five-Year Plan of Rs. 43,825 crore was higher than the Ninth Plan outlay of Rs. 24,908.38 crore by 1.76 times. Rs. 30,000 crore had been provided for the Department of Elementary Education and Literacy and Rs. 13,825 crore for the Department of Secondary and Higher Education. The outlay for Education during 2005-06 was Rs. 12,531.76 crore for the Department of Elementary Education and Literacy and Rs. 2,712.00 crore for the Department of Secondary and Higher Education. The expenditure during the plan periods on the different sectors of education is given Table 11.1.

II. Elementary Education

1. Sarva Shiksha Abhiyan (SSA)

The scheme of Sarva Shiksha Abhiyan (SSA) a national flagship programme, is being implemented in all districts of the country. The aim

Table 11.1: Plan Expenditure on Different Sectors of Education

Sector	First Plan Expdt. 1951-56	Second Plan Expdt. 1956-61	Third Plan Expdt. 1961-66	Plan Holiday Expdt. 1966-69	Fourth Plan Expdt. 1969-74	Fifth Plan Expdt. 1974-79	Sixth Plan Expdt. 1980-85	Seventh Plan Expdt. 1985-90	1990-92 Expdt.	Eighth Plan Expdt. 1992-97	Ninth Plan Outlay (1997-2002) (Central Sector)	Ninth Plan Expdt. (1997-02) (Central Sector)	Tenth Plan Outlay (2002-2007) (Central Sector)
(1)	(2)	(3)	(4)	(5)	(6)	(7)	(8)	(9)	(10)	(11)	(12)	(13)	(14)
Elementary Education	58 (870)	35 (950)	34 (2010)	24 (750)	50 (3743)	52 (5913)	32 (8414)	37 (28494)	37 (17290)	48 (103940)	66 (163696)	65.7 (145233)	65.6 (287500)
Secondary Education	5 (83)	19 (510)	18 (1030)	16 (530)	@	@	20 (5344)	24 (18315)	22 (10530)	24 (52311)	10 (26035)	10.5 (23227)	9.9 (43250)
Adult Education					2 (126)	2 (248)	6 (1533)	6 (4696)	9 (4160)	5 (11421)	3 (6304)	2.4 (5204)	2.9 (12500)
Higher Education	8 (117)	18 (480)	15 (870)	24 (770)	25 (1883)	28 (3188)	21 (5604)	16 (12011)	12 (5880)	10 (20944)	10 (25000)	10.3 (22709	9.5 (41765)
Others	15 (227)	10 (300)	12 (730)	11 (370)	13 (936)	9 (1071)	11 (2729)	3 (1980)	2 (1180)	3 (7398)	2 (4314)	1.6 (3492)	1.4 (6235)
Technical Education	14 (215)	18 (490)	21 (1250)	25 (810)	10 (786)	9 (1015)	10 (2563)	14 (10833)	17 (8230)	10 (21987)	9 (23735)	9.5 (21095)	10.7 (47000)
Total	100 (1512)	100 (2730)	100 (5890)	100 (3230)	100 (7474)	100 (11435)	100 (26187)	100 (76329)	100 (47270)	100 (218001)	100 (249084)	100 (220960)	100 (438250)

Source: Five-Year Plan Documents, Planning Commission and Analysis of Budget Expenditure, Ministry of HRD.

Notes: 1. Figures in parenthesis in millions of rupees.

2. Figures in Col.2 to Col.11 includes the share of States/UTs.

@ Included under Elementary Education.

of SSA is to provide useful and relevant elementary education for all children in the 6-14 age group by 2010. The scheme of Sarva Shiksha Abhiyan (SSA) was launched in 2001. The goals of SSA are as follows: (i) All 6-14 age children in school/EGS (Education Guarantee Scheme) centre/Bridge Course by 2005. (ii) Bridge all gender and social category gaps at primary stage by 2007 and at elementary education level by 2010. (iii) Universal retention by 2010. (iv) Focus on elementary education of satisfactory quality with emphasis on education for life.

The assistance under the programme of Sarva Shiksha Abhiyan was on a 85:15 sharing arrangement during the Ninth Plan, 75:25 sharing arrangement during the Tenth Plan and 50:50 sharing thereafter between the Central Government and the State Government except for 8 NE states, where 15 per cent of the state there met by Ministry of DONER far the two years 2005-06 and 2006-07.

The programme covers the entire country with special focus on educational needs of girls, SCs/STs and other children in difficult circumstances. The programme seeks to open new schools in those place which do not have schooling facilities and strengthen existing school infrastructure through provision of additional class rooms, toilets, drinking water, maintenance grant and school improvement grant. SSA has a special focus on girls and children of weaker sections. A number of initiatives, including distribution of free textbooks, targeting these children is under the programme. The SSA also seeks to provide computer education even in the rural areas.

During 2006-07, the SSA approved 41656 primary school building, 358939 additional classrooms, 6438 drinking water facility, 5634 toilet facility and free textbooks of 6.22 crore children for all 604 districts. A sum of Rs. 10,863.34 crore (up to March 2007) was released by Central Government to the States/UTs.

Till December 2006 almost 1.81 lakh new schools had been opened since the inception of SSA. 149683 new school buildings and 650442 additional classrooms have been constructed or are nearing completion and 8.14 lakh new teachers had been appointed under SSA till 31.3.2007. In the XIth Plan Rs. 27,895.85 crore were provided by Government of India for SSA.

SSA has succeeded in bringing about a huge reduction in the number of out of school children from 320 lakh in 2001-02 to about 70 lakh in March 2007. The enrolment of girls during the same period increased by 19.2 per cent at primary level and 15 per cent at upper primary level. sixty-seven lakh children are presently enrolled in flexible alternative schools that provide access in small, remote habitations and for specific groups of children like working children, children who migrate seasonally with families, urban deprived children etc.

2. *Education Guarantee Scheme and Alternative and Innovative Education*

Education Guarantee Scheme and Alternative and Innovative Education (EGS and AIE) is an important component of Sarva Shiksha Abhiyan (SSA) to bring out-of-school children in the fold of Elementary Education. The scheme envisages that child-wise planning is undertaken for each out-of-school children.

EGS addresses the inaccessible habitation where there is no formal school within the radius of one km and at least 15-25 children of 6-14 years age group who are not going to school are available. In exceptional cases remote habitations in hilly areas even for 20 children an EGS school can be opened.

Alternative Education interventions for specific categories of very deprived children e.g., child labour, street children, migrating children, working children, children living in difficult circumstances and older children in the 9+ age group especially adolescent girls are being supported under EGS and AIE all over the country.

A sizeable number of out-of-school children are in the habitations where schooling facility is available but these children either did not join the school or dropped out before completing their schooling. These children may not fit into the rigid formal system. To bring such children back to school; back to school camp and Bridge Courses strategies have been implemented. Bridge courses and Back to school camps can be residential or non-residential depending upon the need of children.

During 2005-06, Department of Elementary Education and Literacy considered and approved District Plans of 600 districts of 35 States/UTs. The States are participating enthusiastically in the programme.

During 2006-07 the EGS/AIE component helped to provide elementary education to 103.82 lakh children, i.e., 47.71 lakh children who were living in non-accessible habitations were provided elementary education through 1 lakh EGS centres and 31.92 lakh children not going to school were brought into Bridge Courses/ Schools camps.

3. *Mid-Day Meal Scheme*

Background

With a view to enhancing enrolment, retention and attendance and simultaneously improving nutritional levels among children, the National Programme of Nutritional Support to Primary Education (NP-NSPE) was launched as a Centrally Sponsored Scheme on 15th August 1995, initially in 2408 blocks in the country. By the year 1997-98 the NP-NSPE was introduced in all blocks of the county. It was further extended in 2002 to cover not only children in classes I-V of government, government aided and local body schools, but also children studying in

EGS and AIE centres. Central assistance under the scheme consisted of free supply of food grains @ 100 grams per child per school day, and subsidy for transportation of food grains up to a maxim of Rs. 50 per quintal.

In September 2004 the scheme was revised to provide cooked mid-day meal with 300 calories and 8-12 grams of protein to all children studying in classes I-V in Government and aided schools and EGS/AIE centres. In addition to free supply of food grains, the revised scheme provided Central Assistance for (a) Cooking cost @ Re. 1 per child per school day, (b) Transport subsidy was raised from the earlier maximum of Rs. 50 per quintal to Rs. 100 per quintal for special category states, and Rs. 75 per quintal for other states, (c) Management, monitoring and evaluation costs @ 2% of the cost of food grains, transport subsidy and cooking assistance, (d) Provision of mid-day meal during summer vacation in drought affected areas.

In July 2006 the scheme was further revised to provide assistance for cooking cost at the rate of (a) Rs. 1.80 per child/school day for States in the North Eastern Region, provided the NER states contribute Rs. 0.20 per child/school day, and (b) Rs. 1.50 per child/school day for other States and UTs, provided that these States and UTs contribute Rs. 0.50 per child/school day.

Objectives

The objectives of the mid-day meal scheme are:

(i) Improving the nutritional status of children in classes I-V in Government, Local Body and Government aided schools, and EGS and AIE centres.

(ii) Encouraging poor children, belonging to disadvantaged sections, to attend school more regularly and help them concentrate on classroom activities.

(iii) Providing nutritional support to children of primary stage in drought affected areas during summer vacation.

Programme Intervention and Coverage

To achieve the above objectives a cooked mid-day meal with nutritional content as shown in column 3 of the table below will be provided to all children studying in classes I-V:

Nutritional Content	*Norm as per NP-NSPE, 2004*	*Revised Norm as per NP-NSPE, 2006*
Calorie	300	450
Protein	8-12	12
Micronutrients	Not Prescribed	Adequate quantities of micronutrients like iron, folic acid, vitamin-A etc.

Components of the revised scheme

The revised scheme provides for the following components:

(i) Supply of free food grains (wheat/rice) @ 100 grams per child per School Day from the nearest FCI godown:

(ii) Reimbursement of the actual cost incurred in transportation of food grains from nearest FCI godown to the Primary School subject to the following ceiling:

(a) Rs. 100 per Quintal for 11 special category States, viz., Arunachal Pradesh, Assam, Meghalaya, Mizoram, Manipur, Nagaland, Tripura, Sikkim, J&K, Himachal Pradesh and Uttarakhand, and

(b) Rs. 75 per quintal for all other States and UTs.

(iii) Provision of assistance for cooking cost at the following rates:

(a) States in North Eastern Region : @ Rs. 1.80 per child per school day, provided the State Govt. contributes a minimum of 20-paise.

(b) For other States & UTs: @ Rs. 1.50 per child per school day provided the State Govt./UT Admn. contributes a minimum of 50-paise.

State Governments/UT Administrations are required to provide the above minimum contribution in order to be eligible or the enhanced rate of Central assistance mentioned above.

(iv) Provision of assistance for cooked Mid-Day Meal during summer vacations to school children in areas declared by State Governments as "drought-affected".

(v) Provision of assistance to construct kitchen-*cum*-store in a phased manner up to a maximum of Rs. 60,000 per unit. However, as allocations under MDMS for construction of kitchen-*cum*-store for all schools in next 2-3 years may not be adequate. States would be expected to proactively pursue convergence with other development programmes for this purpose.

(vi) Provision of assistance in a phased manner for provisioning and replacement of *kitchen devices* at an average cost of Rs. 5,000 per school. States/UTs Administration will have the flexibility to incur expenditure on the items listed below on the basis of the actual requirements of the school (provided that the overall average for the State/UT administration remains Rs. 5,000 per school).

(a) Cooking devices (Stove, Chulha. etc.)

(b) Containers for storage of food grains and other ingredients.

(c) Utensils for cooking and serving.

(vii) Provision of assistance to States/UTs. for *Management, Monitoring & Evaluation* (*MME*) at the rate of 1.8% of total assistance on (a) free food grains, (b) transport cost, and (c) cooking cost. Another 0.2% of the above amount will be utilised at the Central Government for management, monitoring and evaluation.

Monitoring Mechanism

The Department of School Education and Literacy Ministry of Human

Resource Development has prescribed a comprehensive and elaborate mechanism for monitoring and supervision of the Mid-Day Meal Scheme. The monitoring mechanism includes the following:

(a) *Arrangements for Local Level Monitoring*: Representatives of Gram Panchayats/Gram Sabhas, members of VECS, PTAs, SDMCs as well as Mothers' Committees are required to monitor the (i) regularity and wholesomeness of the mid-day meal served to children, (ii) cleanliness in cooking and serving of the mid-day meal, (iii) timeliness in procurement of good quality ingredients fuel, etc., (iv) implementation of varied menu, (v) social and gender equity. This is required to be done on a daily basis.

(b) *Display of Information under Right to Information Act*: In order to ensure that there is transparency and accountability, all schools and centres where the programme being implemented are required to display information on a *suo-moto*. This includes information on:

(i) Quality of food grains received, date of receipt.
(ii) Quantity of food grains utilised.
(iii) Other ingredients purchased, utilised.
(iv) Number of children given mid-day meal.
(v) Daily Menu.
(vi) Roster of Community Member involved in the programme.

(c) *Inspections by State Government Officers*: Officers of the State Government/UTs belonging to the Departments of Revenue, Rural Development, Education and other related sectors, such as Women and Child Development, Food, Health are also required to inspect schools and centres where the programme is being implemented. It has been recommended that 25 per cent of primary schools/EGS & AIE centres are visited every quarter.

(d) *Responsibility of Food Corporation of India (FCI)*: The FCI is responsible for the continuous availability of adequate food grains in its Depots (and in Principal Distribution Centre in the case of North East Region). It allows lifting of food grains for any month/quarter up to one month in advance so that supply chain of food grains remains uninterrupted.

For the NP-NSPE, 2006, FCI is mandated to issue food grains of best available quality, which will in any case be at least of Fair Average Quality (FAQ). FCI appoints in Nodal Officer for each State to take case of various problems in supply of food grains under the MDM Programme.

The District Collector/CEO of Zila Panchayat ensures that food grains of at least FAQ are issued by FCI after joint inspection by a team consisting of FCI and the nominee of the Collector and/or Chief Executive Officer, District Panchayat, and Confirmation by them that the gain conforms to at least FAQ norms.

(e) *Periodic Returns*: The State Government/UT is also required to submit periodic returns to the Department of School Education and Literacy, Government of India to provide information on (i) coverage of children and institutions, (ii) progress in utilisation of central assistance, including cooking costs, transportation, construction of kitchen sheds and procurement of kitchen devices.

Extension to Upper Primary Stage

The Finance Minister has announced in the Union Budget 2007-08 that the Mid-Day Meal Scheme will be extended to cover children in upper Primary Classes in 3427 Educationally Backward Blocks (EBBs) in 2007-08. A Budget provision of Rs. 7,324 crores has been made for this purpose, representing 37 per cent increase over the budget for 2006-07.

4. District Primary Education Programme

The Centrally-Sponsored Scheme of District Primary Education Programme (DPEP) was launched in 1994 as a major initiative to revitalise the primary education system and to achieve the objective of universalisation of primary education.

DPEP adopts a holistic approach to universalise access, retention and improve learning achievement and to reduce disparities among social groups. Adopting an 'area-specific approach' with district as the unit of planning, the key strategies of the programme have been to retain the sensitivity to local conditions and ensuring full participation of the community. It also seeks to strengthen the capacity of national, state and district institutions and organisations for planning, management and professional support in the field of primary education.

DPEP is based on the principle of 'additionality' and is instructed to fill in the existing gaps by providing inputs over and above the provisions made under Central and State Sector schemes for primary education. The State Governments are required to at least maintain expenditure in real terms at base year level.

The programme components include construction of classrooms and new schools, opening of Non-formal/Alternative Schooling Centres, appointment of new setting up early childhood education centres, strengthening of State Councils of Educational Research and Training (SCERTs)/District Institute of Educational Training (DIETs), setting up of Block Resource Centres/Cluster Resource Centres, teacher training, development of Teaching Learning Material Research based interventions, special interventions for promoting education of disadvantaged groups, girls, SC/ST, etc., initiatives for providing integrated education to disabled children and distance education for teacher training have also been incorporated in the DPEP scheme.

Under the Programme parameters, investment per district is limited to Rs. 40 crore over a project period of 5-7 years. There is ceiling of 33.3 per cent on civil works component and 6 per cent on management cost. The remaining amount is required to be spent on quality improvement activities.

DPEP is an externally aided project 85 per cent of the project cost is met by the Central Government and the remaining 15 per cent is shared by the concerned State Government. The Central Government share is resourced through external assistance. At present External Assistance of about Rs. 6,938 crore composing Rs. 5,137 as credit from IDA and Rs. 1,801 crore as grant from EC/DFID/UNICEF/Netherlands has been tied up for DPEP.

Presently DPEP is in operation in nine States covering 123 districts. DPEP at its peak was operational in 273 districts in 18 Stats. However, with the progressive closure of the programme, it is now existing only in 123 districts.

The programme is supervised through periodic Supervision Missions such as joint review Missions, Project Management Information System (PMIS), Educational Management Informatics System (EMIS), Programme Impact Studies, etc. The reviews and various evaluatory studies of the programme have brought out that the programme has resulted in significant increase in enrolment, improvement in learning achievement, reduction in repetition rates/drop-outs with increased community involvement, improvements in classroom processes, etc.

Major Achievements of DPEP: (i) DPEP has so far opened more than 1,60,000 new schools, including almost 84,000 alternative schooling (AS) centres. The AS centres cover nearly 3.5 million children, while another two lakh children are covered by Bridge Courses of different types, (ii) The school infrastructure created under DPEP has been remarkable. Works either complete or in progress include 52,758 school buildings, 58,604 additional classrooms, 16,619 resource centres, 29,307 repair works, 64,592 toilets, and 24,909 drinking water facilities, (iii) The Gross Enrolment Ratio (GER) for Phase-I states was around 93 to 95 per cent for the last three years. After the adjustment for the Alternative Schools/Education Guarantee Centres enrolment, the GER in the 2001-02 works out above 100 per cent. In the districts covered under subsequent phases of DPEP, the GER including enrolment of AS/EGS was above 85 per cent; (iv) The enrolment of girls has shown significant improvement. In DPEP-I districts, the share of girls enrolment in relation to total enrolment has increased from 48 per cent to 49 per cent, while this increase in the subsequent phases of DPEP districts has been from 46 per cent to 47 per cent; (v) The total number of differently-abled children enrolled is now more than 4,20,203 which represents almost 76 per cent of the nearly 5,53,844 differently-abled children identified in the DPEP States; (vi) Village Education Committees/School Management Committees have been set up in almost all project villages/habitations/schools, (vii) About 1,77,000 teachers, including para-teachers/Shiksha Karmis have been appointed; (viii) About 3,380 resource centres at block level and 29,725 centres at cluster level have been set-up for providing academic support and teacher training facilities.

5. Mahila Samakhya Scheme

Pursuant to the objectives of the NPE, 1986, the Mahila Samakhya Scheme was started in 1989 to translate the goals enshrined in the NPE into a concrete programme for the education and empowerment 6l women in rural areas particularly those from socially and economically marginalised groups. The MS scheme recognises the centrality of education in empowering women to achieve equality. The Mahila Sanghas or women's collectives at the village level provide the women a space to meet, reflect, ask questions and articulate their thoughts and needs and make informed choices.

The Mahila Sanghas though various programmes and awareness campaigns have brought about a change in the outlook of rural women and the effects can how be seen in various facets of life at home within the family, the community and at the block and panchayat levels. The programme has also focussed on awareness of the need to educate the children, especially girls, to give the equal status and opportunities which has resulted in a direct impact on enrolment and retention of girls in schools.

The Mahila Samakhya Scheme is currently being implemented in nine States viz., Andhra Pradesh, Assam, Bihar, Jharkhand, Karnataka, Kerala, Gujarat, Uttar Pradesh and Uttarakhand spread over 83 districts and covering more than 21,000 villages. From the current financial year the programme is being extended to two new States i.e. Madhya Pradesh and Chhatisgarh. The budgetary allocation for the Scheme for the current financial year i.e. 2007-08 is Rs. 34.00 crores.

6. Right to Education

The Constitution (86th Amendment) Act 2002, enacted in December 2002 seeks to make free and compulsory education a Fundamental Right for all children in the age group 6-14 years by inserting a new Article 21-A in Part III ("Fundamental Right") of the Constitution. Article 21-A of the Constitution says that:-

'The State shall provide free and compulsory education to all children of the age of six to fourteen years in such manner as the State may by law, determine".

The Government is committed to facilitate the enactment of an appropriate law that would enable the realisation of making education a fundamental right as required the constitution. Necessary action is being taken to put in place a suitable legislation envisaged under Article 21-A of the Constitution.

7. Prarambhik Shiksha Kosh

A two per cent Education Cess was levied on all major Central taxes through the Finance (No.2) Act, 2004, to help finance government's commitment to quality basic education. In order to receive the proceeds of this Education Cess, the creation of a dedicated non-lapsable fund called Prarambhik Shiksha Kosh (PSK) in the Public Account was approved by Government on 6-10-2005. Formal orders constituting PSK were issued on 14-11-2005. After presentation of the Union Budget (2006-07) on 28-2-2006, PSK became a separate line item. A provision of Rs. 8,746 crores for the initial transfer to the newly created PSK was made in the Union Budget 2006-07 against estimated receipts of Education Cess. Subsequently, in the 3rd batch of Supplementary Demand for Grants, a provision of Rs. 189 crores was made for additional transfer to PSK based an additional estimated collection of education cess of 2% during 2006-07. The funds available in the PSK were utilised exclusively for Sarva Shiksha Abhiyan (SSA) and National Programme for Nutritional Support of Primary Education (MDM Scheme). The levy of education cess is a concrete step towards providing assured funding for elementary education.

8. Teacher Education Scheme

I. Centrally sponsored scheme of Teacher Education was launched in 1987-88 with *inter-alia*, the following components:
   1. Establishment of District Institute of Education & Training (DIETs) by upgradation of existing Elementary Teacher Education Institutions (ETEIs) wherever possible, and establishment of new DIET where necessary.
   2. Upgradation of selected Secondary Teacher Education Institutions (STETIs) into:
      (a) Colleges of Teacher Education (CTEs) and
      (b) Institutes of Advanced Study in Education (IASEs).
   3. Strengthening of State Council of Educational Research and Training (SCERTs).

II. The Scheme was revised in 2003 and the revised guidelines were issued in January 2004 the main objectives of the Teacher Education Scheme are as follows:
   1. Speedy completion of DIET/CTE/IASE/SCERT projects sanctioned but not completed up to the end of the IX Plan period.
   2. Making DIETs, IASEs sanctioned (and SCERTs strengthened) up to the IX Plan period, optimally functional and operational.
   3. Sanction and implementation of fresh DIET/CTE/IASE/SCERT projects to the extent necessary.
   4. Improvement in the quality of programmes to be undertaken by DIETs, etc. especially those of pre-service and in-service training, so as to enable them to effectively play their nodal role of improving quality of elementary and secondary education in their respective jurisdiction, as measured in terms of levels of learner achievements.

III. Criteria for setting up of DIETs/District Resource Centre (DRC) are:
   1. One DIET for each district having a minimum of 2,500 teachers. If there is an existing Government ETEI in the district, it would

be upgraded into a DIET. If no Government ETEI exists in the district, a new institution (DIET) will be established.

2. District Resource Centres in districts with less than 2,500 teachers. If a Government ETEI exists in the district, it would be upgraded into a DRC. Otherwise, a new DRC would be established in which case it would not conduct pre-service course.
3. If in a district with more than 2,500 teachers, State Government wishes to establish a DRC in preference to a DIET, it would be able to do so.

IV. As on 1.4.2002, there were 599 districts in the country. Out of these, DIETs have been established in 571 districts. A total of 512 DIETs are operational. A rigorous follow up is being maintained with the States concerned to make the remaining CTEs and all of them are functional. There are 31 IASEs and all of them are functional.

The NCTE has issued new norms and standards for various teacher training programmes like C.Ed, D.Ed, B.Ed., DP.Ed, and MP.Ed. The new norm have been introduced to improve the quality of teacher programmes and to strengthen the infrastructural and the facilities in teacher training institutions.

9. National Literacy Mission

The National Literacy Mission set up in May 1988 aims to attain a sustainable threshold level of 75 per cent literacy by 2007 by imparting functional literacy to non-literates in the age group of 15-35 years, which is the productive and reproductive age group and constitutes a major segment of the work force. Apart from predetermined levels of reading, writing and numeracy with comprehension, functional literacy includes imbibing values of national integration, conservation of environment women's equality, observance of small family norms, etc. Literacy, as enunciated in NLM, is not an end in itself but has to be an active and potent instrument of change ensuring achievement of these social objectives and creation of a learning society.

Special interventions for Female Literacy: As per Census, 2001, 47 districts in the country have a female literacy rate below 30 per cent. Hence, dealing with low female literacy is of immense concern to the National Literacy Mission and it was decided to target the 47 low female literacy districts for improvement. As most of the these districts are concentrated in the States of Uttar Pradesh, Bihar, Orissa and Jharkhand, special innovative programmes have been taken up in these districts for promoting female literacy. The programme in Uttar Pradesh and Bihar has been completed and externally evaluated.

Nine districts in Orissa, which have low female literacy rates, have been covered under Special Project for Accelerated Female Literacy Programme. The programme was assigned to a network of 117 NGOs targeting 10.43 lakh non-literate women in 15-35 age group. The programme is being evaluated by external evaluation agencies.

The special female literacy programme has also been implemented in five low literacy districts of Jharkhand. Around five lakh women illiterates in 15-35 age group have been covered under the programme. The programme has been completed and the external evaluation is awaited from two districts.

Projects for Residual Illiteracy: Although the Total Literacy Campaigns took the form of mass movement and spread throughout the country in many cases a number of campaigns stagnated due to natural calamites, lack of political will, etc. Despite success of literacy phase, there are still pockets of residual illiteracy and low female literacy. To tackle this problem, Projects for Residual Illiteracy (PRI) have been taken up in 9 Districts of Rajasthan covering about 6.60 lakh learners, 10 districts of Andhra Pradesh covering 22.81 lakh learners, 7 districts of Bihar, covering 12.54 lakh learners, 14 districts of Karnataka covering 27.35 lakh learners, 12 districts of Madhya Pradesh covering 7.01 lakh learners, 3 districts of Tripura covering 1.38 lakh learners, 3 district of Jharkhand covering 3.01 lakh learners and 18 districts of Uttar Pradesh covering 36.11 lakh learners, 4 districts of Mizoram covering 0.45 lakh learners, and West Bengal covering 29.54 lakh learners.

Special Literacy Drive: The Council of the NLMA in its meeting held in April 2005 identified 150 districts which have the lowest literacy rates in the country for launching a special literacy drive, with special focus on the minority groups, persons belonging to scheduled castes, scheduled tribes, women and other backward sections of the society by drawing up implementation strategies suited to the specific needs of the group, sections of the society or region. So far, 134 districts in the States of Arunachal Pradesh (7), Andhra Pradesh (8), Bihar (31), Chhatisgarh (2), Jammu and Kashmir (8), Rajasthan (10), Jharkhand (12), Karnataka (2), Madhya Pradesh (9), Meghalaya (3), Nagaland (2), Orissa (8), Punjab (1), Uttar Pradesh (27) and West Bengal (4) have been covered under the Special Literacy Drive.

Jan Shikshan Sansthan: The objective of the Jan Shikshan Sansthan (JSS) is educational, vocational and occupational development of the socio-economically backward and educationally disadvantaged groups of urban/rural population particularly neo-literates, semi-literates, SCs, STs, women and girls, slum dwellers, migrant workers, etc. At present, there are 172 JSSs in the country. Jan Shikshan Sansthans run a number of vocational programmes with varying duration of different skills. More than 250 types of courses and activities are offered by these institutions. The trades/courses for which training is imparted include cutting, tailoring & dress making; knitting and embroidery; beauty culture and health care; handicrafts; art, drawing and painting repair of electrical software, etc.

10. Education of Scheduled Castes and Scheduled Tribes

Constitutional Provisions: Article 46 of the Constitution states that "The State shall promote, with special care, the education and economic interests of the welfare sections of the people, and, in particular of the Scheduled Castes and Scheduled Tribes, and shall protect them from social injustice and all forms of social exploitation". Articles 330, 332, 335, 338 to 342 and the entire Fifth and Sixth Schedules of the Constitution deal with special provisions for implementation of the objectives set forth in Article 46. These provisions need to be utilised for the benefit of these weaker sections in our society.

Commitment in NCMP: The UPA government has set six basic principles for governance. One of them is *To provide for full equality of opportunity, particularly in education and employment for scheduled castes, scheduled tribes, OBCs and religious minorities*. Besides; the National Common Minimum Programme (NCMP) of the UPA Government contains following provisions aimed at the welfare and empowerment of these communities: (a) UPA Government will take immediate steps to reverse the trend of communalisation of education that had set in the past five-years. (b) Steps will be taken to remove the communalisation of the school syllabus that has taken place in the past five-years. A review committee of experts will be se up for this purpose. (c) The UPA will ensure that nobody is denied professional education because he or she is poor. (d) All reservation quotas, including those relating to promotions, will be fulfilled in a time bound manner. To codify all reservations, a Reservation Act will be enacted. (e) The UPA Government is very sensitive to the issue of affirmative action, including reservations, in the private sector.

Special Provisions: After independence, the Government of India has taken number of steps to strengthen the educational base of the persons belonging to the Scheduled Castes and Scheduled Tribes. Pursuant to the National Policy on Education-1986 and the Programme of Action (POA)-1992, the following special provisions for SCs and STs have been incorporated in the existing schemes of the Departments of Elementary Education and Literacy and Secondary and Higher Education: (a) relaxed norms for opening of primary/middle schools; a primary school within one km. walking distance from habitations of population up to 200 instead of habitations of up to 300 population. (b) Abolition of tuition fee in all States in Government Schools at least up to the upper primary level. In fact, most of the states have abolished tuition fees for SC/ST students up to the senior secondary level. (c) Incentives like free textbooks, uniforms, stationery, schools bags, etc., for these students. (d) The Constitutional (86th Amendment) Bill, notified on 13 December 2002, provides for free and compulsory elementary education as a Fundamental Right, for all children in the age group of 6-14 years. (e) Sarva Shiksha Abhiyan (SSA): SSA is a historic stride towards achieving the long cherished goal of

Universalisation of Elementary Education (UEE) through a time bound integrated approach, in partnership with States. SSA which promises to change the face of elementary education sector of the country aims to provide useful and quality elementary education to all children in the 6-14 age group by 2010. The main features of the programme are: (i) Focus on girls, especially belonging to SC/ST communities and minority groups. (ii) Back to school campus for out of school girls. (iii) Free textbooks for girls. (iv) Special coaching remedial classes for girls and a congenial learning environment. (v) Teachers' sensitisation programmes to promote equitable learning opportunities. (vi) Special focus for innovative projects related to girls education. (vii) Recruitment of 50 per cent female teachers.

District Primary Education Programme (*DPEP*): The thrust of the scheme is on disadvantaged groups like girls, SCs/STs; working children, urban deprived children, disabled children, etc. There are specific strategies for girls and SCs/STs; however, physical targets are fixed, in an integrated manner including coverage of these groups as well. According to a study by NIEPA, schools in DPEP districts had more than 60 per cent students belonging to SC/ST communities.

Mahila Samakhya (*MS*): MS addresses traditional gender imbalances in educational access and achievement. This involves enabling women (especially from socially and economically disadvantaged and marginalised groups) to address and deal with problems of isolation and lack of self-confidence, oppressive social customs and struggle for survival, all of which inhibit their empowerment.

National Programme for Education of Girls at Elementary Level (*NPEGEL*): The NPEGL under the existing scheme of Sarva Shiksha Abhiyan (SSA) provides additional components for education of girls underprivileged/disadvantaged at the elementary level. The scheme being implemented in Educationally Backward Blocks (EBBs) where the level of rural female literacy is less than the national average and the gender gap is above the national average, as well as in blocks of districts that have at least 5 per cent SC/ST population and where SC/ST female literacy is below 10 per cent based on 1991.

Shiksha Karmi Project (*SKP*): SKP aims at universalisation and qualitative improvement of primary education in remote, arid and socio-economically backward villages in Rajasthan with primary attention to girls. It is noteworthy that in Shiksha Karmi Schools, most of the students are from SCs, STs and OBCs.

Kasturba Gandhi Balika Vidyalayas: Under the scheme of Kasturba Gandhi Balika Vidyalaya, 750 residential schools are being set up in difficult areas with boarding facilities at elementary level for girls belonging predominantly to the SC, ST, OBC and minorities. The scheme would be applicable only in those identified Educationally Backward Blocks (EBBs) where, as per census data 2001, the rural female literacy is below the national average and gender gap in literacy is more than the national average. Among these blocks, schools may be set up in areas with concentration of tribal population, with low female literacy and/or a large number of girls out of school.

III. Quality Improvement in Schools

During the 10th Five-Year Plan, "Quality Improvement in Schools" was introduced as a composite centrally sponsored scheme having the following components: (i) National Population Education Project, (ii) Environmental Orientation to School Education, (iii) Improvement of Science Education in Schools, (iv) Introduction of Yoga in Schools, and (v) International Science Olympiads. A decision was taken to transfer four of these components to National Council of Educational Research and Training (NCERT) w.e.f. April 2006, except the component of improvement Science Education in school that was transferred to states.

The 10th plan outlay for this scheme is Rs. 115 crore. A budgetary provision of Rs. 7 crore was made for the year 2006-07 for four components that have been transferred to National Council of Educational Research and Training.

1. National Population Education Project

National Population Education Project was launched in April 1982 with the overarching objective of institutionalising population education in the school education and teacher education systems to contribute to the attainment of population and development goals of the country. Up to 2002, this was implemented as externally aided project which was fully funded by the United Nations Population Fund (UNFPA). It was being implemented in the University education and adult education sector as well. In view of the achievements and significance of the Project, Government of India decided to continue in the 10th Five-Year Plan with a more focussed objective of integrating the elements of reconceptualised framework of population education in school curriculum.

Moreover, UNFPA decided to support a concomitant Project focused on adolescent reproductive and sexual health (ARSH) from 2004. For that a budgetary allocation of Rs. 7.29 crore has been made for the period 2004-2007. During 2006-07, the NPEP was implemented as an integral part of Adolescence Education Programme, launched by Ministry of Human Resource Development in 2005 in collaboration with National AIDS Control Organisation (NACO).

2. Environmental Orientation to School Education

The National Policy on Education (NPE)-1986 provides that the protection of environment is a value which, along with certain other values, must form an integral part of curricula at all stages of education. To operationalise this noble objective, the mind and intellect of the students must be sensitised to the hazards inherent in nature upsetting the ecological balance in nature. This step inculcates awareness and respect among students for basic concepts relating to the conservation of environment.

To this end, a Centrally Sponsored Scheme "Environment Orientation to School Education" was initiated in 1988-89. The scheme envisages assistance to voluntary agencies for conduct of experimental and innovative programmes aimed at promoting integration of educational programmes in schools with local environmental conditions. During the year 2006-07, voluntary organisations were provided financial assistance to the extent of Rs. 90 lakh for undertaking innovative and experimental projects in the field of environmental education.

3. Improvement of Science Education in Schools

To improve the quality of science education and to promote the scientific temper as envisaged in the National Policy on Education, 1986, a Centrally Sponsored Scheme; "Improvement of Science Education in Schools" was initiated during 1987-88. Under the scheme financial assistance was being provided to States/UTs and voluntary agencies. While voluntary agencies were provided assistance for conducting experimental and innovative programmes States/Union Territories were assisted for provision of science kits to Upper Primary Schools, setting up of upgradation of science laboratories in Secondary/Senior Secondary Schools, Library facilities in Secondary/Senior Secondary Schools and Training of Science and Mathematics teachers.

One of the important components of this scheme was participation of Indian Students at school level in the International Science Olympiads, viz., International Mathematical Olympiad (since 1989), International Physics Olympiad (since 1998), International Chemistry Olympiad (since 1999) and International Biology Olympiad (since 2000).

4. Introduction of Yoga in Schools

Introduction of Yoga in schools was launched as a Centrally Sponsored Scheme during 1989-90 to provide financial assistance to States/Union Territories/Non-Governmental Organisations. It aimed at giving central assistance for training and research, enrichment of library and construction/expansion of hostels for teacher trainees. It was being implemented through the concerned Departments of Education of States/UTs. It was transferred to NCERT w.e.f. April 2007. NCERT has initiated to review the Scheme in the light of National Curriculum Framework 2005.

During 2006-07, financial assistance (both non-plan and plan) has been provided to NGOs. An amount of Rs. 65 lakh has been given as non-plan grant to one agency and Rs. 26,38,00 to 13 agencies for conducting training and library related activities.

5. International Science Olympiads

With an aim to identify and nurture talents in Mathematics, Physics,

Chemistry and Biology at school level, and International Mathematical Olympiad (IMO), International Physics Olympiad (IPhO), International Chemistry Olympiad (IChO) and International Biology Olympiad (IBO) are held every year. India has been participating country in these Olympiads since 1989, 1998, 1999 and 2000, respectively. Each participating country is required to send a team comprising not more than 6 secondary students contestants to IMO. 5 secondary student contestants at IPhO, 4 contestants to IChO and 4 contestants to IBO apart from a Team Leader and a Deputy Team Leader. Since 2002 Indian team is also participating in international Olympiad in informatics.

As per the exiting financial pattern, the host country pay for the boarding and lodging and transportation of teams during their stay in the nest country, while the international travel cost is borne by the participating countries. The Indian teams in the last Olympiads were jointly sponsored by the Department of Secondary and Bhabha Centre for Science Education (HBCSE)/Bangalore Association for Science Education (BASE)/Indian Association for Research in Computing Science (IARCS) and Central Board of Secondary Education (CASE). The cost of international travel is paid by the Department of Secondary and Higher Education while all other expenses on selection of students internal travel incidental borne by NBHM/HBCSE/IARCS.

At IChO-2005 held at Taipei, Taiwan during July 2005 the Indian Team won 3 silver and 1 Bronze medals. At IPhO-2005 held at Salamanca, Spain during July 2005, the Indian team won 2 gold, 2 silver and 1 bronze medals. At IBO 2005 held at Beijing, China during July 2005 the Indian Team won 1 gold and 3 bronze medals. At IMO-2005 held at Menda, Mexico in July 2005, the Indian Team won 1 silver and 1 bronze medals and 3 honourable mentions. India had also participated in international Olympiad in Informatics (IOI-2005) held in Nowy Sacz, Poland during August 2005.

At IPhO-2006 held at Singapore from July 8-17, 2006 the Indian team won two gold and three bronze medals. At IchO-2006 held at Gyeongsangbuk, Korea from July 2-12, 2006 and Indian team won one gold, two silver and one bronze medals. In the IMO-2006 held at Lublijana, Slovenia from July 6-18, 2006 the Indian team won five bronze medals and one honourable mention. At IBO-2006 held at Jordoba, Argentina from July 9-16, 2006 the Indian team won three silver and a bronze medal.

6. Navodaya Vidyalaya Samiti

The National Policy on Education-1986 envisaged setting up of model school, one in each district of the Country. Accordingly a scheme was formulated under which it was decided to set up co-educational residential schools (now called Jawahar Navodaya Vidyalayas).

Navodaya Vidyalayas are fully residential co-educational institutions providing education up to senior secondary stage. The scheme, which started with only two schools on experimental basis in 1985-86, has grown to 565 schools (as on 31 March 2007) covering as many districts in 34 States/UTs with over 1.93 lakh students on rolls as on 31 March 2007. More than 30,000 new students are admitted every year.

The Vidyalayas envisaged a new style of growth with identification and development of talented, bright and gifted children predominantly from rural areas who may otherwise be denied good educational opportunities. Efforts are made to ensure that at least 33 per cent of the students enrolled are girls.

Migration is a unique feature of Navodaya Vidyalaya scheme whereby 30 per cent of students of Class IX from a Vidyalaya located in Hindi speaking area spend one academic year in a Vidyalaya located in Non-Hindi speaking area and *vice-versa* to promote national integration through understanding of the diversity and plurality of country's people, their language and culture.

7. Kendriya Vidyalaya Sangathan

The Government approved the scheme of Kendriya Vidyalaya Sangathan in 1962, on the recommendations of the Second Pay Commission. Initially, 20 regimental schools in different States were taken over as Central Schools. In 1965, an Autonomous Body called Kendriya Vidyalaya Sangathan was established with the primary objective of setting-up and monitoring Kendriya Vidyalaya to cater to the educational needs of the children of transferable Central Government Employees including Defence Personnel and Para-Military forces by providing common programme of education. At present, there are 931 Kendriya Vidyalayas (as on 17 June 2005) out of which three Kendriya Vidyalayas are abroad i.e. one each in Kathmandu, Moscow and, Tehran. All Kendriya Vidyalayas follow a uniform syllabus.

8. Integrated Education for Disabled Children

The Centrally Sponsored Scheme of Integrated Education for Disabled Children (IEDC) was launched in 1974 by the then Department of Social Welfare and was later transferred to the Department of Education in 1982-83. The Scheme was last revised in 1992. The Scheme provides educational opportunities for disabled children in common schools to facilitate their integration and ultimate retention in the general school system. Under IEDC, 100 per cent assistance is being provided under various components for education of children suffering from mild to moderate disabilities in common schools. The components include educational aids supporting equipments, salaries for special teachers and facilities for children with disability.

By the end of 2005, a total of approximately 2 lakh disabled children have been covered in nearly 85,000 schools. The total budgetary provision during the Tenth Plan is Rs. 200 crore and during the year 2005-06, Rs. 45 crore has been allocated for the implementation of the scheme.

IV. National Council of Educational Research and Training

The National Council of Educational Research and Training (NCERT) is an apex institution which provides technical resource support for school education. The NCERT charter envisages a special place for designing curriculum. NCERT is expected to review school curriculum as a regular activity ensuring the higher standards in education. The National Policy of Education (NPE) 1986 and the Programme of Action (PoA), 1992 assign a special role to NCERT in preparing and promoting a National Curriculum Framework. The NPE views such a task as a means of establishing a national system of education, characterised by certain core values and goals relevant to changing needs of children and society and within the constitutional framework of the country.

National Curriculum Framework: The National Curriculum Framework (NCF) 2005 was the outcome of wide ranging deliberations and collective endeavours. A National Steering Committee was set up under the chairpersonship of Prof. Yash Pal, eminent scientist and scholar. The committee comprised 35 members including scholars from different disciplines, principals and teachers, representatives of well-known NGOs and members of the NCERT. Its work was supported by 21 National Focus Groups, covering major areas of the curriculum, national concerns and systemic issues. Consultations were held across the length and breadth of the country. In addition NCERT held consultations with rural teachers, State Education Secretaries and Principals of private schools. Regional seminars were organised at the Regional Institutes of Education in Ajmer, Bhopal, Bhubaneswar, Mysore and Shillong.

V. Strengthening of Culture and Values in Education

The National Policy on Education, 1986 (revised in 1992) and its Programme of Action-1992 has laid considerable emphasis on value education by highlighting the need to make education a forceful tool for social and moral values.

To fulfil the objectives of the National Policy on Education, a Central Sector Scheme of Assistance for Strengthening of Culture and Values in Education is being implemented. Under this Scheme, financial assistance is given to Governmental and non-Governmental organisations, Panchayati Raj Institutions, etc., to the extent of 100 per cent of grant for the project proposals approved subject to a ceiling of Rs. 10 lakh for strengthening cultural and value education from pre-primary education system to higher education including technical and management education.

VI. Sanskrit Division

Sanskrit has played a vital role in the development of all Indian languages and in the preservation of the cultural heritage of India. The Government of India gives 100 per cent financial assistance through State Governments for: (a) Eminent Sanskrit scholars in Indigent Circumstances; (b) Modernisation of Sanskrit Pathshalas; (c) Providing facilities for teaching Sanskrit in High/Higher Secondary Schools; (d) Scholarship to students studying Sanskrit in High and Higher Secondary Schools; (e) various schemes for the promotion of Sanskrit; and (f) improving the methodology of teaching Sanskrit in schools, Sanskrit Colleges/Vidyapeeths. Presently the Scheme is under revision.

VII. Scholarships

The Ministry of Human Resource Development operates a Centrally Sponsored Scheme viz., National Merit Scholarship Scheme through States/UTs, under which 100 per cent financial assistance is provided to meritorious students from rural areas studying in classes IX and X. Besides scholarship is also provided to all the meritorious students on state-wise merit, including students from rural areas, studying from the post-metric to the post-graduate level. The rate of scholarship varies from Rs. 250 to Rs. 750, depending on course of study. Under the Scheme of Scholarship to Students from Non-Hindi Speaking State-for Post-Matric Studies in Hindi, the rate of scholarship ranges from Rs. 300 to 1,000 per month.

The Government provides scholarship to Indian scholar for Post-Graduate/Research/Post-Doctoral studies road on the basis of offers received from foreign Government under the various Cultural/Educational Exchange Programme. The details of offers and other conditions are given wide publicity in the leading newspapers while inviting applications for scholarship and are available on Department's website www.education.nic.in. The amount and other facilities provided by foreign governments varies from country to country and time-to-time.

VIII. Educational Development in North Eastern Region

The NE Region comprising eight Sates has a high literacy level and is rich in ethnic cultural heritage with linguistic diversity. However, the region lacks infrastructure and facilities in educational institutions across sectors and there is a need to improve the quality of education imparted. The NE States have been provided grants under the Non Lapsable Central Pool of Resources (NLCPR) to improve their infrastructure facilities. The Empowered Committee administering NLCPR has, since its inception in 1998-99, approved proposals worth Rs. 480.68 crore for the development of educational infrastructure in the NER. Funds amounting to Rs. 392.81 crore have also been released as on 30 November 2005. Out of this, Rs. 14.84 crore was released in 2005-06.

In the Central sector, the proposals mainly relate to infrastructure development of Central Institutions like the five central universities in the North East which include construction of staff quarters, academic buildings, library buildings, administrative buildings and purchase of lab equipments, books, etc. These projects are in various stages of implementation. The important Central Sector Institutions in the North East Region are IIT Guwahati; NERIST, Itanagar; NIT Silchar; Regional Centres of IGNOU; Central Universities of Assam; Tezpur, Mizoram, Nagaland and NEHU.

In addition to the funds released under NLCPR, the Department of Secondary and Higher Education also released Rs. 40.42 crore during 2003-04 from its own budget for meeting the committed liability under NLCPR for infrastructure projects of Assam University, Tezpur University, NEHU and JNU (for NER students' hostel).

A provision of Rs. 261.05 crore and Rs. 1,053 crore has been kept for NER under BE 2005-06 for the Department of Secondary and Higher Education and Elementary Education and Literacy respectively. Out of this an amount of Rs. 187.57 crore and Rs. 501.60 crore has been certified for expenditure on various schemes of the Department of Secondary and Higher Education and Elementary Education and Literacy till 31 January 2006.

The Kendriya Vidyalaya Sangathan are running 86 schools in the North East Region.

The Navodaya Vidyalaya Samiti are trying to achieve their goal of opening one JNV in each of the 78 districts of the North Eastern States. Presently 76 JNVs have been sanctioned for the NE Region.

IX. University and Higher Education

Universities and university-level institutions in India include 20 Central Universities, 215 State Universities, 100 Deemed Universities, 5 institutions established under State Act and 13 institutes of national importance apart from around 17,000 colleges including 1800 womens' colleges.

University Grants Commission

The University Grants Commission (UGC) which came into existence on 28 December 1953, became a statutory organisation by an Act of Parliament in 1956. It is a national body for the coordination, determination and maintenance of standards of university education. It serves as a coordinating body between the Union and State Governments and the institutions of higher learning. It also acts as an advisory body to these Governments and institutions on issues relating to higher education.

Section 12 of the UGC Act provides that the Commission shall, in consultation with the universities concerned, takes all such steps as it may think fit for the promotion and coordination of university education and for the maintenance of standards in teaching, examination and research. To teaching and research, extension was added as the third dimension of education by the Commission. For the purpose of performing its functions, the Commission may allocate and disburse, out of the Fund of the Commission, grants to universities and colleges for their maintenance and development; advise the Union Government, State Governments and Institutions of higher learning on the measures necessary for the promotion of university education and make Rules and Regulations consistent with the Act, etc.

The Commission consist of the Chairman, Vice-Chairman and 10 other members appointed by the Government of India. The executive head is Secretary.

The University Grants Commission has its Regional Offices at Hyderabad, Pune, Bhopal, Kolkata, Guwahati and Bangalore. The Northern Regional Office which was earlier located at Ghaziabad has now been functioning from the UGC Head Quarters as Northern Regional Colleges Bureau (NRCB). The UGC has taken up some new initiatives viz.

- Promotion of Entrepreneurship and knowledge based enterprises.
- Protection of Intellectual Property Rights.
- Promotion of Indian Higher Education abroad.
- Training and Development of Academic Administrators.
- Comprehensive Computerisation Initiative.

X. Indira Gandhi National Open University

The Indira Gandhi National Open University (IGNOU) established in September 1985, is responsible for the promotion of Open University and distance education system in the educational pattern of the country and for coordination and determination of standards in such systems. The major objectives of the University include widening access to higher education to larger segments of the populations, organising programmes of continuing education and initiating special programmes of higher education for specific target groups like women, physically challenged and people living in backward regions and hilly areas, such as NE, KBK, and those predominantly inhibited by tribals and SCs.

The IGNOU provide an innovative system for tertiary education and training. The system is flexible and open in regard to methods and pace of learning, combination of courses, eligibility for enrolment, age of entry, method of evaluation, etc. The University has adopted an integrated multimedia instructional strategy consisting of printed materials, audio-visual aids, educational radio and TV, teleconferencing and video conferencing supported by face-to-face counselling sessions through a network of study centre throughout the country. It conducts both continuous evaluation as well as term-end examinations.

The IGNOU introduced its programmes in 1987 and has so far launched 117 programmes consisting of more than 900 courses consisting of Ph.D., Master's Degree Programmes, Advanced/Post-Graduate Diploma, Diploma Programmes and Certificate Programmes etc. During 2005 over 4.60 lakh students were registered for various programmes of study.

The University has established an extensive student support services network consisting of 60 regional centres, 7 sub-regional centres and 1298 study centres situated in different parts of the country. IGNOU has established 269 study centres for women, SC/ST and physically challenged persons. On 26 January 2001 IGNOU launched an education channel Gyandarshan which is now a 24-hour channel and has capacity for six simultaneous telecasts. In November, 2001, IGNOU launched FM Radio Network for providing additional student support. As of now, 17 FM radio stations are functional and this number should increased to 40 FM stations in course of time. The launch of an exclusive educational satellite Edusat is an historic opportunity for the growth and development of distance education to create Educated India and meet the aspirations of our people and empower them through quality education. In the year 2005, the university established 100 Edusat supported Satellite Interactive Terminals (SITs) in its regional/study centres all over the country. Distance Educational Council, established by the University as a statutory authority, is an apex body for coordination and determination of standards in distance education in the country.

XI. Minority Education

The National Policy on Education 1986, updated in 1992 envisages paying greater attention to the education of the educationally backward minorities in the interest of equity and social justice. In pursuance of the revised Programme of Action (POA) 1992, two new Centrally Sponsored Schemes, i.e. (i) Scheme of Area Intensive Programme for Educationally Backward Minorities; and (ii) Scheme of Financial Assistance for Modernisation of Madarsa Education were launched during 1993-94.

Over a time, it has been felt that these schemes need to be implemented in an integrated way so as to have wider coverage, greater thrust and visibility of minority education programme. In the Tenth Plan the aforesaid two schemes have been merged to form the Area Intensive and Madarsa Modernisation Programme.

The National Commission for Minority Educational Institutions 2004 has been set up by an Act of Parliament under which minority education institutions can seek affiliation to Scheduled Universities. University of Delhi, North Eastern Hill University; Pondicherry University; Assam University; Nagaland University and Mizoram University are at present in the Schedule.

XII. Technical Education

The Technical Education System in the country covers courses in engineering, technology, management, architecture, pharmacy, etc. The Ministry of Human Resource Development caters to programmes at undergraduate, post-graduate and research levels. The technical education system at the central level companies, among others, the following: (a) The All India Council for Technical Education (AICTE), which is the statutory body for proper planning and coordinated development of the technical education system; (b) Seven Indian Institutes of Technology (IITs); (c) Six Indian Institutes of Management (IIMs); (d) Indian Institute of Science (IISc), Bangalore; (e) Indian Institute of Information Technology and Management (IIITM), Gwalior; Indian Institute of Information Technology (IIIT), Allahabad; and its Extension Campus at Amethi; and Indian Institute of Information Technology, Design and Manufacturing (IIITDM), Jabalpur; and (f) Eighteen National Institutes of Technology (NITs) (converted from RECs with 100 per cent Central funding).

New initiatives have been taken to promote research and education in basic sciences in the country. The IIS, Bangalore was sanctioned a special grant of Rs.100 crore to upgrade its infrastructure facilities, including laboratories. On the recommendations of the Scientific Advisory Council to the Prime Minister, two Indian Institutes of Science Education and Research have been approved at Pune and Kolkata. These Institutes will combine education in basic sciences at undergraduate and post-graduate level, with world class research facilities.

To enhance research productivity in Science and Technology Education and to improve quality of education, access to electronic journals and databases is being provided to all technical institutions. To benefit from lower costs, AICTE and Indian National Digital Library for Science and Technology (INDEST) have joined hands to form a combined AICTE-INDEST consortium.

During the 10th Plan, there has been a significant increase in the number of Technical Education Institutions and total intake of students. Of the 10th Plan outlay of Rs. 13,825 crore for the Department of Secondary and Higher Education, Rs. 4,700 crore was earmarked to 16 programmes of Technical Education. Of this, the major share goes to the World Bank-aided technical, Educational Quality Improvement Programme (TEQIP) with an outlay of Rs. 900 crore; AICTE with an outlay of Rs. 600 core and IITs with an outlay of Rs. 612 crore. The outlay for Annual Plan 2004-05 for Technical Education was Rs. 750 crore and expenditure Rs. 615.85 crore.

XIII. Indian National Commission for Cooperation with UNESCO (INCCU)

India has been a member of the United Nations' Educational,

Scientific and Cultural Organisation (UNESCO) since 1946. The Government set up an interim National Commission for Cooperation with UNESCO (INCCU) in 1949, which was later put on a permanent footing in 1951. The Commission consists of five Sub-Commissions namely, Education, Natural Science, Social Sciences, Culture and Communication.

The main objective of the Commission is to advise the Government in matters falling in the domain of UNESCO and to play a role in UNESCO's work, particularly in the formation and execution of its programmes. The Minister or Human Resource Development is the President of the Commission and the Secretary of the Government of India in the Department of Secondary and Higher Education is its Secretary of the Government of India in the Department of Secondary an Higher Education is its Secretary General. The membership of the Commission is of two categories: (i) Individual, and (ii) Institutional members distributed among its five Sub-Commissions.

The National Commission acts as an advisory, coordinating and liaison agency at the national level in respect of all matters within the competence of UNESCO. It also collaborates with the National Commissions of the Region and with UNESCO's Regional Offices, for fostering regional sub-regional and bilateral cooperation in education, science, culture and information.

Appendix 1

Committees, Commissions, Policy Statements and Other Significant Documents on Education in India Since Independence

Bibliography

1947

1. Overseas Scholarship Committee, 1947, Ministry of Education, Bureau of Education, Pamphlet No. 62, New Delhi, 1947.

1948

2. Committee on Secondary Education in India, 1948. Ministry of Education, Bureau of Education, Pamphlet No. 52, New Delhi, 1948.

1949

3. Indian University Education Commission, 1948. Manager of Publications, Delhi, 1949.

1950

4. Committee on the Ways and Means of Planning Educational Development in India, 1948. Manager of Publications, Bureau of Education, Pamphlet No. 64, Delhi, 1950.

1951

5. Committee on the Relationship between State Governments and Local Bodies in the Administration of Primary Education, 1951. Manager of Publication, Delhi, 1954.

1952

6. First Five Year Plan, Planning Commission, Government of India, New Delhi, 1952.

1953

7. Secondary Education Commission, 1952-53. Ministry of Education, 1953.

1954

8. Committee on Higher Education for Rural Areas, 1954. Ministry of Education, New Delhi, 1955.

1955

9. Study Team on General Education, 1955.
10. Committee to Study and Report on the Question of Establishing Uniform Standards in Respect of Education and Practice of Vaidas, Hakims and Homeopaths, 1955. Ministry of Health, 1956.

1956

11. Assessment Committee on Basic Education, 1956. Manager of Publications, New Delhi, 1956.
12. Education Committee for the Andaman and Nicobar Islands, 1956. Manager of Publications, Delhi, 1956.
13. Second Five Year Plan, Planning Commission, New Delhi, 1956.
14. Sanskrit Commission, 1956. Manager of Publications, Delhi, 1958.
15. Three-Year Degree Course Committee, 1956. Manager of Publications, Delhi, 1958.

1957

17. Committee on Rural Education, 1957. Ministry of Education, New Delhi, 1959.
18. Examination Committee, 1957. University Grants Commission, New Delhi, 1957.
19. Banaras Hindu University Enquiry Committee, 1957. Ministry of Education, New Delhi, 1957.
20. Committee for the Integration of Post Basic and Multipurpose Schools, 1957. Ministry of Education, New Delhi, 1960.

1958

21. Committee on Fisheries Education, 1958. Ministry of Food and Agriculture, New Delhi, 1959.
22. National Committee on Women's Education, 1958. Manager of Publications, Delhi, 1959.
23. Committee on General Education, 1958. U.G.C., New Delhi, 1961.
24. Special Committee on Commerce Education, 1958. All India Council for Technical Education, New Delhi, 1961.

1959

25. Review Committee for Mathematics in Indian Universities, 1959. U.G.C., New Delhi, 1959.
26. Committee on Religious and Moral Instruction, 1959. Ministry of Education, New Delhi, 1960.
27. Committee for Coordination and Integration of Schemes Operating in the Field of Physical Education, Recreation, and Youth Welfare, 1959. Ministry of Education, New Delhi, 1960.
28. Committee on the Problem of Students Indiscipline in Indian University, 1959. U.G.C., New Delhi, 1960.
29. Committee on Post-graduate Engineering Education and Research, 1959. Ministry of Scientific Research and Current Affairs, New Delhi, 1961.
30. Review Committee on Biochemistry, 1959. U.G.C. New Delhi, 1963.

1960

32. Review Committee for Chemistry in Indian Universities, 1960. U.G.C., New Delhi, 1963.
33. Review Committee for English in Indian Universities, 1960. U.G.C., New Delhi, 1963.

34. Review Committee for Education in Indian Universities, 1960. U.G.C., New Delhi, 1963.
35. Review Committee on Social Work, U.G.C., New Delhi, 1960.

1961

36. Committee on Plan Projects: Study Team for Selected Educational Schemes, 1961. New Delhi, 1963.
37. Committee on Plan Projects: Study Team for Selected Educational Scheme, 1961. Report on Social Education, New Delhi, 1963.
38. Committee on Model Act for Universities, 1961. Ministry of Education, New Delhi, 1961.
39. Expert Committee on Correspondence Courses and Evening Colleges, 1961. Manager of Publications, Delhi, 1961.
40. Review Committee for Philosophy in Indian Universities, 1961. U.G.C., New Delhi, 1961.
41. Review Committee for Sociology in Indian Universities, 1961. U.G.C., New Delhi, 1961.
42. Third Five Year Plan, Planning Commission, New Delhi, 1961.
43. Committee on Plan Projects: Panel for Science Laboratories and Equipment, 1961. New Delhi, 1962.
44. Committee on Differentiation of Curricula for Boys and Girls, 1961. Ministry of Education, New Delhi, 1964.
45. Indian Parliamentary and Scientific Committee, 1961. Manager of Publications, Delhi, 1964.

1962

46. Committee on Residential Accommodation for Students and Teachers, 1962. U.G.C., New Delhi, 1965.

1963

47. Committee on Setting-up a University for the North Eastern Region of India, 1963. U.G.C., New Delhi, 1965.
48. Committee to Look into the Causes for Lack of Public Support Particularly in Rural Areas for Girls Education and to Enlist Public Cooperation, 1963. Ministry of Education, 1965.
49. Committee on Education as on Elective Subject at the Undergraduate Stage, 1963. U.G.C., New Delhi, 1966.

1964

50. Committee on Plan Project Panel for Science Education in Secondary Schools, 1964. Government of India Press, 1964.
51. Mathematics Reforms Committee, 1964. U.G.C., New Delhi, 1966.
52. Education Commission, 1964-66. Manager of Publications, Delhi, 1966.
53. Committee to Examine the Extent of Malpractices in the Universities, 1964. U.G.C., New Delhi, 1967.
54. Committee on Plan Projects: Study Team for Selected Educational Schemes, 1964. Report on Teacher Training, New Delhi, 1969.

1965

55. Committee on Physical Education, 1965. U.G.C., New Delhi, 1965.
56. Report of the Committee on Student Welfare and Allied Matters, 1965, U.G.C., New Delhi, 1967.

1966

57. Committee on Improvement of Art Education, 1966, NCERT, New Delhi, 1967.
58. Review Committee on Political Science in Indian Universities, 1966. U.G.C., New Delhi, 1967.
59. Committee on Examination Reform in Central Universities, 1966. U.G.C., New Delhi, 1969.
60. Committee on School Textbooks, 1966. Ministry of Education, New Delhi, 1969.

1967

61. Committee of Members of Parliament on Education, 1967. Government of India Press, Faridabad, 1969.
62. Committee on Workers Education 1967. Manager of Publications, Delhi, 1968.
63. Committee on Rural Education, 1967. Ministry of Education, New Delhi, 1970.
64. Committee on Audio-Visual Aids in Higher Education, 1967, U.G.C., New Delhi, 1969.

1968

65. Review Committee on Future Development of National Council of Educational Research and Training, 1968. NCERT, New Delhi, 1969.

1969

66. Banaras Hindu University Inquiry Committee, 1969. Ministry of Education and Youth Services, New Delhi, 1969.
67. Study Group on Supervision and Inspection, 1969. NCERT, New Delhi, 1969.
68. Committee on Governance of Universities, 1969. U.G.C., New Delhi, 1971.

1970

69. Fourth Five Year Plan, Planning Commission, New Delhi, 1970.
70. Committee on Examination, 1970. NCERT, New Delhi, 1971.
71. Special Committee on Reorganisation and Development of Polytechnic Education in India, 1970. Ministry of Education, New Delhi, 1971.
72. Committee on School Buildings, 1970. Ministry of Education, New Delhi, 1972.
73. Committee on Calcutta University, 1972. U.G.C., New Delhi, 1972.
74. Review Committee of Regional Engineering Colleges, 1972. Ministry of Education and Social Welfare, New Delhi, 1974.

1974

75. Committee on the Status of Teaching of Sociology and Social

Anthropology, 1974. U.G.C., New Delhi, 1974.

76. Committee on Visva Bharati, 1974. Government of India Press, Faridabad, 1975.
77. Review Committee on the University Grants Commission, 1974. Ministry of Education and Social Welfare, New Delhi, 1977.
78. Fifth Five Year Plan, Planning Commission, New Delhi, 1976.

1977

79. Review Committee—Ishwar Bhai Patel, NCERT, New Delhi, 1977.
80. Working Group on Organisation of Vocational Education, 1977. Ministry of Education, New Delhi, 1977.
81. Working Group on Universalisation of Elementary Education, 1977. Ministry of Education and Social Welfare, New Delhi, 1977.
82. Committee on Adult Education Programmes for Women, 1977. Ministry of Education and Social Welfare, New Delhi, 1977.
83. National Review Committee on Higher Secondary Education with Special Reference to Vocationalisation, 1977. Ministry of Education and Social Welfare, New Delhi, 1978.

1978

84. Development of Higher Education in India—A Policy Framework. U.G.C., New Delhi, 1978.
85. Fourth All India Educational Survey 1978. NCERT, New Delhi, 1982.

1980

86. Sixth Five Year Plan. Planning Commission, 1980.

1981

87. Report on Autonomous Schools. Central Board of Secondary Education, New Delhi, 1981.

1983

88. National Commission on Teachers I (School Teachers), 1983-85. Controller of Publications, Delhi.
89. National Commission on Teachers II (Higher Education), 1983-85. Controller of Publications, Delhi, 1986.

1984

90. Report of the Committee to look into the Working of the Central Universities, U.G.C., New Delhi, 1984.

1985

91. Curriculum Load at the School Level: A Quick Appraisal. NCERT, New Delhi, 1985.
92. Challenge of Education—A Policy Perspective. Ministry of Human Resource Development, Government of India, New Delhi, 1985.
93. Seventh Five Year Plan, Planning Commission, New Delhi, 1985.
94. Report of the U.G.C. Committee on the Involvement of the Universities and Colleges in the Promotion of National Integration, 1985-86, U.G.C., New Delhi, 1986.

1986

95. National Policy on Education, 1986. Ministry of Human Resource

Development, Government of India, New Delhi, 1986.

96. Programme of Action, 1986. Ministry of Human Resource Development, New Delhi, 1986.
97. Report of the Committee on Revision of Pay Scales of Teachers in Universities and Colleges, 1986. U.G.C., New Delhi, 1986.
98. Report of the Committee on Revision of Pay Scales of Librarians and Directors of Physical Education in Universities and Colleges, 1986. U.G.C., New Delhi, 1990.

1987

99. Report of the U.G.C. Committee Towards New Educational Management, 1987. U.G.C., New Delhi, 1990.

1988

100. Report of the Task Force on Performance Appraisal of Teachers, U.G.C., New Delhi, 1988.
101. Report of the Committee on Setting-up State Councils of Higher Education. U.G.C., New Delhi, 1988.
102. National Curriculum for Elementary and Secondary Education: A Framework, NCERT, New Delhi, 1988.

1989

103. Fifth All India Educational Survey: Selected Statistics. NCERT, New Delhi, 1989.
104. Report of the Seventh Plan Visiting Committees for Mid-Term Review of Bihar State Universities, 1989, U.G.C., New Delhi, 1990.

1990

105. Committee for Review on National Policy on Education, 1986, Towards on Enlightened and Humane Society: NPE, 1986, A Review, New Delhi, December 1990.
106. Report of the Committee for Review of National Policy on Education, 1986: Recommendations. Ministry of Human Resource Development, New Delhi, 1990.

1991

107. Report of the Working Group on Adult Education, New Delhi, March, 1991.
108. Report of the Working Group on Elementary Education, New Delhi, March 1991.
109. Report of the Working Group on Policy and Planning, New Delhi, March 1991.
110. Report of the Working Group on Secondary Education, New Delhi, March 1991.
111. Report of the Working Group on Technical Education. New Delhi, March 1991.
112. Report of the Working Group on Education of Women and Other Disadvantaged Groups like SC, ST, Minorities, etc., New Delhi, March 1991.
113. Objectives, Thrusts and Macro-Dimensions of the Eighth Plan. Planning Commission, New Delhi, December, 1991.

1992

114. Report of the CABE Committee on Policy, Department of Education, Ministry of Human Resource Development, Government of India, New Delhi, January 1992.
115. National Policy on Education (NPE), 1986, Revised Policy Formulations. Department of Education, New Delhi, May 1992.
116. Report of the Conference of Chairmen of Board of School Education on Semesterisation and Examination, NCERT, New Delhi, 1992.
117. Report of the National Colloquium on Right to Education as a Fundamental Right, Sponsored by UGC and Association of Indian Universities, September 1992, AIU, 1992, Journal of Higher Education, autumn 1992.
118. Eighth Five Year Plan (1992-97), Planning Commission, New Delhi, 1992.

1993

119. Learning Without Burden: Yash Pal Committee (1993) Report of the National Advisory Committee Appointed by the Ministry of Human Resource Development, Government of India, NCERT, New Delhi, 1993.
120. Decentralisation of Educational Planning: Panchayati Raj: Veerapan Report (1993). Ministry of Human Resource Development, New Delhi, 1993.
121. Report of the Group on the Reduction of Academic Burden on School Education (1993-94), Ministry of Human Resource Development, New Delhi, 1993.
122. Report of the Committee on Vocationalisation of Higher Education, UGC, 1993.
123. Report of the Justice Punnya Committee on UGC Funding of Higher Education (1992-93), UGC, 1993.
124. Performance and Accountability in Higher Education: Discussion Papers and Summary.
125. Record of Discussions on the Workshop, UGC, New Delhi, 1994. UGC Occasional Papers.
126. Resource Mobilisation for EFA. NIEAP, New Delhi, 1993.
127. Report of Expert Committee for Developing a Performance Appraisal System, Ministry of Human Resource Development, Government of India, New Delhi, 1993.

1994

128. Report of the Expert Group on National Literacy Mission (1993-94), Literacy Mission, Ministry of Human Resource Development, New Delhi, 1994.

1995

129. Sixth All India Educational Survey: Provisional Statistics, NCERT, New Delhi, 1995.
130. Report of the IIT Synergy Sub-Group, 1995, Ministry of Human Resource Development, New Delhi, 1995.

1996

131. Curriculum Framework for Teacher Education—Discussion Document, National Council for Teacher Education, New Delhi, 1996.

1997

132. Report of the Committee of State Education Ministers on Implications of the Proposal to make Elementary Education a Fundamental Right, Ministry of Human Resource Development, New Delhi, 1997.

1998

133. Restructuring and Revitalising Teacher Education (National Report on the Role of CTE/IASES), National Council of Teacher Education, New Delhi (1998).

1999

134. Expert Group Report on Financial Requirements for Making Elementary Education a Fundamental Right. Ministry of Human Resource Development, New Delhi, 1999.
135. Report of the Chief Justice J.S. Verma Committee to Operationalize the suggestions to teach the Fundamental Rights to the Citizens of India, New Delhi, 1999.
136. Human Values in Education: Chavan Committee Report, Rajya Sabha Secretariat, Eighty First Report on Value Based Education, New Delhi, 1999.
137. Ninth Five Year Plan on Education (1997-2000). Planning Committee, New Delhi, 1999.

2000

138. National Curriculum Framework for School Education: A Discussion Paper, NCERT, New Delhi, 2000.
139. National Curriculum Framework for School Education, NCERT, New Delhi, 2000.
140. Census of India, 2001. Registrar, General and Census Commissioner, India, Census of India, 2001, Delhi.

2002

141. Education Rights of Minorities: Supreme Court Judgment (2002), P.D. Mathews, S.J. Indian Social Institute, New Delhi, 2002.
142. Tenth Five Year Plan (2002-2007), Planning Commission.
143. The Constitution (Eighty-Sixth Amendment) Act, 2002.

2005

144. Draft National Curriculum Framework, 2005, NCERT, New Delhi, 2005.
145. National Curriculum Framework, 2005.

2006

146. Report on the Social Economic and Educational Status of the Muslim Community in India or Sachar Committee Report, 2006.
147. National Knowledge Commission (NKC), 2006.

Appendix 2

Towards EFA: The Quality Imperative: Mirror of Equity

Whether a particular education system is of high of low quality can be judged only in terms of the extent of which its objectives are being met. Quality must also be judged in the mirror of equity. An education system in which there is gender inequality or discrimination against particular groups on ethical or cultural grounds is not a high-quality system. A shift towards equity represents, in itself, an improvement in the quality of education.

From a policy perspective, one fundamental reason why simply focusing upon the quantitative dimension of UPE and the other goals will not deliver EFA is that, in many parts of the world, an enormous gap prevails between the numbers graduating from schools and those among them who can master a minimum set of cognitive skills.

Governments committed to improving learning outcomes face difficult choices, but policies exist that are not necessarily beyond the reach the most resource-constrained countries. They start with a focus on the learner and place emphasis on the dynamics of teaching and learning, supported by a growing body of research on what makes schools and teachers effective.

Links among different parts of the education sector can help improve quality but they are often hidden or ignored by the compartmentalized machinery of government. ECCE helps with subsequent achievement in school and further lifelong learning. Literacy improves adults' commitment to their children's education and is desirable in its own right. Gender-sensitive and inclusive policies directly improve the quality and outcomes of education.

Successful qualitative reforms require government to pay a strong leading role. Although external assistance can boost resource levels and help in managing school systems, it cannot make up for the absence of a societal project for education improvement. Accordingly, the domestic political process is ultimately the guarantor of successful reform. If it favours educational change, the chances that external assistance will facilitate a move towards higher-quality universal education are profoundly better than is the case where such political circumstances are absent.

Strong impact on children's education. Yet the world counts about

800 million illiterate adults (Adapted from 'EFA Global Monitoring Report, 2005', UNESCO); 70% of them living in just nine countries belonging mostly to sub-Saharan Africa and East, South and West Asia.

Introduced in the 2003 EFA Global Monitoring Report, the Education for All Development Index (EDI) provides a summary quantitative measure of the extent to which countries are meeting four of the six EFA goals (UPE, gender, literacy and quality). It shows that massive educational deprivation continues to be concentrated in sub-Saharan Africa, some of the Arab States and South and West Asia. Progress between 1998 and 2001 was widespread but not universal. About three-quarters of the seventy-four countries having the data registered a modest increase in their index value but at a rate insufficient to reach the EFA goals.

Adapted from 'EFA Global Monitoring Reports, 2005, UNESCO

Table 1: Expenditure on Education Public

S. No.	*Country*	*As % of GDP*
1.	Australia	4.6
2.	Bangladesh	2.3
3.	Barbados	7.8
4.	Bhutan	5.2
5.	Canada	5.2
6.	Cuba	8.5
7.	Germany	4.6
8.	India	4.1
9.	Indonesia	1.3
10.	Iran, Islamic Republic of	5.0
11.	Israel	6.3
12.	Japan	3.6
13.	Korea, Republic of	3.6
14.	Malaysia	7.9
15.	Myanmar	4.1
16.	Nepal	3.4
17.	New Zealand	6.6
18.	Norway	6.8
19.	Pakistan	1.8
20.	Russian Federation	3.1
21.	South Africa	5.7
22.	Sri Lanka	1.3
23.	Sweden	7.6
24.	Switzerland	5.8
25.	United Kingdom	4.6
26.	United States	5.6

Source: 'Human Development Report, 2004' UNDP.

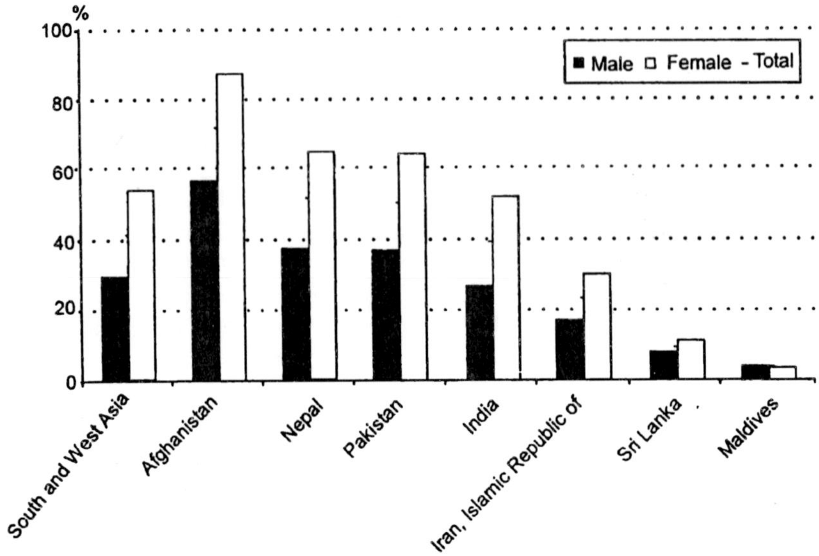

Illiteracy Rate by Sex in South and West Asia 2000-2004

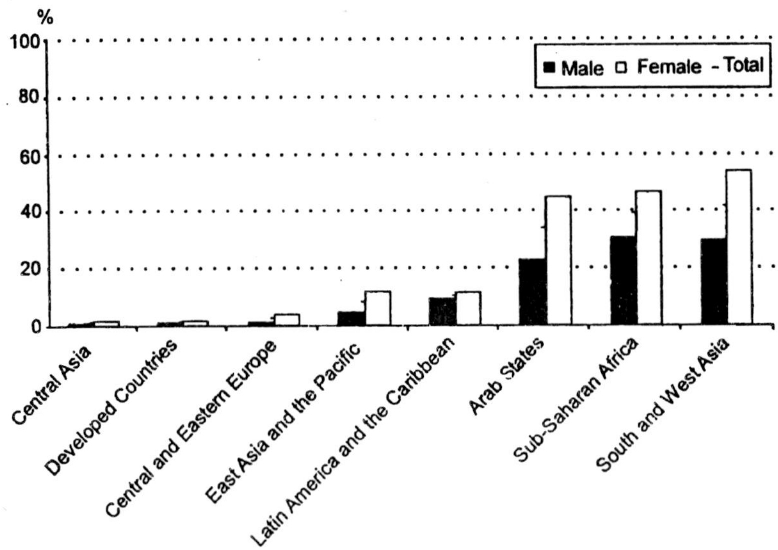

World Illiteracy Rates by Region and Sex 2000-2004

Appendix 3

Basic Indicators including Education

Countries and Territories	*Total Population (thousands) 2004*	*GNI per Capita (US$) 2004*	*Life Expectancy at Birth (years) 2004*	*Total Adult Literacy Rate 2000-2004**	*Net Primary School Enrolment/ Attendance (%) 1996-2004**	*% of Primary School Entrants Reaching Grade 5 Survey Data 1997-2004*	*Secondary School Enrolment Ratio*	
							Male	*Female*
(1)	(2)	(3)	(4)	(5)	(6)	(7)	(8)	(9)
Afghanistan	28574	250	46	-	53	92	-	-
Australia	19942	26900	81	-	97	-	87	89
Bhutan	2116	760	63	-	-	-	-	-
Brazil	183913	3090	71	88	95	84x	72	78
Canada	31958	28390	80	-	100	-	97	98
China	1307989	1290	72	91	99	-	-	-
Cuba	11245	1170	78	100	93	99	86	86
Denmark	5414	40650	77	-	100	-	94	98
Egypt	72642	1310	70	56	83	99	83	79
Ethiopia	75600	110	48	42	31	65	23	13
Finland	5235	32790	79	-	100	-	94	95
France	60257	30090	80	-	99	-	93	95
Germany	82645	30120	79	-	83	-	88	88
Ghana	21664	380	57	54	61	98	39	33
India	1087124	620	64	61	77	95	-	-

(1)	(2)	(3)	(4)	(5)	(6)	(7)	(8)	(9)
Indonesia	220077	1140	67	88	94	97	54	54
Iran (Islamic Republic of)	68803	2300	71	77	86	-	-	-
Iraq	28057	2170	59	-	78	88	40	26
Ireland	4080	34280	78	-	96	-	80	87
Israel	6601	17380	80	97	99	-	89	89
Italy	58033	26120	80	-	99	-	91	92
Japan	127923	37180	82	-	100	-	99	100
Kenya	33467	460	48	74	78	98	25	24
Korea, Democratic People's Republic of	22384	a	63	-	-	-	-	-
Korea, Republic of	47645	13980	77	-	100	-	88	88
Malaysia	24894	4650	73	89	93	-	66	74
Myanmar	50004	220	61	90	80	78	36	34
Nepal	26591	260	62	49	74	92	-	-
New Zealand	3989	20310	79	-	100	-	91	93
Nigeria	128709	390	43	67	62	97	32	26
Oman	2534	7830	74	74	72	-	69	70
Pakistan	154794	600	63	49	56	90	-	-
Philippines	81617	1170	71	93	88	93	54	65
Russian Federation	143899	3410	65	99	90	-	-	-
Saudi Arabia	23950	10430	72	79	54	-	54	52
Singapore	4273	24220	79	93	-	-	-	-
South Africa	47208	3630	47	82	89	99	63	68
Sri Lanka	20570	1010	74	90	-	-	-	-
Sweden	9008	35770	80	-	100	-	99	100
Switzerland	7240	48230	81	-	99	-	89	84
Thailand	63694	2540	70	93	85	-	-	-
United Arab Emirates	4284	18060	78	77	83	-	70	72
United Kingdom	59479	33940	79	-	100	-	94	97

(1)	(2)	(3)	(4)	(5)	(6)	(7)	(8)	(9)
United States	295410	41400	78	-	92	-	88	89
Zambia	11479	450	38	68	68	88	25	21
Zimbabwe	12936	480	37	90	79	94	35	33
SUMMARY INDICATORS								
Sub-Saharan Africa	697561	611	46	60	60	84	29	24
Eastern and Southern Africa	348833	836	46	63	65	81	29	25
Middle East and North Africa	371384	2308	68	67	79	90	60	55
East Asia and Pacific	1937058	1686	71	90	96	-	54	55
CEE/CIS	404154	2667	67	97	88	96	-	-
Industrialized countries	956315	32232	79	-	95	-	91	92
Developing countries	5166574	1524	65	77	80	90	50	49
Least developed countries	741597	345	52	54	60	80	30	26
World	6374050	6298	67	78	82	90	60	60

Definitions of the Indicators

- **Adult literacy rate** — Percentage of persons ages 15 and over who can read and write.
- **Net secondary school enrolment ratio** — The number of children enrolled in secondary school who belong to the age group that officially corresponds to secondary schooling, divided by the total population of the same age group.
- **Primary school entrants reaching grade five** — Percentage of children entering the first grade of primary school who eventually reach grade five.

Source: 'The State of World's Children 2006', UNICEF.